T4-AHW-046

Norms over Force

The Sciences Po Series in International Relations and Political Economy

Series Editor, Christophe Jaffrelot

This series consists of works emanating from the foremost French researchers from Sciences Po, Paris. Sciences Po was founded in 1872 and is today one of the most prestigious universities for teaching and research in social sciences in France, recognized worldwide.

This series focuses on the transformations of the international arena, in a world where the state, though its sovereignty is questioned, reinvents itself. The series explores the effects on international relations and the world economy of regionalization, globalization (not only of trade and finance but also of culture), and transnational flows at large. This evolution in world affairs sustains a variety of networks from the ideological to the criminal or terrorist. Besides the geopolitical transformations of the globalized planet, the new political economy of the world has a decided impact on its destiny as well, and this series hopes to uncover what that is.

Published by Palgrave Macmillan:

Politics In China: Moving Frontiers
edited by Françoise Mengin and Jean-Louis Rocca

Tropical Forests, International Jungle: The Underside of Global Ecopolitics
by Marie-Claude Smouts, translated by Cynthia Schoch

The Political Economy of Emerging Markets: Actors, Institutions and Financial Crises in Latin America
by Javier Santiso

Cyber China: Reshaping National Identities in the Age of Information
edited by Françoise Mengin

With Us or Against Us: Studies in Global Anti-Americanism
edited by Denis Lacorne and Tony Judt

Vietnam's New Order: International Perspectives on the State and Reform in Vietnam
edited by Stéphanie Balme and Mark Sidel

Equality and Transparency: A Strategic Perspective on Affirmative Action in American Law
by Daniel Sabbagh, translation by Cynthia Schoch and John Atherton

Moralizing International Relations: Called to Account
by Ariel Colonomos, translated by Chris Turner

Norms over Force: The Enigma of European Power
by Zaki Laïdi, translated from the French by Cynthia Schoch

Norms over Force

The Enigma of European Power

Zaki Laïdi

translated from the French
by Cynthia Schoch

palgrave
macmillan

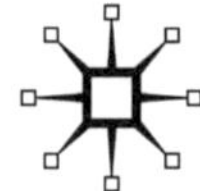

NORMS OVER FORCE

La Norme sans la force was first published by Presses de Sciences Po, Paris.

First published in 2008 by
PALGRAVE MACMILLAN®
in the US—a division of St. Martin's Press LLC,
175 Fifth Avenue, New York, NY 10010.

Where this book is distributed in the UK, Europe and the rest of the world, this is by Palgrave Macmillan, a division of Macmillan Publishers Limited, registered in England, company number 785998, of Houndmills, Basingstoke, Hampshire RG21 6XS.

Palgrave Macmillan is the global academic imprint of the above companies and has companies and representatives throughout the world.

Palgrave® and Macmillan® are registered trademarks in the United States, the United Kingdom, Europe and other countries.

ISBN-13: 978–0–230–60460–5
ISBN-10: 0–230–60460–9

Library of Congress Cataloging-in-Publication Data

Laïdi, Zaki.
[Norme sans la force. English]
Norms over force : the enigma of European power / by Zaki Laïdi; translated from the French by Cynthia Schoch.
p. cm.—(The Sciences Po series in international relations and political economy)
Includes bibliographical references and index.
ISBN 0–230–60460–9
1. Europe—Politics and government—21st century. 2. World politics—21st century. I. Title.

D2024.L3513 2008
303.48′24—dc22 2007052405

"Ouvrage publié avec l'aide du Ministère français chargé de la culture. Centre national du livre" (Published with the support of the French Minister of Culture. Centre National du Livre).

A catalogue record of the book is available from the British Library.

Design by Newgen Imaging Systems (P) Ltd., Chennai, India.

First edition: August 2008

10 9 8 7 6 5 4 3 2 1

Printed in the United States of America.

CONTENTS

TABLES

INTRODUCTION

It may seem strange to take an interest in the power of Europe at a time when Europe more than ever seems to be a vulnerable political entity. But I will respond to this irrefutable observation in two ways: first, by considering that crises provide stimulation and justify in-depth questioning and, second because the failure of the constitutional treaty does not prefigure Europe's demise. If this were the case, it would mean that the foundations on which Europe has been built since 1957 are incredibly fragile. It is unimaginable that the *acquis communautaire*, which remains considerable whatever people might say, could dissolve due to the failure of a text that in fact introduced no major innovation. From this standpoint, the comparison between the failure of the Constitutional Treaty and that of the European Defense Community (EDC) in 1954 does not hold water. Admittedly, the failure of the EDC delayed the idea of a European defense for over 40 years. But the project in itself was a historical gamble, a leap into the unknown that grew out of nothing other than the idea that war was the evil that Europe needed to shake if it wanted to survive. The Constitutional Treaty is backed by 45 years of slow, gradual, erratic but real construction work that has significant results to show for its efforts: peace, prosperity, the rule of law, a single market, and the communitarization of certain public policies. Seen from Europe, the result may seem modest. Seen from the rest of the world, the achievement is obvious. For even if the political integration of Europe is stalled, even if its growth has not improved, and even if globalization has eroded the social protection of European citizens, Europe still has very strong trump cards in its hand. And the fact that so many states are seeking to join the European Union is, from this standpoint, an important promotional argument. Building the rule of law, protecting civil liberties, guaranteeing the free functioning of the market, preventing the risk of war are all essential components of the European project. The fact that these *acquis* are fragile or perceived as not inspiring enough in no way makes them less important. Actually, it is highly likely that Europe's main difficulty derives from the fact that it lacks self-confidence and that the confidence deficit reflects a problem of identity. Europeans certainly have no trouble defining themselves with respect to the rest of the world. But they have a lot more trouble thinking of themselves in new terms and according to new categories, ones that would enable them to combine national identity and European identity. Naturally, the easy answer is to say that these dimensions are complementary and compatible, and that they are a source of enrichment. But, as usual, the reality is more complex than that. For between European citizens, who can view themselves from multiple angles, and Europe, comes the great survivor that is the nation-state. The prospect of its demise, always announced and systematically belied, is disturbing, either because its existence no longer seems guaranteed (wherefore the announcement of its demise), or because it seems incontrovertible (wherefore the announcement of its return). Such that the European project basically experiences itself as a project that both wants to get beyond nation-states and still keeps them alive without really knowing how to go about it.

From this historic ambivalence flows what I will call here the enigma of European power. In many regards, Europe "looks like a power" and tries to assume this appearance. But its power is not one of a nation-state. One might be tempted to discount this objection by pointing out that in the world today, there are numerous forms and modalities of wielding power that do not avail themselves of a state apparatus: multinationals know it well. But there again, nothing is simple. For although Europe in no way aspires to become a super state, on a world scale it is striving to obtain recognition as a "de facto super state" on which the classic attributes of power would be conferred.

Nothing offends Europeans more than to see Europe reduced to the rank of mere regional organization. But Europeans are even more offended when they are asked one way or another to sweep their particularism under the carpet of European unity. Thus there is a basic contradiction in European power. But rather than seek to overcome it, it should be investigated. Unfortunately, political analyses of Europe have not necessarily always given themselves the means to do so. Traditionally, analysis of European power has been the privilege of either foreign-policy specialists or public policy analysts. Analyses that seek to study the connection between European defense, its trade policy, and its environmental strategy are few and far between. Worse yet, analysis of social preferences is disconnected from that of the European Union's external action. Such that it is often weighed down by a considerable handicap: institutional formalism. In many analyses, investigating Europe's role in the world still means examining the constitutional and legal framework of Europe's foreign policy, at the risk of succumbing to a fascination for microdecisions that would yield very meager results.

Now that is exactly the habit that needs to be broken. I do not mean that institutions are not fundamental, but that institutions only have the meaning we are willing to give them. Such that without first examining the contents of the choices and preferences of Europe, an analysis of its institutions remains a infertile exercise. Moreover, separating external policy from Europe's social, economic, and cultural preferences is untenable. For if globalization makes any sense, it is in the shattering of the hermetic compartments of Europe's action in the world. Certainly, trade is not diplomacy, and the issue of arms sales to China is not on the same level as that of respect for basic social norms that are at odds with this same China. But never has the gap between these various problems been so small. For how can we convince China not to rely too much on its competitive edge if we do not have more political cards to constrain it to make an effort in this direction? For the United States, such an approach makes sense because it is a state. But can Europe do the same?

The point is not to confuse matters, but to try to connect everything by attempting to answer this simple question: What does Europe really want? What worldview does it hold? What preferences does it defend? What likelihood is there of its being able to share them with the rest of the world?

Such are the questions this book will address, not by providing abstract or idealized answers, but by suggesting an analytical framework that aims to consider Europe in the context of globalization, beyond the microdisciplinary segmentations that it is sometimes subject to.

In an attempt to rise to this challenge, I will thus submit to the reader four sets of questions that actually are more open avenues than sort of closed-circuit conceptualizations.

The first has to do with the meaning of European power. Is it a deceptive power, merely a civilian power, or a superpower in gestation that simply needs to be given time to mature? My hypothesis is that Europe will not be a superpower as long as it is not the ultimate guarantor of its own security. Therefore, as long as European Union defense policy does not tackle this problem, its meaning will remain unchanged. This is why it is reasonable to think that Europe will remain a soft power, but a soft power that must be taken seriously.

So if the power does not have the strength to make itself heard, what instruments does it have? My second hypothesis, which consists in thinking that the power of Europe is based on what I will call the *preference for norms*, addresses this question.

Assuming that this preference is a trademark of European power, what ethical, political, social, and cultural preferences does it express?

Taking that question as a starting point, I will try to show how the European model of preference for norms is confronted today with the resistance of political state sovereignties—particularly the most powerful of them, the United States.

I will conclude by discussing the implications that the European preference for norms can have on the world system. Two paths can be imagined. The first involves thinking that with the rise in new powers such as China and India, the world checkerboard will tend to be rearranged around the classic interstate game in which realpolitik will win over regulation by norms. In this hypothesis, there will be a real race between Europe and the rest of the world. With Europe seeking to standardize the world system, the other powers will try to delay or chip away at this normative system. The consequences of this competition will, of course, be considerable.

For either Europe wins, and its model will come out strengthened, or else Europe loses, and its model will suffer, inciting the most powerful European states to try to strike out on their own in a big geopolitical negotiating game. In the most extreme case, the European project will come apart on its own, except perhaps in the field of trade, the transnational functioning of which does not bother realpolitik theoreticians.

To thwart this possibility, which could be fatal, Europe could then attempt to force the hand of destiny by moving toward what I call a constitutionalization of the world order. Norms would be not only global but also legally guaranteed. That would be the logical response in the face of the return of world realpolitik.

Yet if Europe has everything to lose in a comeback of realpolitik, it has nothing to win from a constitutionalization of the world order. For to constitutionalize the world order means, in a way, seeking to draw out of norms the very essence of politics. This is the crux of the criticism that the United States addresses to Europe in a sometimes brutal manner. Europe does not have to agree with this analysis, but it cannot ignore it. Not only because the United States matters, but also because the relationship between norms and politics poses problems in Europe as well. Wherefore the need to cross over the hump that will prevent Europe from falling into the trap in which it has historically fallen (realpolitik), while avoiding succumbing to another temptation that historically it has not always resisted either: confusing the defense of its interests with those of universal morality.

CHAPTER 1

Why Europe Cannot Be a Superpower

Much plethora of research has been conducted on Europe's power.[1] But aside from the fact that it tends to concentrate particularly on procedures and discourses, it winds up stumbling upon the same enigma: Can Europe be a superpower? This question in turn raises two new questions: Is it conceivable for a political actor that is not a state—even if it seeks de facto acknowledgment as such, particularly by international institutions—to rise to the rank of a superpower? Even more fundamentally, is the European project compatible with the very idea of power? As we will see, these questions are essential. And the fact that they are posed with regard to Europe and not China, India, Brazil, or Russia shows that Europe is indeed a specific case. Its specificity is twofold. Not only because Europe's political structure has no historical equivalent—it is not a state, even a federal one (and nothing indicates that it is on the way to becoming one)—but also because, like it or not, the philosophy of the European project is historically dominated by a refusal of power: "Cooperation between nations," wrote Jean Monnet, "solves nothing. What we need to strive for is to merge European interests and not simply to balance them."[2] This very definition contains an explicit desire to get beyond the traditional balance of power (in fact, invented by the Europeans) and the ambition to draw out common European interests that amount to more than the sum of national interests.

This enigma of European power—which arises from both the refusal to accept power and the inability to ignore it totally in a world where such refusal is perceived or experienced as powerlessness and where, moreover, the pooling of forces almost automatically produces power—is something I shall return to at length.

What Is a Superpower?

At this stage, I shall begin by formulating a hypothesis: Europe has several instruments of power, including the instruments of a superpower. But it has little chance of achieving the rank of superpower, not because it does not have a military force—as it is too often claimed—but because, basically, *Europeans do not see themselves as the ultimate guarantors of their own security.* That is a fundamental starting point.

In the hierarchy of important actors in the world system, Europe shares this particularity with Japan; this is obviously no coincidence. After 1945, Japan sought to turn its back on its imperialistic past. As for Europe, it wanted to break the endless cycle of confrontation between nations at a time, moreover, when it had exhausted its needs for imperial conquest. The Rome Treaty followed on the heels of the Franco-British debacle in Suez. The hypothesis may seem chancy, but it nevertheless seems temporarily to hold true: The major *soft powers* are striving to disown part of their history. In the case of Europe, there is an additional challenge: to turn its back on a history of wars between European nations without quashing them. *Hard powers* see themselves differently. They want to break with their history not to create a new one, but to pursue or revive it.[3] However, making a clean break with one's past is not an easy task, for it fundamentally deprives the actor of an historic depth of field. Europe, where the modern notion of political sovereignty of states was founded, has for fifty years been trying to circumvent it, sublime at, and share it without wanting or being able to get beyond it.

Thus all the other major actors such as the United States, China, Russia, India, and even Brazil see themselves as the ultimate guarantors of their own security. Saying that does not mean that all these states actually have the means to ensure their own security, even though their morphology is a considerable contributing factor.

They are all indeed vast states that make territorial conquest difficult to undertake, whereas Europe does not have the same expanse to protect it.[4] That means that these states view the world "as if" it will always be their duty to carry the ultimate responsibility of ensuring their security. Now, the fact of perceiving oneself as the ultimate guarantor of one's own security has incommensurable consequences on the way an actor looks at the world and, in a mirror effect, on the way the world looks at it.

To be the ultimate guarantor of one's own security means constantly speculating about the conditions for one's survival, the extreme situations that could jeopardize it, and the tight interweaving of the various dimensions of power—political-military power, economic power, and identitarian power, taken to mean the ideas and values to which a human collectivity connects its survival. To be a superpower is to believe that "the world order," with its codes and rules, could one day or another come into contradiction with one's own survival, which implies, in this event, either pulling out of the game or changing the rules.

Being a superpower also means integrating the fact that one's survival is at stake almost on a daily basis. Let us take an example suggested by recent current events. In the past few years, the energy question has returned to the forefront. The rise in power of China as well as India, coupled with the usual U.S. demand for Fuel, has led to increased energy demand and a subsequent rise in price across the globe. As a result, all these countries are trying to develop veritable energy supply strategies. The most spectacular form of this approach has been the Chinese takeover bid on an American mini-major corporation—Unocal.[5] Like other big consumers, China is also trying to acquire oil reserves through the stock market, with India following in its wake. It is moreover obvious that these two countries place considerable importance on energy supply security in their overall political strategy.

All this may appear in a way to be perfectly natural and rather trite. Except that a country such as Japan that is even more dependent than India and China in terms of energy does not behave at all in the same way. It has no major oil company and conducts a very passive supply policy that keeps it in a position of very high dependency with respect to Middle Eastern oil. But it does not seek any political outlet to this situation. Its oil dependence is experienced as a mere constraint that has prompted it to keep a low profile in the Middle East.

What does all this tell us about nations' relationship to power? The lesson is fundamental. Japan deliberately strives not to transform its energy supply security into a political issue, because it intensely associates the "aggressive" search for oil with war. Tokyo attacked Pearl Harbor when the United States suspended their exports. With regard to its history, Tokyo associates the quest for oil with recourse to force. It is, therefore, not inclined to treat its energy supply security in political or strategic terms.[6] Europe's approach is different from Japan's, but it also appears inspired more by a sustainable logic of interdependence than by a power strategy. In the next 20 years, Europe's energy dependence will represent two-thirds of its needs as opposed to only half of them today. And to meet them, it has chosen recourse to natural gas (to protect its environment), which, unlike oil, requires lasting commitments in terms of infrastructure on the part of both importers and exporters. The role of a guaranteed supplier is mainly played by Russia. Politically, this means that Europe is structurally impelled to seek political accommodation with Russia.[7] Naturally, there is nothing automatic about Europe's conduct of its policy that prompts us to believe that its natural gas dependence requires it to refrain from criticizing Russia about Chechnya or other human rights abuses. Certain observers do not exclude such a relationship, pointing out a coincidence between Euro-Russian negotiations on energy supply and the Union's commitment to extend its *Tacis* program to Chechnya, a commitment that could hardly be considered as anything but an implicit support for the Russian policy of "normalization."[8] But all this is a matter of perspective. When looking at Russia, the gaze European Union casts is one that can mainly be qualified as a "gaze of interdependency."[9]

The second case study deals with the EU's energy policy. In this context, the stakes of the Energy Charter are highly revealing of Europe's preference for norms and the resistance it faces. Initiated by the Commission in 1994, signed in 1998 but not ratified since then, this charter explicitly states that its fundamental role is to "strengthen the rule of law on energy issues, by creating a level playing field of rules to be observed by all participating governments, thus minimizing the risks associated with energy-related investments and trade."[10] In addition, it provides for a characteristic element of governance by norms: the setting up of a dispute-resolution mechanism. Through this entire system, Europe is basically seeking to engage Russia in a partnership that will make it very difficult for Russia to interrupt natural gas delivery to Europe, particular by depriving it of a monopoly over the gas distribution network.[11] The energy issue confronts Europe with not only realist issues (energy supply involves interests that can be qualified as highly sensitive, even vital), but also arbitration, because it just so happens precisely that its main suppliers, Russia and Algeria, are fiercely hostile to any idea of political conditionality.[12]

But the energy issue does not stop there. It poses a more general problem: how does Europe envisage regulation of the energy market on a global scale? Should the EU think of it in terms of regulation through the market and institutions or should it on the contrary reason in terms of classic geopolitics?[13]

The first alternative reflects the hypothesis of governance through norms that Europe prefers over realpolitik, whereas the second fits into a classic geopolitical framework in which a dominant actor uses energy as the instrument of state power, has little sympathy for world regulation, but is highly reactive to political considerations. Naturally, these two options leave room for uncertainty in the middle. It remains to be seen how the EU will manage to handle it. It is conceivable that the EU will be entrusted with the governance aspect, whereas the geopolitical aspect will remain in the hands of member states—a division of roles that naturally carries a risk of incoherence.

Power is indeed a way of viewing and acting in the world and this independently of any objective consideration. In paroxystic manner, a superpower seeks to "create reality" and not react to it. This is the meaning of George Bush's remarks when he said, "We're an empire now, and when we act, we create our own reality. And while you're studying that reality . . ., we'll act again, creating other new realities."[14] Hard power can be considered as the actor potentially trying to fashion a world reality in its own image, whereas soft power does its best to influence it.[15] Hard power is one that describes the world in political terms; soft power is one that is subjected to it to varying degrees. The Solana report, which set out to define Europe's security strategy, is an illustration of this approach.[16] The global threats it identifies are about the same as those identified by the United States. This coincidence is not surprising in itself. But it is significant to note that this report uses the same terminology as the Americans, particularly the controversial notion of failed states, and offers nothing original or European in origin. It is moreover striking to see that this document practically entirely evacuates issues of global governance and European approaches in this regard. All this starkly points up the European Union's lack of strategic coherence as a world actor. From this a twofold observation can be drawn: the conclusion that the document is a sort of broad enough compromise to accommodate convergent European positions. Europe can be said to style itself on the U.S. world agenda but suggests more cooperative and less conflictual solutions for implementing it.

In any event, hard power also spends its time sending out signals to the other dominant actors to indicate that it shares the codes of power with them, and only them. Thus, when India reveals plans to put in orbit a satellite that will enable it to observe the moon's surface, no one seriously thinks that it will obtain results that will be any different from those brought back by the Apollo missions nearly 30 years ago. On the other hand, everyone understands that India is seeking to endow itself with the status of a superpower, forcing China to launch a program so as not to seem to lag behind its regional competitor.[17]

Power Avoidance

This naturally brings us straight to Europe. Like Japan, it is weighed down by the memory of war. Such that each time confrontation is involved when issues of power are at stake, it will do everything to sublime them or remove them from the center. And like Japan, it will attempt to conceive its dependence in terms of interdependence rather than survival. A superpower has a natural tendency to pose the stakes of the world in terms of a zero-sum game, which a lesser power seeks precisely to avoid. And it is precisely because superpowers view the world in the form of a potential zero-sum game that they are prompted to up the ante: to ensure its survival it must ensure its *supremacy*. Hard power implicitly conveys a dominant instinct, even if its sphere of domination is only regional, as is the case with Brazil and India. Soft power discards this idea, even on an economic level. When the Europeans launched the Lisbon strategy in the year 2000 to make the European Union the most competitive region in the world, no one read the declaration as a claim for world leadership. Its aim was much more to galvanize Europeans by encouraging them to reform their economies to close the gap between the United States and Europe, particularly in the field of innovation and research.

It is thus understandable that an actor that is not the ultimate guarantor of its security will behave differently. It will by nature be less assured, less determined, and more diversified. It will naturally start by thinking about the conditions that will allow it to overcome this weakness or deficiency in order precisely to become the ultimate guarantor of its security. But this assumes a keen intentionality, backed not only by discourse but also by strong choices.

Now, even for the two political-military powers that are France and Great Britain, the ultimate guarantee of their own security has not been posed in exclusively national terms since 1945. France, which pursued the game of strategic national autonomy the furthest, conceived it only with respect to the U.S. strategic guarantee in Europe. And even if it tried to develop an autonomous strategic culture in Europe that in the long run would lead to Europe's ensuring its own defense, it did not manage to achieve this. The real but modest progress that can be noted as regards European defense has been possible only by cooperating with Great Britain, which itself is fiercely hostile to any idea of strategic decoupling between Europe and the United States. The immense majority of Europeans do not view themselves as the ultimate guarantors of their own security. And with European enlargement, this outlook can only be reinforced because the countries of "new Europe" still sense a potential threat to their sovereignty that no European force today can protect against, and also because, paradoxically, they fear a slump in the vigor of the U.S. guarantee.

In fact, up until 1989, U.S. defense implicated defending Europe.

Since the end of the cold war, and especially since September 11, 2001, which the Americans call the "*11/9–9/11 sequence*" (November 9, 1989–September 11, 2001), this strategy has become "globalized" in that it is no longer a question of defending a territory (Europe) better to defend its own territory, but of seeing how the Europeans can contribute to what is now a deterritorialized strategy. Strategically, there is less U.S. interest in thinking about Europe as a whole, as it did during the cold war, because today it is less a matter of fighting a battle on European soil to prevent a subsequent attack against the American territory, than of seeking allies in a more global combat. In order for them to remain "in the area," to use NATO jargon, the United States demands of their allies an engagement outside of Europe, in other words "out of the area."[18] The United States moreover is seeking to release NATO from majority rule, because, particularly since the war in Kosovo, they have been able to measure just how much it can limit their own margin for the maneuver.[19]

The Americans want to act locally in Europe in order to picture themselves globally in the world.[20] And in this perspective, it is less Europe as such that interests them than the EU member states taken separately. To this end, they are absolutely determined to weigh their engagement in Europe very carefully. Their stand against Germany being granted a permanent seat on the UN Security Council to punish it for its nonalignment during the war in Iraq, and so as not to rile London, shows that the question of the U.S. preference for a strong or weak Europe is purely academic. Between a Europe united behind them and a Europe divided, the United States will always prefer a united Europe. But if this united Europe came to view itself in terms of a "counterweight," an American preference for disunity would win out. To be convinced of this, suffice it to examine how the United States did everything in its power to prevent the European Galileo satellite project from getting off the ground, in order to maintain the asymmetrical relationship between the United States and Europe as regards satellite communications.[21] They fear that in the long run Europe will have its own instruments, particularly for military intelligence, which is obviously not without consequence with regard to the controversy on weapons of mass destruction in Iraq. Countries such as France and Germany cast doubt on the way the Americans interpreted satellite photos, but they had no counterproof to back up their suspicions.

The first option offered to European power is thus that of *implementing* its strategy with all the limits that we have briefly mentioned. But this choice is only one among others. It is possible to imagine—and in the case of Europe, the hypothesis is borne out—that an actor that is not the ultimate guarantor of its own security practices *avoidance* or, in other words, the more or less pronounced refusal to take an interest in the consequences of this lack of autonomy. Avoidance can be interpreted as the accepted interiorization of this inferiority or dependence with respect to the ultimate guarantor of one's security.

Lastly, there is a third approach that involves changing the refusal of power into a virtue, in other words, instead of avoiding power, *diverting* it. Europe's entire approach to security could be considered to involve rephrasing the question of "world order" in terms of the ultimate security guarantee not only of each nation, but of the human species more than ever caught up in webs of interdependence. Taken even further, this approach can seek to banalize classical forms of national and military security and promote postmodern approaches to security, for instance, in the fields of the environment, health, or society.

In observing the political reality of Europe, fragments of these three dimensions are easy to spot: fragments of the quest for power (including from a military standpoint), a persistent refusal of power, and innovation to shift the power center toward civilian and societal areas. If Europe indeed wields power, it is *composite* to say the least. Such that when one denies that Europe has any "features" of power, it is not difficult to find counterexamples to this overly abrupt assertion. But on the other hand, in attempting to rationalize power to the point of trying to compare it to others, considerable power "deficits" can be identified. This is why thinking about European power does not boil down to piercing its "enigma" but to conceptualizing it.

This enigmatic power naturally affects how the rest of the world looks at it. Some may see a power in gestation, others the construction of a market in which only nation-states are worth considering; still others an original form of civilian or normative power. The vast array of possible ways of considering Europe naturally depends on which actor is looking at it. The fact that Europe is not a hard power is likely to make it more acceptable, less threatening, and therefore an entity easier to associate in the eyes of the rest of the world. Protest against Europe as such is a rare phenomenon indeed. An international opinion survey conducted in 18 non-European countries shows that in nearly all of them the European Union is perceived in a positive light. But certain details of the survey warrant a closer look. In Latin America, where pro-European sentiment is yet generally symmetrical to anti-American sentiment, there is one notable exception: Brazil, where European agricultural protectionism is obviously perceived as a hindrance to its power. In Asia, pro-European sentiment stands out, but what dominates in a country such as India or the Philippines is indifference toward Europe, reflected in the high rate of no-answers.[22] From indifference it is easy to slide toward a certain disdain, either because "norms over force" hardly seems a credible stance, or because it is perceived as "a second-rank player" (the strategic choices being made by its protectors—in this case the United States), or, finally, because Europe is seen only through its member states, each having specific interests and practices far removed from the principles defended by Europe. The more one touches on questions of strategy and security, the more crucial this dimension would appear.

A country such as India, for instance, has considerable trouble picturing the EU as an international actor, to such an extent that European Commissioner Mandelson has publicly expressed concerns about it: "Just as Europe should take India seriously, I want India to take Europe seriously.... I read recently a report that Indians do not think very much about the European Union. This is a shame if it is true."[23] This statement implicitly addresses a key issue: that of state sovereignty. Not only India, but also China, Russia, and

Brazil, not to mention the United States, seem to identify power only with a national power. An Indian forecasting report drafted in 2005 imagines in 2035 a tripolar world made up of the United States, India, and China. He arrives at this conclusion via a fairly simple methodology taking into account population, GDP, and per capita GDP.[24] Now if Joschka Fischer is to be believed, this is precisely the scenario the Americans are working from.[25] What is interesting in the Indian report is to see the treatment reserved for Europe. Two hypotheses are envisaged. The first is based on surrendering half the sovereignty of European states to the benefit of the European Union and to the detriment of its member states. In this case, Europe would become the fourth pillar of the world system. The second imagines a much more moderate surrender of member state sovereignty (one-fourth). In this case, the power of the European Union in 2035 would represent either 25 percent of the American power, as opposed to 50 percent in the first scenario.[26] Notwithstanding any reservations one might have with regard to a quantitative approach to power, it is interesting to see that the Indians stick to an extremely classic vision of sovereignty and power, and with regard to Europe its entire dynamic is seen from the angle of a zero-sum game between member states and the EU.

The question of sovereignty, in fact, rebounds on all aspects of Euro-Indian relations in that the Indians cannot help but be wary of a European project that seeks to erode the sovereignty of its members—and thus of its partners—whereas India is striving by all possible means to enhance its power as a nation.[27] For the Indians, for instance, the notion of "shared sovereignty" is simply synonymous with "intergovernmental cooperation."[28] This explains the obvious misunderstanding about the shared European and Indian attachment to multilateralism. For the European Union, multilateralism constitutes a regulatory instrument aiming to advance "the common good," whereas for the Indians, it primarily represents a resource to gain U.S. recognition as a full-fledged major power.

To conceptualize Europe's power, three possible directions can be taken: that of power *achievement*, which would inevitably transform Europe from a commercial power into a global power; that of power *avoidance*, which would involve not posing the ultimate security question; and that of *diverting* it, which would involve shifting the way the world game is organized in such a way that the issue of ultimate security is no longer posed in the same terms. We must then try to ponder these three dimensions simultaneously rather than to choose one of them over the other, according to one's preferences or prejudices.

Hard Power and Soft Power

Let it be admitted, then, that Europe has constructed itself as a composite power made up of contradictory elements. But what is power? To analyze "power," Joseph Nye forged a useful classification that divides power into two categories: hard power and soft power.[29] This simple distinction has met with considerable success. But it rests rather firmly on a misunderstanding. In the current meaning given to the terms "hard power" and "soft power," the former is usually identified with military power and the second with civilian power. Naturally, a military power can also be a civilian power. This is particularly the case of the United States. In this commonly accepted meaning, military power lends credibility to civilian power, which does not have the resources to make itself heard or respected if its resources as a civilian power turn out to be insufficient. It acts as a multiplier on the content of power. This is evidenced by the fact that Europe and the United States are virtually equal in economic terms but the political statuses they enjoy are incomparable. Speaking along the same lines, it can be said that the congenital weakness of European power is, incapacity to combine the attributes of hard power with its soft power resources. And to remedy this, the creation of a European military instrument is seen by some as a decisive stage in achieving power.

Naturally, like all commonsense interpretations, this one holds several grains of truth. But its mechanistic interpretation ("let's give Europe military power in order to make it a superpower") stumbles upon countless methodical and implemental difficulties. I shall return to this later. Let us try, at this stage, to understand the distinction between hard and soft power and how it might apply to Europe.

Table 1.1 Nye's distinction between hard and soft power

	Hard power	*Soft power*
Behaviors	Command, coercion	Inducement, attraction, cooptation
Resources	Use of force, sanctions	Institutions, values, culture policies

Source: Adapted from Joseph Nye, *Soft Power. The Means to Success in World Politics*, New York, Public Affairs, 2004.

Actually, on reading Nye a little more carefully, his distinction between hard and soft power appears to cover only very imperfectly the distinction between civilian power and military power (see table 1.1). For Nye, a hard power is an actor capable of resorting not only to force but also to coercion, whereas a soft power is an actor capable of reducing and convincing other actors to accept its own preferences. A hard power inspires fear, whereas a soft power uses attraction instead of fear. Nye associates different behaviors and resources with the wielding of hard and soft power, while pointing out that hard and soft power are more complementary than opposite.[30]

Attraction and Coercion

Nye has the merit of identifying hard power not only with military power but also with coercion. The dividing line between hard and soft power is thus not recourse to force, but the passage from attraction to coercion. Naturally, at a very general level, the definition makes sense. But as soon as one tries to delve a little deeper into things, one realizes that it raises more problems than it solves. Take, for example, the matter of attractivity, it remains a very ambivalent concept. The United States attracts by the considerable opportunities that it offers individuals, by creating a climate of liberty and the opportunity to accumulate wealth quickly by working and to become part of the political community without giving up one's own origins. In this regard, it is very clearly different from continental Europe where a real wariness remains toward immigrants despite the growing demographic deficit, where the obstacles to integration are more tangible, especially in European countries that are historically fairly closed to immigration, where the procedures for starting a business are longer, and so on. Nothing better illustrates America's attractiveness from this standpoint than the phenomenon of Hollywood, which symbolizes the image that America has of itself, an image that, as everyone knows, is very largely produced by artists who very often come from abroad. The same phenomenon can be found on American university campuses, the power and influence are largely related to their capacity to attract foreign talent.[31]

But at the same time it is easy to see that the social attractiveness of the United States does not mechanically produce support for American policies. Robert Cooper pointed out rather humorously that Saddam Hussein enjoyed Hollywood movies.[32] We might even add that these same films draw their strength not so much from any automatic support they induce for the American model, but from the capacity they offer individual viewers to identify with their narratives. A filmmaker of Indian stock put down the unusual success of *Titanic* in India—unusual because Indian national film production is substantial—not so much to a fascination for America, but to the fact that the film mobilizes human resources such as emotion that Indian audiences especially value.[33] Hence there is sometimes an undeniable naïveté among certain "realists" in seeing any vehicle of American origin as potential source of American influence. Simultaneously, there is equally great naïveté among certain authors, including Nye, in analyzing "attractiveness" outside of any reference to a power struggle in which coercion still plays an essential role. If tomorrow the European Union adopts accounting norms that are much closer to the Anglo-American model than the continental model, it would not be because the former would magically be more "attractive," but because they have been defined by mainly Anglo-Saxon private actors who are concerned much more with a need to financialize economies than with outlining a less volatile conception of accounting.[34] Aware of the enormous stakes involved in implementing these new norms, the Commission in Brussels finally took charge of the dossier to renegotiate the terms of applying these new norms on the European continent. There is in fact a whole gray zone between functional attractiveness and the political pressure that is found for instance in the globalization of American legal practices.[35]

Associating the intangibility of created wealth such as information, for instance, with a mere logic of attractiveness as does Nye is thus disarmingly naïve,[36] as if there were a cause-and-effect relationship between the intangibility of a product and the stakes of power and strength attached to them. If American films take up 70 percent of European screens although European film production is numerically greater than American production,[37] it is primarily because the advertising budgets of U.S. films are now as high as their production costs and incomparably higher than European film budgets. A French film costs on the average $6.6 million to produce compared to $63.6 million for an American film. If an American film can bear such costs, it is first and foremost because production costs for a film are practically instantly recovered on the American market, with a potential $1.7 billion in tickets sales for a monolingual audience before it is even distributed in Europe. European films cannot possibly enjoy such an advantage simply because there is not the same European market for films as there is for goods. Theoretically, there is nothing to counter free circulation of artistic works. But the cultural and linguistic segmentation of Europe remains considerable. Furthermore, the fact that 80 percent of the world market for American films is dominated by seven American majors enables it to set the rules of supply: for instance, to the distribution rights for *Titanic* may be attached the purchase of rights to six other much less interesting films as a package deal.[38] This is thus a far cry from the principle of attractiveness based on the intrinsic merits of a work. And the fact remains that the proportion of American films is smaller in France than in Spain, both on the big and little screens, which shows that the discriminating variable is not attractiveness but the variety of the supply, itself made possible by the existence of a concerted policy of support for French films.[39] The political opposition demonstrated by the United States with regard to cultural diversity well indicates that "cultural attractiveness" is not independent from the economic context in which it develops. Thus if the Spanish watch many more

American films than the French do, it is because France has the means to encourage its own production and offset the American cultural influence and not because the Spanish "like" American films more than the French do.[40]

All the above goes to demonstrate, then, that it is difficult to dissociate the notion of attractiveness from power struggles and thus from a potential or actual power of coercion.

I would add a second reservation, just as important as the first. Attractiveness only very rarely refers to a homogenous or coherent representation. In the case of the United States, the attraction of the American model or American society is clearly offset by a marked hostility toward American power by virtue of the very fact that it is a power. Certainly, the sources and forms of what is called by simplification anti-Americanism are numerous and highly complex.[41]

In any event, in Europe the image of the United States has deteriorated considerably, a phenomenon that probably began with the American refusal to ratify the Kyoto protocol and amplified after the American invasion of Iraq. The most notable fact of this evolution is that it only slightly receded with the events of September 11, 2001, which should have, logically, created a sense of Atlantic solidarity in the face of terrorism.

Thus, of all the EU countries taken into account in this international opinion survey on the United States conducted by the Pew Research Center in 2006 (see table 1.2), four of them have a negative image of the United States (France, the Netherlands, Germany, and Spain) compared to two others—one that has a rather positive image (Great Britain), and the other a very positive image (Poland).

It thus appears clear that these representations result more from the conduct of American policy and from a depreciation of the American cultural model. They, therefore, have a strong potential for reversal.

In any event, the idea of attractiveness that Nye refers to in defining soft power turns out to be relatively fragile when confronted with the facts.

I have discussed attractiveness as a modality of soft power. It is time now to turn to the notion of coercion as an expression

Table 1.2 Opinions favorable to the United States in Europe (percentage of opinions expressed)

	2000	*2006*
Poland	NA	62*
Great Britain	83	56
The Netherlands	NA	45
France	62	39
Germany	78	37
Spain	50	23

Source: Figures from *The Pew Global Attitudes Project*, June 13, 2006 (www.pewglobal.org).
*2005 figures.

of hard power. As already mentioned, the field of coercion is in no way limited to the field of military power. There are some extremely powerful forms of civilian coercion, just as there are noncoercive or only slightly coercive forms of military power. Microsoft has a much stronger power of coercion than a military peacekeeping mission in Macedonia. In matters of economic coercion, Europe has undeniable resources. Because it is constituted as a unified market with codified rules, it has a great power of attraction for the major world economic players, particularly the American ones. Despite the reigning Euroskepticism, the European continent continues to be the most attractive area in the world for foreign investors.[42] This attraction as a unified market in return lends an exceptional power of legal extraterritoriality that it shares so to speak only with the United States. Thus the Commission in Brussels managed to block the merger of the two American giants, General Electrics and Honeywell Bull, by arguing that such a merger would put them in a dominant position that would harm free competition. Behind this case, like that of Microsoft sued by Europe for abuse of dominant position, lurk two conceptions of regulation and thus of international norms: one, American, privileging consumer interests; the other, European, taking into account the interests of all actors in the market. The fact remains that this economic hard power within the single market has a hard power extension in trade that is just as effective because it is also founded on the collective power invested in the Commission. That is why even when European Union defense spending is aggregated, we come up with a figure that reflects absolutely no effectiveness in terms of power. On the other hand, when Europe is said to be the largest trading power in the world (20 percent of world trade), the aggregation of national powers makes sense even naturally in terms of hard power: Europe has a power of trade coercion that is guaranteed and circumscribed by the WTO, but enhanced by its economic effectiveness. This is why the debate between hard power and soft power can be summarized as follows: hard power is a power that is feared; soft power is a power that is not feared. Often fear is prompted by military might, but the array of resources available to soft power is much broader than that. Europe has at its disposal two instruments of "fear" and thus two resources of hard power: conditional access to its market (because highly regulated) and conditional access to its institutional system through the process of accession.

The Impossible American Parallel

From there, a new question arises: isn't Europe inexorably bound to become a hard power, different from the United States but nevertheless comparable to it?

At first glance, there is no reason it should not. In fifty years of existence, Europe has figured out that it can better "make itself heard" by "speaking with one voice." The fact that the Rome Treaty provided for a de facto communitarization of Europe's trade policies points to the difficulty of escaping from the wheels of power. The fact that Airbus and Ariane, and next Galileo, are identified not only as European "achievements" but also as expressions of European power again indicates Europe's permeability to the challenges of power, with all the implications of competition, rivalry, and confrontation. It remains to be seen whether these fragments are *conductive beams* of power, taken in the sense of world power as defined above, or mere kernels of power that resist fusion. Some analysts believe they have the answer to this question. For instance, Charles Kupchan sees Europe calmly advancing on the road to a centralized authority comparable to American centralization in the nineteenth century.[43] He interprets Javier Solana's nomination as High Representative for the Common Foreign and Security Policy as the birth of European diplomacy—whereas the means available to him are trifling and his power purely rhetorical—and credulously takes all the professions of faith made by European leaders literally, however contradictory they may be to or cruelly belied by the facts. Joschka Fischer's famous appeal in 2001 in favor of a European federation signaling the demise of the Monnet method and calling for a leap toward political integration is naively deemed congruent with Tony Blair's message regarding a strong Great Britain in a strong Europe.[44] Oddly enough, such a declaration is seen as nothing short of the emergence of "supranationalism" in which states and institutions would "coexist comfortably."[45] The call of power is supposedly irresistible due to its alleged correspondence with European well-understood interests.[46] Wherefore the "tipping point" rhetoric that now supposedly obliges Europe to choose between "power" and "impotence" whereas it is constantly maneuvering so as not to have to take this route without for all that relinquishing the idea of making headway. If there is any lesson to be drawn from the failure of the constitutional treaty, it is indeed Europeans' reluctance to conceive of Europe beyond the "concrete achievements" creating a "de facto solidarity" that Schuman mentioned in a famous speech, achievements he contrasted with what he called "a single plan."[47]

In an equally optimistic but perhaps less rigorous vein, Jeremy Rifkin also sees in the defunct Constitutional Treaty "the first transnational government in history whose regulatory powers supercede the territorial powers of the members that make it up."[48] At the price of a terrible misinterpretation, he likens this document to the creation of a transnational political institution designed to make the European Union function like a state.[49]

Thus, Europe is said to be on the road to political unity because the stakes are too high for national resistance to sabotage it.[50] The teleology of European integration seems alive and well even if the clichés used to express it are apparently more often uttered by "benevolent" Americans than wary Europeans.

Rifkin rightly recalls that the European approach differs from the American approach. But by presenting the Constitutional Treaty as "something quite new in human history," a document that can "build a perpetual peace, and nurture a global consciousness,"[51] one can legitimately ask whether the author has not finally left the ground of analytical rigor for ideological fantasy. In the face of an American political elite that is deeply skeptical of Europe's ability to assert itself but at the same time determined to prevent it from doing so, American Europhiles are seeking to rehabilitate Europe and encouraging Americans to take it seriously. This is what Kupchan and Rifkin basically mean. They must hence be taken for what they are: pro-European professions of faith aimed to counterbalance the Europe-bashing that Republicans are so fond of.[52] In addition, analyses of power have trouble shedding the state schema. That means that if power no longer lies with the state, then it can be only a super state power. And if it is not a super state, then Europe has no other choice then to unite on the model of a super state, maybe not like others, but a super state all the same. In short, if Europe wants to make itself heard, it cannot escape some degree of political centralism. True, nonstate forms of power exist that have been well identified in the literature on transnationalism. But there are loci of power where circumventing the nation-state as a form is simply impossible because international reality remains at least in part so highly structured by states. Germany's demand for a permanent seat on the UN Security Council could, for instance, be viewed as preposterous with respect to other power issues. But as long as it has not been explained why a supposedly preposterous question of status continues to be seen as essential by a state and its population, people will analyze international reality the way they want it to be and not the way it is.[53] Therein lies the problem of defining Europe as a potentially diverse actor. Diversity naturally has a number of advantages. But in terms of power, it is undeniably a hindrance.[54]

Wherefore the tempting parallel made with the political structure of the United States, a parallel that American international relations specialists cannot help but make, especially when their subjectivity leads them to "support" the European project.

Yet between the American and European approach, there are glaring differences. The most fundamental of them has to do with the fact that the building of the American nation started with the existence of an American *demos* (the American people), whereas in Europe this assumption is neither made nor intended. Joseph Weiler even takes this a step further in saying that starting with the Rome Treaty, Europeans rejected the federal state model when speaking of an "ever closer union of European people."[55] True, there is a descending order of norms that legally corresponds fairly well with the American federal model. But the parallel existence of an authority with ascending power sets it radically apart.[56] Intellectually, European integration is thus destabilizing, because it creates a hierarchy of norms that clearly subordinate juridical monopoly of states to a European norm without creating a corresponding political community.[57] Europe has managed to create a body of norms that govern it and on which it is based, but not an entity capable of symbolizing it.

There is no doubt that certain European federalists have been tempted to or have tried to take advantage of the debate surrounding the constitution precisely to take that symbolic step toward a European *demos.* But besides the fact that European member states put a brake on such ardors during the Intergovernmental Conference, it must be pointed out that the advocates of a constitutionalization of Europe—at least on the books—were not necessarily in favor of European federalism. Valéry Giscard d'Estaing for instance was both a champion of the "constitutionalization of Europe" and at the same time the greatest partisan of an intergovernmental Europe that we now know is impracticable in a Europe with 25 members. And this is indeed the conception that finally won out because ratification of the Constitutional Treaty has remained subject to the principle of unanimity, whereas the Constitution of the United States came into force even before the state of New York had ratified it.[58] That means that the U.S. Constitution had posited from the start the existence of an American *demos* that transcended the sovereignty of the various states, whereas Europe has refused such a perspective and seems likely to refuse it for a long time to come.

To understand Europe, one must, therefore, try to refrain from comparing it too hastily to the United States.

If Europe can thus not be thought of in American terms, then what terms should be used to analyze it? The commonsense answer is to say that there is no model for Europe and that it constitutes a sui generis construction. The argument is impossible to counter, except that Europe is caught up in a world game that forces it to position itself with respect to extant forms of political organization that are comparable by definition and, especially, finite in number. There are yardsticks of power against which it is simply impossible not to measure oneself unless one admits to one's inferiority. Europeans can always argue that their power is not like the power of others, but at the UN, the WTO, the IMF, or on battlefields it is obliged to choose between unity and plurality. There is, at the base of it, a contradiction between an international system whose raw logics understand only binary terms (power versus impotence) and an aesthetics of European power that seeks to get beyond this duality without being sure it wants to or without always knowing how to go about it.

Power with No Anchoring Point

Can Europe pull out of this dilemma and this difficulty? Probably not, because as long as there is no European *demos*, there can hardly be a European power in the traditional sense of the term. From that perspective, the rejections of the Constitutional Treaty can be interpreted as another refusal of Europeans to conceive of themselves as a *demos* even if, paradoxically, the draft text hardly went in this direction. It was closer to "rules of association" than a foundational act. Introducing the very word "Constitution," to which we associate belonging to a people, exacerbated the fears of those who were afraid of losing their identity as a "national people."[59] For lack of a European *demos*, Europe is thus not in a position to construct a new postnational historical narrative. Certainly, after the war, it managed to produce a narrative structured around the "memory of the war." But this remarkably effective narrative has run out of steam. Not that peace is naturally lasting. But the idea that there is a very slim chance of the peoples of the European Union ever going to war against one another has undeniably been internalized. "Up to now, it was enough to say that European integration was a guarantee of peace. But this argument leaves the younger generation cold. A dream come true no longer makes people dream."[60]

The memory of war thus is not enough to foster the progress of Europe. What is more, the "memory of the war" did not imply the emergence of a European *demos*. It merely aspired to the fact that the *demoi* of Europe would no longer make war on each other. This is why the ritual and sometimes overwhelming appeals for the emergence of a new European narrative are thus at risk of continuing to spin in a void if the question of a European *demos* is not raised. Europe lacks a strong symbol, a basic signifier that gives meaning to and anchors the multiple signifieds Europe produces, though not without some degree of success in fact: peace, stability, prosperity, networks, governance, and so on. The result is a discursive deficit that recalls what Lacan called the *point de capiton*, the anchoring point:

> Whether it be a sacred text, a novel, a play, a monologue, or any conversation whatsoever, allow me to represent the function of the signifier by a spatializing device... I shall call the *anchoring point* this point around which any concrete analysis of discourse must operate.[61]

Is there a means for Europe to find itself an anchoring point without a common *demos*? The question is thus posed. The fact remains that the absence of a European *demos* must be the starting point to understand the unlikely conversion of Europe to the logic of a hard power.

If Europe does not constitute a *demos*, it has no reason to conceive of its security and survival in identical terms. Certainly, there are joint threats and common challenges Europe must face, globalization being one of them. And as we shall see, it is at this level that Europe can be a useful and effective actor. But global threats in no way diminish local threats. Globalism does not destroy localism. A good grasp on postmodernity does not involve thinking that political forms succeed one another on a stage where the actors' business is clearly blocked out. On the contrary, they are constantly intertwined. Nothing prevents a Lithuanian from feeling concerned by the greenhouse effect, while considering that its neighbor Russia will continue to threaten its independence for a long time to come. Under such conditions, it has no need to choose between the global and the local and consequently, between Europe—for its prosperity—and NATO—for its security. But what is true for a Lithuanian is not necessarily so for a Spaniard or a French person. European peoples do not weigh threats the same way, which means that a common, integrated defense seems very remote indeed.

Europeans Don't Share the Same History

Naturally, it is not impossible that these scales of risks will become closer and better harmonized in the long run. But for the moment, and particularly since the enlargement of Europe to the East, heterogeneity prevails, precisely because Europeans do not share the same history. Enlargement pointed up a certain heterogeneity in political timeframes in Europe that the accession mechanism alone cannot compress. The incorporation of the *acquis communautaire* does not have that function, and it would be unwise for this process to appear as an eraser of history. As a result, these societies have different relationships to security. The Central and Eastern European countries see their accession to Europe as a means of reuniting not only with their European past but also with their national history left in deep-freeze by communism. Accession to the European Union is certainly in no way contradictory with this plan. But the consequences they lead to in terms of sovereignty are not at all the same as those that prevailed at the time of the Treaty of Rome. For them, the idea of sharing their sovereignty does not make sense because they feel that their return to Europe should hail the recovery of their sovereignty. For them, membership in the Europe Union means recovering not only dignity and prosperity, but sovereignty as well. This very different relationship to sovereignty is often seriously misunderstood in "old Europe," where for some the sovereignty issue may seem obsolete.[62] But this lack of understanding has paradoxically been maintained by certain Central European leaders such as Vaclav Havel, who always expressed a preference for a Kantian postnational Europe. His article "Kosovo and the End of the Nation-State" is the strongest illustration of this.[63] Vaclav Havel's point of view, however respectable it may be, probably remains in the minority. His successor as Czech head of state, Vaclav Klaus, in some ways seems more representative of a "neoliberal sovereignism" dominant in the East that demands more political sovereignty and more neoliberalism, probably in reaction to the Soviet system. Carried to its extreme, this vision leads to a rejection of Europe because Europe is viewed as a machine to share sovereignties and regulate economies, to prevent too much social deregulation. But there are an infinite number of beliefs—including those in the East—many of which hold accession to Europe to be compatible with their recovered national sovereignty. The only point common to all these beliefs is the fact that they are not spontaneously receptive to the idea of Europe as a power precisely because they may see therein a form of federalist power in contradiction to their sovereignty. They are even less in favor of it if such power is conceived as a means of emancipating Europe with respect to the United States. For them, everything possible should be done to prevent an American withdrawal from Europe and everything should be undertaken to grant the United States the real or symbolic quid pro quos that it demands in exchange (e.g., support for sending troops to Iraq). Under such conditions, being pro-European and pro-American is in no way contradictory, but on the contrary perfectly complementary: Europe is supposed to bring them prosperity, and America, security.[64]

It could certainly be argued that this reality is not set in stone and is thus transitory. I will not disagree with that, with the caveat that in the long run, accession to Europe will necessarily lead to a French-style European power. It must, however, not be believed that this resistance to Europe as a power, with all the voluntarism and distantiation from the United States that it implies, constitutes a mark of defiance to France alone. Nothing guarantees that British calls for "liberal European imperialism" receive any real assent in Eastern or Northern Europe.[65] The Central and Eastern European countries' backing of Washington in Iraq seems to be guided more by a very narrow nationalistic calculation than by some political-ideological messianism. The gradual withdrawal of East European troops from Iraq confirms this hypothesis.

For there too, one of the lessons of the Dutch referendum was the reactiviation of national sentiment, against all expectations, in countries thought to be "sated" and already postnational since they have been engaged in European integration for over 50 years. Naturally, the Dutch sovereignist reaction does not have at all the same connotations as Czech or Polish sovereignism. With the Dutch, like with other Northern Europeans, sovereignty refers to a peaceful, liberal lifestyle, particularly jealous of its protection from "political" interferences. To them it is Europe and not NATO that would appear to jeopardize such sovereignty.

For the French in particular, it may seem strange for Europe to be identified with an erosion of sovereignty and NATO with its preservation. But that is nevertheless the way the vast majority of countries in Central, Eastern, and Northern Europe as well as the United Kingdom—all for different reasons—view things. And that is why Europe's conversion into a hard power in the sense given here seems unlikely, even supposing it were desirable.

This state of things is apparently contradicted by European opinion polls that regularly highlight the rise in demand for a common foreign and security policy for all Europeans.[66] But these professions of faith should be read with caution. First, because, out of principle, few Europeans have any reason to be against common action on the world scene. Second, because setting up a common foreign and security policy takes on meaning only when it involves real arbitrations for the European member states: between European sovereignty and national sovereignty, or between military spending and civil spending. Now on these two planes, the slim margin for European states to conduct such dual arbitrations is continually narrowing.

Structurally, all European member state apparatuses are reluctant to see themselves stripped of their political sovereignty, especially if these resources are residual. Even if it may seem that it is absurd for Europe to maintain 21 navies and 22 armies, which of these will be sacrificed? Here we enter registers where the symbolic is totally impermeable to Community method or a military reorganization rationale modeled on industrial reorganizations.[67]

The difficulty is compounded when converting to power involves real financial arbitrations. Even Germany, which owing to the Iraq crisis gave a spectacular demonstration of its political and affective dissociation from the United States, seems to have no desire to draw lessons from this emancipation to rethink its relationship to power from a military standpoint, for instance.

However, because Europe remains an open, diverse, and pluralistic space, it is by definition laced with contradictory forces.

European armies cannot be rationalized merely from a managerial perspective. But the power of the economic constraints that military programs are up against can lead to the rationalization of national arms production programs and their interoperability and possibly to common doctrines for using these forces. This is the context in which to interpret the creation of a European Defense Agency or the Franco-British project to build an aircraft carrier, which should enable both states to have two aircrafts carriers constructed jointly in order to reduce the prohibitive costs of such projects. Thus the harmonization of equipment programs and the pooling of military research programs would constitute considerable progress on the road to European defense. It would reflect the "concrete solidarities"—the only ones that have proven their effectiveness in Europe in the past 50 years—and would offer tangible advantages to each state.

Furthermore, even if the French discourse on Europe as a power remains misunderstood—or rejected because too well understood—European opinions and elites seem more sensitive to the need to act in the world, including via military action, as long as this projection does not fit within any strategy of power or domination (Germany) or if it intervenes in areas where the United States has only secondary interests (Macedonia, Africa).

The organization of 13 battle groups to be set up by 2007—able to deploy European forces within 10 days as far as 6,000 km from Europe's borders for as long as 120 days, which has been approved by 20 member states of the EU[68]—attests to the will to extend European power mentioned above. But the existence of fragments of military power is not the premonitory sign of a European power in gestation and even less so of a superpower.

All the same, it is highly likely that in the coming years the requirements of the fight against terrorism will probably relegate the urgency for a common defense policy to the back burner, even if the two priorities are not incompatible. But in this area, sharing sovereignty proves to be an extremely thorny problem. Differences in legislation and the interpretation of individual rights have already reduced the effectiveness of the European arrest warrant.[69] Moreover, the European member states seem extremely reluctant to share intelligence in the fight against terrorism, reducing the European antiterrorism coordinator's role to one of a mere facilitator.[70] On the other hand, major states such as France seem to have a preference for intergovernmental cooperation; it has, in fact, established extremely close relations with the United States in this area.[71]

CHAPTER 2

Norms over Power

It is generally acknowledged that Europe will not be a superpower in the sense of a political-military ensemble on an equal footing with the United States or China. Europeans reject this possibility across the board. Moreover, even if they wanted to go that route, would it not expose them to reproducing on a European scale what they have struggled to combat amongst themselves: the idea of becoming a great power with all the attributes of force and supremacy that such a project implies?[1]

So if Europe will not be a superpower, how can it be a power at all? Probably by reinforcing what remains its major political resource: its capacity to produce and set up at the global level a system of norms as broad-sweeping as possible to organize the world, discipline the interplay of its actors, introduce predictability in their behavior, develop among them a sense of collective responsibility, and offer those who engage on this path, particularly the weakest, at least some possibility of using these norms as an argument against all, including the world's most powerful.

The task may seem colossal, even outrageous. It probably is, but does Europe have any other choice but to assume its responsibility as a normative power? Probably not.

Normative Power: The Genealogy of a Concept

The academic debate on European power has been and remains closely indexed on commonsense representations of this power as well as on the dominant interpretations or those in vogue in the international system. Between the abortive attempt of the EDC (European Defense Community) in the early 1950s and the early 1970s, this question was virtually absent from the debate simply because the instruments for action outside of Europe were limited to its trade and development aid policies. These instruments were not yet perceived as a palpable source of decline in state sovereignty and even less so as a source of internal social debates, as trade policy has become since the creation of the WTO. The issue did not reemerge until the early 1970s with the publication of works by François Duchêne and Johan Galtung.[2] Several explanations contribute to understanding this relative resurgence of interest:

The first is a result of the initial enlargement in which the major European powers (France, Great Britain) would coexist in a common political framework. The second is the opening of the East-West corset in the wake of détente and the Chinese-American rapprochement. And last, the energy crisis confronted Europe with its first major test of cohesion reflected not only in the difficulty Europeans had in defining a common strategy, but also in the United States' irritation at seeing one emerge. This was the context in which Kissinger made his famous complaint about the lack of a "telephone number for Europe," and this is still the image that is used symbolically every time the definition of a common European policy crops up again. These empirical facts about the changing international system are confirmed on an academic level by the emergence of a whole body of interdependentist literature that emphasizes the retreat of interstate dynamics giving way to economic interactions and insists on the growing obsolescence of military tools.[3]

Even if Duchêne's and Galtung's definitions rest on very different premises, they agree on two essential points: Europe is destined to be a power, but it can achieve this only via means that differ from those used historically by European nation-states and on different terms than those of the two superpowers of the period.

According to Duchêne, the axis of European power can only be one of a civil power, in other words, only as an actor capable of contractualizing world relations on the basis of treaties and conventions that would reduce the benefit of resorting to force. According to him, Europe's contribution to international politics should be a sense of shared responsibility and structures of political contractualization.[4] In his mind, Europe cannot be a military power because such a perspective is so entirely antithetical to the project of its founders. He sees in what was not yet called the European Union a driving idea, the "power over opinion," oddly borrowed from Edwar Carr, the father of realism in international relations theory, but who already in 1962 placed this form of power on the same lines as military or economic power.[5] The power of ideas is also very present in Galtung's writing, in which the underlying Marxist idealism leads this scholar to conceptualize the power of ideas through ideology. In Galtung's mind, Europe is not inclined to either reward or punish (classic attributes of power) but to influence the world with its ideas. Europe would thus constitute a third way between the United States and the USSR. The possibility of becoming a power by taking another route than the Westphalian path it has usually followed thus fueled early discussion on Europe's place in the world.

In the early 1980s, it was an article by Hedley Bull—father of the British realist school and Carr's successor—that rekindled the debate, this time on more Manichean bases. In Bull's mind, to talk about civilian power is a contradiction in terms, for there can be no power without military power.[6] But this verdict needs to be contextualized. In the early 1980s, Europe once again became a sensitive issue in East-West rivalry due to the deployment of Euromissiles. Bull argued in favor of a European military power that would be capable of preventing an American withdrawal and neutralizing the continent. But he did not at all discuss the issue of the communitarization of this policy. For Bull, the priority was to make way for a middle road between Atlanticism and neutralism.[7]

This return to Europe's geopolitical realities was not to last. The gradual weakening followed by the collapse of the USSR on the contrary reinvigorated interdependentist and post-Westphalian interpretations of the international system and Europe's place in this new process.[8]

In 1990, Maull reintroduced the concept of civilian power in the debate, using a comparison between Germany and Japan.[9] Not only in Maull, but also in Twichett, who picked up on Duchêne's idea in 1976,[10] the definition of civilian power, however, remains very classical: a preference for peaceful conflict settlement and the use of a binding multilateral framework to organize the international system.

It was not really until after the Maastricht Treaty was signed that the question of a community actor in international politics was again raised, this time with an intention to consider the way in which a sui generis actor that is less than a state but much more than an interstate organization can act on the world scene. It was Christopher Hill who paved the way to reconsider this in clear opposition to Bull's remarks when, 10 years earlier, he indicated that Europe "is not an actor in international affairs, and does not seem likely to become one."[11] Christopher Hill primarily set out to take the then European Community seriously by identifying the areas in which it could become a power as an actor in its own right, and different from the member states. There is, of course, nothing original about the areas in which Hill imagined a specific action on the part of the European Community, all the more so since they were dealt with too succinctly to be assessed properly.[12] This attempt at formalization, however, contains two new ideas. The first, an unusual position for a British academic to hold, is to view Europe as a counterweight to the United States after the collapse of the USSR. The second is to conceive of the European Community as a specific actor toward which strong demands converge emanating from countries outside of it and which, by this very fact, finds itself confronted with the challenge of a disproportion between these demands and the means at its disposal.[13] Thus we clearly enter into a phase in which Europe is now seen as a specific actor, even if this specific actor is perceived, rightly so, not as a state in its holistic form, but as a system that for a long time to come will combine national policies, intergovernmental policies, and common policies.[14]

Nonetheless, for a long time fairly little research was done on external EU action and in any case it remained incomparably weak with regard to the immense body of literature devoted to the political integration of Europe. Moreover, even when it exists, it seems much more interested in the procedural dimensions of Europe's external action than in its content or its finalities.[15]

Finally, it was not until Ian Manners's article on normative power published in 2002 that the academic debate got rolling again.[16] Manners in fact takes as a starting point a definition given a few years earlier by Rosencrance, who defined Europe as a normative rather than an empirical power. For Rosencrance, *normative power* refers to the idea of setting world standards, in contrast to *empirical power*, which imposes itself by conquest or physical domination.[17]

Manners thus starts with the assumption, that the specificity of the European Union rests on post-Westphalian norms, in other words, he shifts the focus for assessing and interpretating Europe's role beyond the usual focus on means of power.[18] What Manners suggests, and therein lies his originality, is that Europe's role in the world cannot be understood by simply comparing it to other states. As it is assumed to be post-Westphalian, it makes no sense to compare Europe to Westphalian states. Manners considers this preference for norms with respect to the principles on which the political integration of Europe has been based since 1950: peace, freedom, and defense of human rights (to which he adds, on a more minor note, social solidarity, the rejection of discrimination, and sustainable development).[19] Prior to Manners, Christiansen had also mentioned the normative foundations of Europe, while Weiler referred to its founding ideals and Laffan to its normative pillar.[20] How are these values placed in the service of EU external action and how do they manage to become performative, that is, capable of exerting a concrete effect on global political processes beyond national frameworks? In other words, the question Manners poses is to know how a post-Westphalian actor can actually promote post-Westphalian norms. Manners then tries to resolve this general question empirically by showing how the fight against the death penalty, widely promoted by the European Union, ended up emerging as a global standard.[21]

The set of issues surrounding normative power provided a means of rekindling the debate on the role of the European Union in the world by shifting the grounds of analysis. And present research places itself on these new grounds. However, I believe that Manners's approach—confirmed by other research—has revealed its true limits in that it simply leads to equating Europe's normative action on the global scene with the ideals on which Europe integration is based.

The Conceptual Foundations of Normative Power

Whatever its limits may be, I find the concept of normative power highly valuable, for it indeed corresponds to a certain vision of the world. This vision is inspired by what is known as the "constructivist" school of thought. Given the extent to which it conditions Europe's worldview, it is useful to say a few words about it here. Constructivism is based on the Weberian idea that human beings are cultural beings that have the capacity and desire to give meaning to the world. Unlike facts of nature (water, mountains, population, or the law of gravity) that exist independent of the meaning given to them, social facts (such as money, property rights, sovereignty, marriage, sports scores, celebrations, processions, or rituals) exist only with respect to the meaning conferred on them and the shared social significations regarding these facts. Thus they are by definition "constructed," not natural. Behind all these facts there is a sort of collective intentionality.

Applied to the international system, constructivism naturally conceives international reality as being constructed on the basis of material facts (wealth, strength) as well as values that reflect a collective intentionality. Such that from a constructivist perspective the very purpose of studying international relations involves analyzing state identities and interests by trying to determine how these identities and interests are socially constructed.[22] Constructivism for instance would have a great deal of difficulty accepting the fact that realpolitik constitutes a sort of natural law of international relations. It would instead see them as the effect of shared beliefs.[23] Because it believes that social reality is manufactured, constructivism naturally ends up attaching a particular importance to the institutions in which social norms are devised. Through socialization, negotiation, and consultation, institutions produce norms, rules, and procedures that which constrain the behavior of states toward convergence. Constructivism and institutionalism thus quite naturally overlap.[24] For constructivists, states are "social actors" and not "cold monsters." Realists naturally do not share this interpretation precisely because they do view states as "cold monsters" whose behaviors and identities are supposedly stable over time.[25]

Realists consider the world order as an anarchic order that is pointless to seek to tame via norms because of the radical discontinuity between internal order and external order. In this perspective, the focal element is not the underlying norms and institutional processes but the distribution of capacities among dominant actors.[26] They attach only secondary importance to the way in which state interests are constructed or altered. These are assumed to be stable, even intangible, as a result.

However summary, this overview of the contrasting theories shows which direction Europe leans toward. Europe by definition cannot see itself in the "realist" terms of power politics because it is not a state. It is itself a highly institutionalized political construct that from the start has rejected realistic determinism. In fact, a realist view of Europe in the aftermath of the Second World War would have led to supposing that the Franco-German antagonism would one day be revived because the interests of the two states were mechanically opposed. Now it is precisely to counter this deterministic and realistic mechanism that Jean Monnet envisaged an economic and institutional system capable of releasing France and Germany from this "inevitable polarization." There was hardly anything idealistic and even less so unrealistic about Monnet's constructivism, because it functioned on very concrete bases. But it provided proof that there was nothing intangible about the supposed realism of states. Even when they are "realist," states can conceive of "realism" in different ways.

At this stage in my reasoning, it is easy to understand that European power draws its meaning in a constructivist view of the world order—an order in which processes matter as much as structures.

Behind the idea of process, there is a close association between norms and institutions. This association is highly understandable. Institutions are real or symbolic spaces in which rules and practices common to all actors involved in a given game (WTO rules, for instance) will be manufactured and legitimated to produce norms.

I define norms here as the basis for standards of behavior admitted by the actors of the game. International relations theorists, always fond of subtle categorizations, tend to distinguish three types of norms: *regulating norms*, those that generate collective discipline (trade rules or respect for procedures in the areas of nuclear proliferation, for instance); *constitutive norms,* those that create new categories of actors or action (greenhouse gas emission permits as provided by the Kyoto Protocol); and *prescriptive norms* that indicate what should be done in the name of admitted principles.[27] This formalism is not necessarily pointless. But in reality, these three types of norms overlap considerably. All international social norms have a prescriptive dimension. In recommending what should be done, they implicitly define what should not be done. Moreover, as soon as a norm tries to discipline actors in a new area, it perforce generates new actors, new interests, or new categories of action. If one adheres to the Kyoto Protocol, then one adheres to prescriptive norms (reduce greenhouse gas emissions), regulating norms (states are bound to a certain discipline), and constitutive norms (a market for greenhouse gas emissions will be created).

This is not the only way of distinguishing between norms. A distinction can be introduced also between procedural norms—those that indicate steps to take—and behavioral norms—those that are concerned with the content of action. Lastly, we can distinguish between norms that are binding or not. From the viewpoint of a norm's effectiveness, that is a decisive criterion. In a highly norm-based world system in which the production of norms moreover leads to setting up implementation mechanisms and sanctions, norms can make a difference. On the other hand, in a world system in which the control and sanction mechanisms are weak, the value of norms is reduced. This naturally poses the crucial question of a norm's legitimacy.[28] In evaluating Europe's performance as a normative power, this point is essential. I shall return to it.

What Is a Normative Power?

The notion of normative power, popularized by Ian Manners, is actually not very far from the notion of civilian power defined by François Duchêne.[29] The first to talk about normative power is Robert Rosencrance, for whom Europe, after having been imperialist, has sought to influence the world through a certain number of driving ideas.[30] A normative power is, therefore, a power that has its identity and strategy grounded on a preference for overarching rules of behavior applicable—largely but not exclusively—to states and that has three essential characteristics: to have been negotiated and not imposed; to have been legitimated equally by representative international bodies; and to be enforceable on all actors of the international system notwithstanding their rank within it. Normative power thus seeks the integration of a world order based on the legitimacy of rules, the predictability of behavior, and especially the enforceability of accepted principles. Naturally, European power is not a de facto power able to achieve these three aims, but it is by reference to this ideal type that it situates itself as a power. What are these norms? They are constructed on the principles of democracy, the rule of law, social justice, and human rights. These principles are said to have been laid down in 1973 during the European summit in Copenhagen, which was one of the first to take an interest in the international identity of what was not yet called the European Union.[31] These principles were expanded, again in Copenhagen, in 1993. At that time, the issue was to define accession criteria to the European Union, which even today are the primary features of Europe's international identity, with the only caveat being that they have no geographic limitation: market economy, democracy, respect for human rights and minorities, respect for the rule of law. In addition to these principles, Ian Manners adds social solidarity, the fight against all forms of discrimination, and sustainable development.[32]

In a way, Romano Prodi truly summarized the idea of normative power when he said, "It is not imperialism to want to spread these principles and to share our model of society with the peoples of Southern and Eastern Europe who aspire to peace, justice and freedom. Indeed, Europe must go further. We must aim to become a global civil power at the service of sustainable global development."[33]

It is obvious that all these ideas and all these discourses are important to understand the power of Europe. Speech is constitutive of reality and that should be taken seriously into account. The risk, and it is a real one, is nevertheless to confuse "normative power" with the power of an idea—in other words, "ideal power," in which everything would be a matter of values and principles and never one of interests.

Ian Manners, for instance, presents sustainable development as a normative reference for Europe—which is hardly debatable—but never questions the whys and wherefores of this preference. European norms are seen as transcendental values overarching European societies. As a consequence there is a considerable risk of idealizing Europe, all the more so since the question of the effectiveness of norms has not really been posed. Manners dwells on Europe's influence on the movement to abolish the death penalty throughout the world.[34] But although the issue is symbolically powerful, it is admittedly perhaps not the best illustration of what could be called a normative power.

For this reason, while I consider the relationship to norms essential to understanding the enigma of European power, I believe it is indispensable to qualify this preference over and above any sort of idealization. To do so, I will proceed in two stages. The first involves exploring why Europe prefers norms. The second, understanding what concrete social preferences these norms reflect.

Why Does Europe Prefer Norms?

Norms are a core feature of European integration because they constitute the only tool for States trying to share their sovereignty the main. Norms are what enable Europe to go beyond individual state sovereignty without abolishing it.[35] In this regard, there is an indissociable relationship between norm and sovereignty. The more a European norm is binding, the more state sovereignty is weakened, even if it is the states themselves that have manufactured this norm and have no qualms about releasing themselves from its bonds if they become too constricting. The various metamorphoses of the Stability Pact demonstrate this.

In building Europe, the preeminence of norms answers three concerns. The first has to do with neutralizing the most conflictual aspects of state political sovereignty to replace them with a stable, lasting, and predictable cooperative model that should gradually lead these very European states to stop thinking of their interests in terms of a zero-sum game. Already starting with the ECSC (European Coal and Steel Community), the European project was a model of decentering the honor of European nations. At first, the point was to destroy the bellicose instinct that had torn apart European nations. But for all that, the disappearance of this instinct did not anesthetize state self-centeredness. Such that with each new stage of European integration, new norms had to be invented to discipline states, without making them formally give up their sovereignty. Norms in Europe have always tried to circumvent state sovereignty. The example of the euro illustrates this rather well.

When the ECB (European Central Bank) was set up, the countries in the euro zone deliberately gave it a very narrow mandate: to ensure price stability. This narrow mandate contrasts with the U.S. Federal Reserve for which the fight against inflation has never been an end in itself, but the condition for growth.[36] Thus on one hand, there is the ECB, dogmatically attached to enforcing a norm imposed by the member states (no more than 2 percent inflation per year); on the other hand, an American fed for which the main thing is not to enforce a norm but to achieve a balance between expected results and risks taken.[37]

Why then do we have, on one hand, an American monetary policy based on weighing risks and, on the other, a European policy constructed on scrupulous respect for norms? The answer is simple. The case of the United States involves an independent institution of a single state. In the case of the ECB, there is a single currency but it comes under several sovereign states. The latter agreed to give up their monetary sovereignty only on condition that the ensuing loss was closely framed. A central bank that would fight against inflation was acceptable, but not a central bank that might end up supervising the economic policy of all the countries in the euro zone. Thus the norm here aims to limit the ECB's authority to prevent it from intruding in budgetary policies, which have remained national.

However, it was quickly realized that a monetary policy that did not take budgetary policies into account contained a threat of economic paralysis, even more so since controlling inflation without controlling budgetary overspending is a very delicate exercise. So what did Europe do? It could have broadened the ECB's mandate following the Fed model. But the European states would not hear of it. How could they reconcile budgetary sovereignty and budgetary discipline? By creating a new norm, enshrined in the Stability and Growth Pact. This pact prohibits states from exceeding a budgetary deficit of 3 percent in all cases other than "exceptional circumstances." In a unified state, these circumstances would be submitted to deliberation. But in Europe, such an approach is hardly possible because either the responsibility would be entrusted to the Commission, for instance, at the risk of dispossessing states, or the states would be allowed to discuss the matter, which is obviously not without risk. So it was decided to circumvent the political problem by creating a new norm, one that would define what exceptional circumstances meant in budgetary matters.[38] Here we can clearly see that every time Europe comes up against a policy that is uncertain or unpredictable and touches on sovereignty, it manufactures a norm. Such an exercise obviously carries certain risks and has already demonstrated its real limits. For although it generates collective discipline, it also produces political rigidity and especially pits norms against politics. Norms thus appear as a sort of metavalue aimed to tame indisciplined states. Taken to its logical conclusion, this reasoning leads to considering that policy constraints—including national ones—are unhealthy constraints that one must break free of in order to enable a supposedly superior European rationality to triumph. The whole question is to know what legitimacy principle this supposedly superior rationality obeys, especially if it implicitly aims to devalue national legitimacies that nevertheless have the benefit of having been approved by democratic vote.

The desire to circumvent politics, or more precisely the constraints of politics, largely explains the decisive role that norms play in the political integration of Europe. But this essential factor does not explain everything. It also has to do with the way in which Europe has been built as a legal construction. Indeed, right from the start, implementation of the four freedoms (free circulation of goods, capital, services, and workers) has given rise to a body of rules laid down by the Commission, themselves complemented by a sizable body of European Community case law.[39] Furthermore, in a process built on chain-type model, norms beget norms, either to specify what was not made explicit in the first place, or to solve a problem that did not previously exist, or to deal with a related sector. Moreover, as states gradually agreed to extend the EU's competences, Europe's normative provisions naturally had to be extended as well.

European Governance and Global Governance

European governance is thus dominated by the centrality of norms. But it is not reduced to that. Added to that is a three-tiered method of governance. First are "communitarized" policies, in other words, those placed under the Commission's responsibility. Then come harmonized policies that obligate EU member states to harmonize but not unify their norms, which are designed on the state's initiative. It is especially the stock of harmonized norms that makes up the bulk of the *acquis communautaire*. Lastly, there is the strategy invented at the Lisbon conference, the open method of coordination (OMC). The level of constraint imposed on member states is much lower than in the preceding two levels. It involves simply setting common policy goals in the areas of research or employment, for instance, it being up to each state to implement them with the means at its disposal.

The central question of sovereignty can be found at each of the three levels. At the level of common policies state subordination to the Commission is accepted; at the harmonization level, we are in the realm of shared competencies; and in the open method of coordination, states remain in control of the game. Moreover, the fact that the OMC was invented in Europe shows plainly that the EU member states have no desire to go any further in economic or political integration, which explains the rough-and-ready settlement between a European "benchmarking" that is supposed to stimulate "laggards" and the freedom of initiative left to the states to achieve it.

This European construction is in fairly close symbiosis with systems of world governance in which basically the same configuration can be found: (1) global public goods subject to the establishment of supranational and not only intergovernmental systems; (2) the whole array of areas affected by world regulation that requires intense cooperation between states in order to produce common and harmonized rules, such as the WTO; and (3) areas of action in which states commit to common objectives but where there is no one to control them, monitor them, and even less punish them. Europe's way of seeking to "sell" the idea of governments on the world scale contains all the arguments that are precisely at the heart of European governance: the first of them involves saying that norms are negotiated among political actors having different degrees of power (Luxembourg is not Germany), thus serving as an equalizer in terms of power. The second is to insist on the fact that they are negotiated within the framework of international bodies that thereby have a certain degree of legitimacy. Lastly, that these norms are enforceable on all, including the most powerful, should incite even the weakest to support them. The whole European discourse at the WTO thus aims to convince developing countries that it is in their interest to participate in a norm-based rationale of governance and that it alone can protect them from market and deregulation excesses.[40]

There is obviously a certain degree of porosity between European governance and global governance (see table 2.1),

Table 2.1 European governance and global governance

European governance	*Modalities*	*Global governance*
Common policies (agriculture, competition, external trade)	Mobilization of common resources managed by superstate bodies	Management of global public goods (the environment, water, health, education, etc.)
Policy harmonization (health, the environment, taxation)	Increase policy convergence without doing away with national differences	Policy harmonization (taxation, intellectual property, trade policy)
Open Method of Coordination (employment, social policy, research, etc.)	Collective commitments made to achieve common goals while respecting each country's sovereignty	Tangible public commitments (public aid, fight against poverty, debt reduction, etc.)

simply because both of them seek to solve problems that states can no longer solve on their own. But states can hardly be said to submit to the principle of responsibility—as opposed to the principle of sovereignty—harmoniously and even less so naturally. But in both cases can be found this attempt to manufacture collective norms to make progress in decision making by going beyond traditional intergovernmental agreements. The most fundamental consequence of globalization is to have highlighted problems that traditional intergovernmental cooperation can no longer handle. And on this level, Europe undeniably has considerable experience.[41]

Certainly the European model of governance cannot simply be transposed to the world scale. However, certain European collective methods of action might well prove useful for global governance. For this reason it seems more apt to talk about a European toolbox or laboratory rather than a European model.[42] This laboratory has three distinctive features that help understand why the European Union manages perhaps better than other regionalized areas to assert its citizens' social preferences over and above the channels offered by nation-states.

Europe first of all has at its disposal fragments of a public space, one of the most important of which is perhaps the European Parliament. It is after all the only transnational parliament that exists in the world, and it has limited but not marginal prerogatives. It is in any event at least an echo chamber that is particularly receptive to interests that do not directly involve states, whether they are economic, environmental, or cultural groups. The European Parliament acts as a counterweight to the EU Council and thus to state power, even if the two institutions are disproportionate in strength.

The second factor likely to explain the porosity between European societal and political preferences has to do with the need European institutions—particularly the Commission—have to constantly find resources to legitimate themselves in order to alleviate what is commonly called the "democratic deficit." Since it does not derive its power from the "European people," the Commission needs to demonstrate in concrete terms that it is acting in the general interest and that it is able to do so in areas in which the social demand for regulation through norms is strong, that is, in areas such as environmental protection, food safety, or the precautionary principle.[43]

The third European specificity has to do with the way its public action is financed. For some 20 years now, most or nearly all the European member states have chosen to fund political parties out of the public coffers. This has not entirely eliminated political party dependence on sponsors, but it has decreased it. The United States has basically taken the opposite route. The dependence of central political figures on financial powers has increased considerably. This is very apparent, for instance, in U.S. policy choices and in its trade priorities. Europe as an international actor, in fact, better reflects the societal concerns of its inhabitants on the world level than does the United States.

CHAPTER 3

Norms for What Preferences?

To grasp the meaning of European power, a normative approach is thus essential. But it must be realized that norms, especially constructed norms, reflect the economic, social, and cultural preferences that are at stake. Once again, globalization plays a fundamental role. For as long as we are moving in a global economy in which competition and trade relations are intensifying, the terms of the debate are altered. Unlike the practice of the past 40 years, it is no longer simply a matter of lowering tariff and nontariff barriers between countries to trade peacefully on the basis of well-understood mutual interests. The stakes are much higher than that. They involve exploring the possibility of harmonizing social systems. There is a risk of not understanding the real issues of globalization if it is not clear that what is now at stake is no longer simple competition between economies, but competition between social systems. For as soon as tariff barriers are lifted, the question posed becomes one of harmonizing the social conditions of trade. That implies everything that takes part in the social construction of trade: wages, social protection, legal systems of property, property rights, educational systems, trade union rights, environmental protection, and so on. It is everything that is socially upstream of trade exchanges that is thus brought into play and becomes involved in the issue of globalization.

To take the environment as an example, over the past decade Europe has developed very high standards that European economic agents, such as automobile manufacturers, must integrate.

This results in additional costs compared to their competitors' who are not bound by such constraints. How, then, can environmental protection standards be reconciled with economic constraints without transforming this qualitative preference into a competitive disadvantage? To do so, Europe must make sure it obtains guarantees, either by encouraging its competitors to adopt the same standards as it has or by closing its borders to products that do not respect certain environmental norms.

An important element of analysis flows from what precedes: To understand Europe as a world actor today, one must understand what collective preferences it is striving to promote and how it goes about obtaining recognition for them. There is too much of a tendency, when speaking about Europe, to wonder what values it projects in the world. But the question can hardly be posed in these terms. On one hand, because, in the world today, few peoples or nations hold any expectations that some external model might release them from their constraints and, on otherhand, because Europe is in a much more defensive position than one might believe. Despite its very high standard of living and its state of economic advancement, the nature and quality of its collective preferences place it in an original but isolated situation. It has preferences on a par with its wealth and its protection system. Its priority is thus not to export its values in the name of some outmoded messianic mission, but to obtain recognition from the international system for the preferences on which its originality is based. This task is obviously not an easy one.

On the basis of this assumption, six major preferences can be identified that are shared by European societies and promoted by the European Union. These preferences are

1. the rejection of realpolitik,
2. the belief in a civilizing power of trade,
3. attachment to nonmarket social values,
4. the primacy of shared responsibility over national sovereignty,
5. serious consideration for individual rights and the desire to expand them,
6. political compassion with respect to world social imbalances.

As stated earlier, these collective preferences are not simply abstract or idealistic preferences. They draw from the source of European political history, its level of development, the constraints of its environment, the expectations of its citizens, and interests of its inhabitants. Historical-social determinants always underlie these preferences, constraints related to the European experience and social interests in the broad sense.

Collective preferences thus reflect a floating combination of *legacies*, *experience*, and *interests*, drawing their legitimacy from the fact that they emanate from democratic societies endowed with deliberation processes and representative institutions. But there is no doubt that all these preferences reflect a liberal worldview in the philosophical sense of the term, in that they attach considerable importance to individual preferences as well as to the institutional frameworks on which they are based and in that they deeply believe in the continuity between internal state norms and their extension to the international sphere.[1] Not all these preferences will be developed here; I will concentrate on the first four, as they provide the most tangible illustration of the European difference.

The Rejection of Realpolitik

The realist worldview (commonly called realpolitik) is by definition the one espoused by hard powers. It rests on five assumptions with which the European Union is at odds. The extent of disagreement may be variable, but there can be no doubt about its existence.

The first assumption states that nation-states remain the principle actors in the international system. Europe is in an ambivalent position with regard to this proposition. It naturally cannot reject this idea wholesale, because the European Union in no way defines itself as a federal entity. Moreover, most member states are for various reasons prepared to admit the "realist" postulate. Countries with a strong realist tradition such as France or Great Britain remain, as we have seen, highly state-centered. For them intergovernmentalism remains the ideal form of European integration, as their joint concern to weaken the European Commission indicates, for instance. For obvious historical reasons, Germany, of all the great European nations, has been the least "realist" in that it has agreed to give up areas of sovereignty due to the need to get beyond the nation-state. This Habermas-inspired "postnational" ideology is not, contrary to what one would think, purely rhetorical. By giving up the deutschemark, Germany accepted a sacrifice in the name of a postnational political reality. Joschka Fischer's famous speech on May 12, 2000 regarding the finality of European integration was unofficially perceived in France, particularly by the Foreign Affairs Ministry, as a sort of declaration of war on the European nation-state, a sign of the desire to dissolve Germany into a European federal ensemble.[2] In fact, it is interesting to see how the Maastricht Treaty gave rise to different legal interpretations in France and Germany. In France, the Constitutional Council has always refused to approve the principle of transfer of sovereignty because constitutionally, sovereignty is inalienable. In Germany, the Constitutional Court in Karlsruhe has never made use of such an argument. The only condition it sets on the principle of sovereignty is that it be framed by democratic legitimacy.[3] Of course, German policy cannot be confined to this example. Germany, like every other county, seeks to promote its own interests by several means, including striving for recognition as a "major power" by securing its status of permanent member of the Security Council. Europe is thus very far from being engaged in the postnational era. That does not mean that its political horizon is reducible to that of its component nation-states. It is actually in a historically undetermined gray zone where three competing rationales are at work: (1) a rationale of classic competition between European states, (2) a rationale of competitive cooperation between European states taken individually as such and the European Commission in all areas of shared competence, and (3) a rationale of assertion of individual rights expressed by European citizens who rely on the body of European law to exercise their rights, including those against the states themselves.

The very idea of "collective preferences" basically rests on "antirealist" postulates, in that it considers that the latter fundamentally emanate from rational individuals who are sensitive to the risks, whose expectations, rooted in their experiences, are constantly renegotiated.[4] The best example, to which I shall return, in fact, is the environment. Some 15 years ago, European environmental standards were well below American standards. Since then, the relationship to risk has been inverted. Here is an example of reversible collective preferences, based in the evolution of perceptions of risk in Europe. Now this idea is durably opposed to "realist" theories of the international system, which reason less in terms of preferences than in terms of interests and which postulate that these interests are stable over time.

Certainly, Europe will easily concede that in security matters, states play a decisive, even exclusive role. But given that it refuses to view the world from the classic angle of security, once again it is a more pluralistic vision of the world system and its decisive actors that prevails.

The second realist hypothesis involves thinking that the international system severely penalizes states that do not protect their vital interests or that pursue objectives beyond their means. States are thus assumed to be sensitive to costs and behave as rational actors.[5] The second assumption is not part of Europe's culture. Certainly, it has "vital interests" to protect like any other actor in the world system. But the notion of "vital interests" is at the very heart of the definition of hard power, because it implicitly presupposes that there is a breaking point at which the threat to vital interests calls for retaliation that can easily be conceived as military. The *National Security Strategy of the United States of America* put out in September 2002 is moreover very explicit in this regard when it says that "defending our Nation against its enemies is the first and fundamental commitment of the Federal Government."[6] Here we are in an entirely realist framework in which a territorialized actor seeks to dissuade or combat its enemies. No similar reasoning can be found in the Solana Report, for instance, which is meant to explore Europe's world strategy. The document talks about "threats" but not about enemies.[7] What is more, it implicitly rejects the notion of defending a territory besieged by enemies. On the contrary, it emphasizes the fact that "no single country is able to tackle today's complex problems on its own." Defending one's soil against an enemy is precisely at the crux of Schmittian theory that has always argued that the political order is a spatial order before being a normative order.[8] Schmitt does not refute norms but subordinates them to the defense of territory. He favors *topia* ("the taking of lands") over *utopia* (perpetual peace).[9] In this regard, Europe is undeniably Kantian and anti-Schmittian.

Indeed, Kant, in his project for *Perpetual Peace*, which is supposed to lead to a cosmopolitical order, privileges values over territoriality. Two factors were essential in his mind: the pacific nature of republics and the civilizing power of trade. The Solana Report takes up these two elements practically word for word. He notes that "the quality of international society depends on the quality of governments: the best protection for our security is a world of well-governed democratic states" and adds that "trade and development policies can be powerful tools for promoting reforms."[10] Even more significant is the latest report of the European Defence Agency devoted to Europe and its strategic environment.[11] It is striking to read the importance given to public opinion in the perception of any military operation ("the political outcome will be determined not just by the achievement of military objectives but by the manner in which operations are conducted or are perceived to be conducted").[12] There again we find something akin to the Kantian reference to the existence of a public space exercising a critical and disciplinary function in view of building Perpetual Peace.[13] But what seems even more revealing in this document is precisely the refusal to conceive of military intervention in terms of a zero-sum game between friend and enemy. Political leaders in the Commission talk about partners, not allies. And even if they talk about "friends," they never mention enemies but noncooperative states.[14] Significantly, the EDA report states: "The objective is not 'victory' as traditionally understood, but moderation, balance of interests and peaceful resolution of conflicts."[15] The European Union adheres to visions of peacekeeping based on very strict rules of engagement, privileging contact with civilian populations and reducing recourse to force as much as possible.[16] For Europeans, military force is clearly not to be used as an instrument of hard power. Its primary goal is one of reconciliation and pacification, not punishment.[17]

Furthermore, the idea that world actors operate only on the basis of a cost/benefit assessment seems somewhat removed from a European vision that emphasizes socially based collective preferences. Naturally, even when it promotes environmental values, for instance, Europe reasons in terms of costs and benefits. But even if the Europeans have ratified the Kyoto Protocol whereas the Americans have not, it is not because the former ignore the costs and the latter overestimate them. It is simply because their individual assessments of the costs and benefits differ. This boils down to saying that, in this case, "sensitivity to costs" can be interpreted in different ways and result in highly varied strategies. The Americans measure environmental costs in the short term and on a national basis. Europeans instead have a tendency to measure costs in the long term and strive to share them in the name of an interdependent world vision.

The third assumption in the realist theory believes that anarchy, in other words, the lack of a world government, forms the guiding principle of the international system as well as the primary motive for state action.[18] There again, this idea is vastly remote from the European vision that seeks precisely to reduce the anarchic structure of the international system through rationales of global governance. The whole philosophy of governance via norms aims to frame the actors of the international system within a web of norms that is both closely woven and if possible binding. It is moreover around this question of international anarchy that the confrontation of European and American theories with regard to Iraq crystallized.

In a famous article, Robert Kagan explained the Euro-American conflict over Iraq as a conflict between two worldviews: the Americans view inspired by Hobbes and the European view inspired by Kant.[19] In Kagan's mind, the United States views the world as an anarchic space dominated by the state of nature and the condition of war of "every man against every man." This prompts him to use the figure of Leviathan—in other words, the state—which prosaically is supposed to prevent men if not from living in perfect harmony, then at least from killing one another. Transposed to the international scale, Kagan's analysis consists in saying that in a world without order, the United States plays the role of Leviathan, a Leviathan powerful enough to be credible but democratic enough in its values to be accepted as world regulator. Hobbes saw in the Leviathan a myth that was able to strike a subject's imagination, maintain affects, and hold him in awe.[20] The expression Hobbes uses, "to keep them in awe," turns up as a verb in a military strategy known as "shock and awe," recently employed by the U.S. military in Iraq.

This obviously cannot be Europe's vision, inspired more by Kantian principles based on conflict prevention precisely through rationales of interdependence. For Kant, a cosmopolitical order would be reached by achieving three conditions that are as many beliefs: the peaceful nature of republics, the civilizing power of trade, and the critical and disciplinary function of public space.[21] There is no doubt that from this standpoint, the European idea remains profoundly Kantian, because it believes in the possible advent of world political order built on rules that organize the interdependence of nations. But contrary to what one might believe, the Kantian vision of the world implies losses and gains of state sovereignty because, as Habermas reminds us, the cosmopolitical union is a federation of states and not a federation of cosmopolitans.[22] In other words, Europe is so Kantian that it has managed to get beyond violent conflicts between states without abolishing state sovereignty, which, in fact, is what Habermas seems to criticize Kant For.[23] In any event, there can be no doubt that the Euro-Kantian vision is indeed constructed on the will to transcend the anarchic character of the international order.

The fourth realist assumption follows directly from the third. In an anarchic world in which the principal issues are those of power and security, states have a predisposition for conflict, even in situations where they might have common interests.[24] There again, the whole European philosophy seems constructed in opposition to this idea, because world governance precisely involves saying that global problems require global solutions and these have a tendency to call for contractual solutions. Europe's wager of governance aims to foil the realist logic, because it believes that interdependence should encourage states to cooperate rather than tear each other apart.

The realist theory of international relations contains one more hypothesis: that international institutions only marginally affect the perspectives for cooperation between states. This points up a strong and long-standing line of cleavage between the absolutist visions of the state and its sovereignty and the liberal, pluralistic visions of the state. The former place the state above everything else and analyze the challenges that arise in terms of possible confrontations, whereas the latter strive to put the role of the state and society in perspective and thereby mobilize the dynamics capable of defusing conflicts. Traces of this difference in interpretation of the social order can be found in the work of Carl Schmitt and in the decisive critique he makes of the pluralistic visions defended by Cole and Laski.[25] I will not rehash the details of the controversy here, particularly since I will return to Carl Schmitt's philosophy to explore it as a veritable counter-model of Europe today, suffice to say for the moment, to evoke his critique of liberal and pluralistic visions. For Schmitt, the essence of politics rests on the distinction between friend and enemy.[26] But for such polarization to be operational, by definition he has to reduce all forms of pluralization that might affect the friend's unity against its enemy. This is why every political community must be able to diminish the pluralisms within it and substitute simple and existential antagonisms that are in turn exploited by states. A state's task is thus not to complicate the world but, on the contrary, to simplify it by reducing it to a powerful and necessarily simplistic line of cleavage.[27] Schmitt's critique of the liberal premises of Cole and Laski are thus only natural, for they, on the contrary, seek to qualify state sovereignty by considering it as one of many actors, invested with the function of governance and transaction among different actors. Europe's political system is, in fact, often defined in these terms. It is also with reference to this idea of plurality that Europe approaches the question of global governance.[28] It can certainly be argued that governance by norms can reduce pluralism. Legal positivists such as Kelsen for instance propose a single normative system, itself anchored to a central point disseminating norms that have been brought down to the very lowest baseline.[29] But this is not the European approach to governance. In fact, to my knowledge there is no theory of governance that aims to reduce pluralism in the name of a procedural vision of the international legal order. The immense majority of plans for world governance seek to organize pluralism rather than to tame it. Moreover, what is put forward is a rationale of transaction among actors rather than one of hierarchy.

This explains the importance of institutions in charge of organizing pluralism, in other words, an institutional process by which the hierarchy of norms is structured and legitimated rather than imposed merely as a result of a power struggle or a legal and institutional void. When Europe calls for an examination of the coherence between WTO rules and multilateral environmental accords, it is seeking to obtain recognition for environmental norms and their enforceability on free trade, and this is due to lack of support for endeavors to establish a World Environment Organization. Unlike realist theories, Europe thus does not believe that international institutions only marginally affect state behavior. It believes, on the contrary, that these institutions are a decisive tool for normifying the world system.

Belief in the Civilizing Power of Trade

Europe is convinced, as Adam Smith was, that trade soothes the savage breast. The more people trade, the less people will make war. Interdependence through trade is at the heart of the European project. But this preference is not purely abstract or ideal. Europe is in favor of trade and opening markets because it conditions the well-being of its inhabitants. Europe is in fact the largest exporter and the second largest investor in the world. Moreover, much more than the United States, it has always been dependent on trade for its development. The downturn in Europe's growth rate over the past 10 years has heightened this dependence. Europe thus has a vital interest in the development of an integrated world economy through trade, especially to enhance its comparative advantage in the area of services. These represent two-thirds of its GNP and the jobs in Europe but only 20 percent of world trade.[30] It thus has every interest in removing obstacles to the liberalization of services. And in that regard, it basically shares the same goals as the United States.

But there are several impediments to achieving this "offensive" goal, which are in fact much more sociopolitical than strictly commercial. For a long time, even a very long time, Europeans mainly traded among themselves. That means they are used to trading with countries that have the same level of development, the same regulatory structure. The harmonization of the single market considerably strengthened this tendency, to such an extent that the very notions of import and export within the EU have become merely a matter for balance sheets.

Not counting the European Union, it is with the United States that Europe has the strongest trade relations. This, in fact, explains why most of Europe's disputes at the WTO involve the United States.[31] But this fact should not be misinterpreted. Euro-American conflicts nevertheless oppose countries having a comparable level of development and similar interests. For this reason, the so-called regulatory conflicts pitting the EU against the United States have tended to diminish, which suggests that their interpretations of WTO rules are beginning to converge.[32] Most of the differences opposing them have to do with the legality of protection measures (safeguard clauses, antidumping measures) in sensitive sectors. The only unusual dimension in Euro-American conflicts has to do with issues that we could call "societal" and that refer to conflicts over social preferences, such as conflicts regarding the use of hormones in beef or GMOs. I shall return to that subject.

At this stage, it is important to understand that Europe's vital necessity to obtain new outlets for its industrial products and especially its services, is confronted with new trends that are all converging toward a rising demand for norms on the part of Europe.

Europeans have a tendency to trade less and less among themselves and more and more with the rest of the world. For Germany, for instance, the decrease in intra-European trade in its overall trade figures is spectacular. In 10 years, it went from 65 percent to 50 percent, a considerable drop. For Belgium, the figures are even more drastic: the proportion of its intra-European trade has gone from 80 percent to 65 percent. What makes this redeployment of trade toward emerging countries significant? It is the fact that it represents a shift toward emerging countries where the social and environmental norms are incomparably lower than they are in Europe and that these countries, at the same time, are catching up to developing nations very, very quickly.[33]

For a long time, international division of labor was explained from the perspective of the division of labor between Europe, which would sell Airbus, and China, which would sell garments. This is not a false view of reality, but it is changing so fast that there is a risk of seeing countries such as China compete with Europe in high value-added markets without allowing rise in quality products to produce a similar rise in wages. In other words, it may well be that in certain areas, China can sell high-technology products to Europe produced at much lower wages. Europe's comparative advantage does not reside only in the fact that it sells high-technology products, but also in the fact that it sells "expensive labor."[34] This "expensive labor" is the reflection of both the high technological level reached in Europe and the high level of social protection supporting it. In the face of China, then, the issue is not to get it to open its market. This has already been achieved and, to a large extent, much more so than in countries with a similar level of development. However, as regards trade regulation, everything remains to be done: assurances are needed that access to the Chinese market is more transparent, that protection against corruption is better guaranteed, that the rules of intellectual property are better complied with, that Chinese development fits in with the logic of sustainable development so that China does not exert further pressure on the raw materials market, so that it does not increase its comparative advantage without integrating environmental constraints, and especially so that it does not use wage repression to increase its advantage. Like the United States, China is in the process of becoming an economic power that by its very morphology will have systemic effects on the whole world regulation system, not only on trade. The EU-China relationship can be seen as a perfect illustration of Europe's interest in normifying globalization. For by acting the way it does, it is primarily seeking to protect its social model.

Consequently, the meaning of its attachment to socialization through trade is altered. The question is not only to wager on the fact that trade will soothe the savage beast to prevent war, but also to wager that societies having neither the level of development nor the regulatory culture of developed countries (nor even the same priorities) can take part in a global game of which the rules have been made together.

From that standpoint, is the WTO the most conducive structure for promoting Europe's regulatory vision? The answer is clearly yes, and this for at least three reasons: the first is that, in general, when Europe files a complaint or is accused, the WTO overwhelmingly finds favor with it. Between 1999 and 2004, Europe won 13 disputes brought before WTO panels and lost only 4 of them,[35] all of these against developing countries.[36] The second is that the European Union does not have any real alternative to the multilateral system to promote its normative view. The United States clearly plays the bilateral card to promote respect for basic social or environmental norms when necessary because it has noncommercial political assets in its hand.[37] Europe does not enjoy such room to maneuver. For it, the challenge comes from China and India. Only a multilateral framework is likely to influence these huge states. A third reason explains and justifies the European preference for regulation through the WTO. This organization is potentially seen as a "disciplinary institution" that enjoys a real legitimacy to convince countries, particularly developing countries, to convert not only to free trade but also to its regulations. It is very eager to see sensitive problems such as corruption handled at a multilateral rather than a bilateral level.[38] Europe views the WTO as an institution able to "soften" the binding character some of its social preferences may have on export strategies in developing countries. That said, the results obtained by Europe on the multilateral level are far from spectacular. The example of core labor standards attests to this. For Europe, the main thing is to avoid both a "social race to the bottom" and to increase the legitimacy of the WTO by encouraging it to take into account social questions and by strengthening the social image of the European Union on the world stage. At the WTO conference in Singapore in 1996, the principle of respect for core labor standards was accepted on condition that these norms would not be used for protectionist purposes.[39]

At the Doha conference in 2001, the Europeans tried to place the subject on the agenda once again, this time on their own. But they came up against the hostility of developing countries, particularly India, which threatened not to sign the final declaration if this question was tabled again.[40] Developing countries combat the issue of core labor standards as much due to considerations of political sovereignty as due to economic questions because such standards do not take into account labor costs. They view them as a remnant of a neocolonialist ideology.[41] Actually, considerable doubt subsists as to the effectiveness of core labor standards, even if European public opinion and trade unions attach great importance to them. Indeed, if the defense of labor standards is perfectly in line with a rationale of protecting human rights, it has never been proven that violating them has constituted a comparative advantage or has sparked a "race to the bottom." Without trade unions, Chinese wages have quadrupled in 30 years, whereas with powerful trade unions, Brazilian wages have stagnated.[42]

The call for a joint organization combining the ILO and the WTO has had little success. Having had their fingers burned with the failure of Seattle, the United States now privileges a bilateral framework to promote its interests in this area.[43] As a result, the Europeans have ended up being much more stigmatized by developing countries than the United States, for Europeans are the ones who prove to be the most demanding as regards the setting up of a multilateral normativity in environmental matters and labor standards.[44] It should nevertheless be noted that sustained European interest in this question is due to the fact that Europe continues to have an industrial base that is in competition with emerging countries. Its industrial specialization is not flexible enough. It is built on static positions, the search for sources of income and exploitation of existing areas of specialization. This is what distinguishes it from the United States, which is more flexible, especially in the area of technology and service industries.[45]

As a consequence, Europe is obliged to revise its goals downward and fall back on a bilateral strategy, at least as regards core labor standards, the defense of which is now integrated into the broader framework of the fight for "decent work." Europe prides itself in having sanctioned Belarus and Myanmar for violating core labour standards. But these are isolated and largely disqualified regimes that do not constitute a threat to European interests. Europe thus gives the impression of levying sanctions only on states that can do it no harm.

The Norms Europe Stands For

Europe's capacity to establish and export norms should not be underestimated. On the contrary, with the expansion of the European common market, Europe has adopted even stricter norms that pertain not only to its member states but also to all the economic agents that want to get into the EU market.

The EU's economic partners are forced to adapt to those norms, since the European market is one of the largest and since norms concerning environment, health, and sustainable development are becoming more and more compelling. In those fields, European norms are becoming the highest in the world and, therefore, Europe is the norm-setter at the global level.[46] A country exporting agricultural products will be very careful in introducing massive use of GMOs if it knows that Europeans will not tolerate them.

This role of *norm-setter* was long fulfilled by the United States. Today, Europe has taken over from it.[47] Two factors account for this: Europe is the most integrated market in the world and it is the one with the highest norms. To demonstrate this, I will provide three examples. They concern what is known as *e-waste* (*WEEE*—Waste Electrical and Electronic Equipment), restrictions on the use of hazardous substances (RoHS) in electrical and electronic equipment, and finally the regulation, registration, evaluation, and authorization of chemicals (REACH).

WEEE is designed to increase recovery and recycling of electrical and electronic equipment by extending producer responsibilities, since consumers can return free of charge all regulated equipment for reprocessing and recycling in exchange for incentives to produce environmentally friendly equipment. Under REACH legislation, chemical products will undergo a registration procedure followed by a safety evaluation.[48]

The WEEE, RoHS, and REACH programs are already influencing other actors. RoHS for example is regarded by the United States as the biggest change in electronics in the past 50 years.[49] REACH also constitutes a source of enormous change for U.S. firms, which must now comply with European regulation. But at the same time, REACH is extremely influential in the sense that it has forced the U.S. Congress to work on national legislation on issues drawn from the European experience. In the United States, the influence of the EU is visible in the action of the various member states, such as their support for the Kyoto protocol. Many states, influenced by European laws, have adopted more compelling legislation than what federal laws require on the issue of the *e-waste.* Nevertheless, this has not prevented the American government from using diplomatic means to combat the realization of REACH. They fear that such legislation constitutes an obstacle to free trade. Actually, the American position mirrors that of American business, which does not want to adapt to European constraints.[50] The European common market is a considerable source of normative influence, provided Europe has a homogeneous rule system and an attractive market. This passive and almost mechanical influence does not exclude the development of a more active policy of norms exportation.

In this regard, competition policy is one of the most powerful instruments in the hands of the EU. Strictly speaking competition policy refers to the rules that are designed to prevent market players from forming cartels. In fact, in a broader sense, for a given market, it refers to provisions intended to distinguish between economic agents by means of innumerable regulatory obstacles. Respect for competitive rules is thus an issue in Europe's internal market as well as for its trade policy.

The stakes are high since Europe is not only the largest solvent market in the world and the leading economic power, but also the first in world investments.

A genuine risk of cartelization does exist because most global investing is done through mergers and acquisitions, thereby automatically increasing the likelihood of market concentration. Faced with this risk, Europe has considerable means at its disposal; their import was evident on two different occasions involving two different issues: when in 2001 a European court, on the basis of extraterritorial powers, effectively prohibited the merger of two American companies (General Electric and Honeywell Bull); and in 2007 when this same court condemned Microsoft for having eliminated its competitors from the operating systems market by denying them access to technical information on Windows. What stands out in this affair is both the fact that Microsoft was condemned in Europe but not in the United States, and also that it was an American company that brought charges against Microsoft in Europe as if it considered it would be easier to do so in Europe than in the United States.[51]

The condemnation of Microsoft is evidence of a European conception of competition that is today different from that of the United States. In Europe's eyes, competition must not only provide an advantage for the consumer but also ensure the continued existence of market competitors. In other words, there can be no genuine competition in the absence of genuine competitors; whereas for Americans the competitive structure of the market itself is of less importance than the advantages to be derived by the consumer. Microsoft's quasi-monopoly would, in the latter perspective, have been acceptable if the consumer were to benefit from a steady price reduction.

The other aspect of competition has to do with the rules guaranteeing fair competition between economic actors. For Europe this aspect—at a time when its trading patterns have been changing radically and rapidly—has become increasingly important. As long as Europe remained an introverted economic area, the rules of competition concerned only countries with strict norms. Conforming to rules governing intellectual property, for instance, had never been a major issue for Europe as long as it traded within its borders or with the United States and Japan. Today the situation is entirely different since trade has been expanding with emerging countries whose norms are looser. Europe thus has an impressive roster of normative cases to settle, one that is closely linked to its commercial policy.

In fact, until around 2005, Europe tried to put through its normative agenda via a multilateral channel known as the "Singapore issues" (investment protection, competition, transparency, and trade facilitation). But after the 2004 failure in Cancun and the deadlock in the WTO multilateral negotiations, Europe—without admitting as much—decided to explore bilateral ways to advance its normative agenda. And it is obvious why. When 80 percent of imitations intercepted in Europe are of Chinese origin, it would appear legitimate to address China directly, rather than waiting for a multilateral solution. All the more so in that the issue in this case was less the drawing up of new rules than their effective application. Europe willingly admits that, when it comes to issues other than tariffs, it has more success in bilateral than in multilateral negotiations. Moreover, Europe is in the process of tightening provisions concerning intellectual property in its bilateral agreements, coming closer to the United States that has always considered that, in such matters, bilateralism was more effective than multilateralism.

Since 2006, Europe's trade policy has taken a bilateral turn so as to take root in emerging countries, particularly China that is its leading commercial partner.

Faced with public scepticism as to the advantages of globalization, Europe knows that it can prove its effectiveness and its legitimacy only by demonstrating that the opening of new markets will lead to the creation of jobs in Europe.

Today it is countries with high growth potential that Europe is most interested in. To meet its objective Europe intends to deploy its battery of norms in the key areas of respect for intellectual property, access to government markets, and discrimination against foreign investors, not to speak of the fundamental social norms concerning environment, energy efficiency, and human rights. There is, of course, the risk that its commercial policy will then be overburdened with conditions, all the more restrictive when the balance of power is in Europe's favour. The issue should be squarely faced, all the more so in that it is clear that Europe has no intention through these agreements of relaxing its control over sensitive aspects of agricultural production and even less so over the movement of people.

The Defense of Nonmarket Values

Globalization, as we have seen, has a powerful ability to reveal social preferences. It highlights what societies are attached to when they find themselves confronted with dynamics of openness. And this is precisely what has happened in recent years. Europe has thus been forced to realize that opening up markets clashes with collective choices it was attached to, whether they pertain to agriculture, the environment, food safety, or its social model. In other words, the defense of nonmarket values boils down to considering that free trade does not necessarily produce well-being (see table 3.1).

Enforcing moral, social, cultural, or religious values on the opening of markets is not in itself a new phenomenon. In 1927, the International Convention on the Abolition of Import and Export Prohibitions and Restrictions explicitly examined the subject. Moreover, the GATT and the later WTO accords include a considerable number of provisions allowing them to suspend imports of a given product that is harmful to health, the environment, or the preservation of rare species, provided that scientific evidence has been demonstrated. The three best known mechanisms are the SPS accord (Sanitary and Phytosanitary Measures), the TBT (Technical Barriers to Trade), and article 20 of the GATT that allows each state to develop its own rules in terms of health and the environment as long as these protection measures are not discriminatory or used as disguised trade barriers. In fact, WTO case law has had a tendency to base its analysis—through its panels—on this very article 20 and hand down its decisions in reference to it when conflicts opposing free trade and environmental preservation were brought before it.

Table 3.1 Europe's nonmarket preferences

- enforceability of environmental rules on opening markets
- use of the precautionary principle
- multifunctionality of agriculture
- respect for core labor standards
- respect for cultural diversity

The two most famous panels in this area are the Shrimp-Sea Turtle Panel and the Gasoline Panel. Europe was not involved in these two emblematic panels, because in both cases the complaint was lodged by the United States, against Asian countries in the shrimp-sea turtle dispute and against Latin American countries in the case of gasoline. Europe nevertheless paid close attention to the WTO ruling because it set a precedent that could be very instructive for it. In the shrimp dispute, the United States justified closing their market to shrimp imports by the fact that the rules regarding the type of nets used in Asian countries endangered the conservation of sea turtles that were caught in these nets. In the gasoline case, the United States claimed that Latin American oil products did not comply with American environmental legislation. Certainly, in both cases, the ruling was not directly in favor of the United States.[52] But in substance, the WTO acknowledged the legitimacy of using environmental laws to prohibit imports. The European Union saw this as moving in the right direction in that the WTO now seemed prepared to take environmental concerns more into account.[53]

The Environmental Preference

Why then does Europe insist so much on better coupling of trade and environmental protection when provisions whenthat can protect the environment and, moreover, WTO case law seems to be going "in the right direction"? Because it believes that WTO provisions such as SPS and its precedents are insufficient to provide a stable and lasting guarantee for its environmental preference. Therefore, it would like to see the WTO also enact clear trade restrictions in the name of environmental protection, as is the case in Community law, thus moving beyond raising environmental issues in panels with a fluctuating jurisprudence. At the Doha conference, in eleventh-hour negotiations, Europe managed to put examination of the consistency of Multilateral Environmental Agreements (MEAs) with WTO rules on the agenda.[54]

The second reason has to do with the fact that social pressure in favor of stricter environmental rules has intensified. In 1991, when the predecessor to the WTO—the GATT—had to settle a famous dispute (tuna-dolphins) in many ways similar to the shrimp-sea issue, the ruling was not in favor of the United States. At that time, Europeans applauded the GATT decision because it refused to link trade and the environment.[55] In ten years, a real Euro-American *chassé-croisé* has taken place in environmental matters. The United States has tended to lower its requirements in this regard while the Europeans have had a tendency to raise them. Why? There are several explanations.

The first is institutional in nature. Environmental issues in a broad sense have gradually been integrated into the sphere of Community jurisdiction. This "communitarization" has systematically worked in the direction of higher standards, beginning with the Single European Act, which came into force in 1987. It provided a legal support to environmental preservation and harmonization of standards on the basis of a high level of protection. In 1993, the Maastricht Treaty for the first time ratified the precautionary principle as a guiding principle for EU action. The Amsterdam Treaty in 1997 confirmed Europe's concern for environmental questions, calling on the EU Council and Parliament to attain high standards in the areas of health, food safety, protection of the environment, and consumer rights. These questions entered the sphere of co-decision, thus reinforcing the influence of European citizens in the field of European decision making.[56] And so, institutional and political logics conjugated with an outcome that considerably raised the environmental stakes in Europe. Since there are now only European consumers, sanitary and environmental regulations necessarily end up engaged in a process of strong harmonization. It is in the interest of economic agents to limit the obstacles to the penetration of their products, while citizens are entitled to demand similar health and environmental guarantees once products are freely circulating, bearing in mind that risks disregard borders.

The second explanation is a result of the demand for increased democratization of European institutions, a demand constantly reiterated since the Maastricht Treaty. This trend has been confirmed by implicating Parliament in environmental choices. In fact, between 1984 and 1994, the precautionary principle was enshrined in 27 European Parliament resolutions.[57] The European Commission was not to be outdone. In February 2000, it called for the precautionary principle to be extended to health risks on the basis of scientific evidence, an examination of the potential benefits and costs of action (or of lack of action), and the level of risk that the European public was prepared to tolerate.[58]

In December 2000, the Nice Summit confirmed the new European philosophy as regards precaution while modifying it on two points. For one, it noted that it may not always be possible to make accurate risk assessments due to lack of scientific evidence or due to averred and immediate risk. It also emphasized social acceptability of risks and consequently the necessity to integrate public acceptability of risks at each stage.[59]

The environment thus became a major political issue in Europe. Three essential factors institutionally favored its rise in importance: It is one of the areas that best lends itself to the production of norms because there is a need to constantly set rules, ceilings, quotas, and other such parameters.

It is also an area in which European political integration can gain in legitimacy as long as it allows the production of high-standards goods and services. No one in Europe can complain about the Europeanization of health and environmental norms, except, of course, social groups or professions who want to take advantage of low standards. Lastly, the environment is the ideal area for sharing sovereignty, obliging Europe to speak and act with one voice once a collective decision has been made. Unlike a nation-state—such as the United States—that can change its mind, the Community rationale "locks" its various member states into choices that it can repudiate only at prohibitive cost. As a political ensemble, the European Union by definition has greater trouble than a nation-state in defining a common position. But once this position is adopted, the unified position exerts a "mass effect" both by the aggregation of forces and by the impossibility of pulling out of the agreement. Moreover, due to the logic of integration, even in the absence of an identical risk assessment in all countries, European legislation tends to align itself along the countries that are the most demanding in terms of risk assessment.[60]

The environment, and more especially climate change, is not only a part of Europe's political agenda but also participates in the construction of its international political identity. It offers the Commission an opportunity to consolidate its legitimacy not only among the member states, but also among the European public, which is particularly sensitive to this topic. It is also by its nature—a public good—a political object that lends itself to the logic of de facto communitarization through European policy. And finally, it is an instrument of political distinction enabling the EU to structure its difference, particularly with regard to the United States.

However, Europe committed itself in April 2007 to reduce by 20 percent its emissions of greenhouse gases by 2020 (and even by 30 percent if a reduction of this kind was accepted by the other states) and then by 50 percent before 2050, keeping 1990 as the reference year. In the Kyoto agreement, the reduction of GHG for Europe was fixed at 8 percent between 2008 and 2012. By being the first geopolitical region to commit itself to After-Kyoto targets, the European Union effectively fixed the norm that was to be central in the international negotiations held in Bali in December 2007. But Europe must meet two challenges. The first is to be exemplary in environmental matters, not simply in rhetoric but in practice. Yet on this score the results are not yet in.

In 2010, according to the Commission's own estimates, GHG emissions in Europe of the 15 will only have been reduced by 0.6 percent below the 1990 level, whereas Kyoto stipulated an 8 percent reduction by 2012. For Europe of the 25, the outlook is more encouraging, but not necessarily significant; the former Eastern Bloc states are closing out the polluting factories left over from the Soviet era. In 2004, the GHG emission levels for Europe's 25 were at their highest since the adoption of the Kyoto Protocol in 1997. The black spot for Europe remains road and air traffic. In addition, the proportion of European exports with high carbon intensity is superior to that of the United States or China, which renders attempts at tax importations of polluting countries hardly credible.

For Europe, to set an example is a crucial issue, but the outcome remains uncertain. A political strategy capable of inciting the emerging countries to share this approach is needed, not to speak of the fact that the United States might be reluctant to see these countries absolved from taking meaningful steps before 2020 as proposed in the latest UN development report. It will be most difficult. Yet it is only by such criteria that European nations can continue priding themselves on being "a green power."

Europe thus has a comparative political advantage in environmental matters, first, because it enjoys undeniable leadership—based on its know-how; second, because it is for Europe that the adjustment to climate change is the least costly (the European Union contributes only one-sixth of the greenhouse gas emissions although it represents 25 percent of the world GDP); last, because it probably enjoys an economic advantage in the area of clean technology it can likely capitalize on. It remains for Europe to convince the other world actors to enter the playing field as soon as possible so that its political advantage is not minimized by a short-term economic advantage if it happened to be the only one to embark on a bold environmental policy.

The institutional dynamic is, however, not the central explanation. If Europe has managed to wrest leadership from the United States in environmental matters, it is basically because the various member states have acquired a common environmental awareness that, in fact, has arisen from very different experiences. Conversely, the United States is confronted with an "environmental counter-revolution" that encourages political, economic, and even religious forces to see environmental protection either as a new form of paganism (Pat Robertson), or as the greatest threat to Texas after illegal immigrants (DeLay), or, more prosaically, as a lack of income for the oil industry or as an attack on the American way of life based on wanton consumption of nonrenewable resources.[61] In fact, American environmental groups seem more than ever on the defensive, ascribing their decline to that of liberal American values. "Our death is a symptom of the exhaustion of the liberal project."[62] There is thus indeed a certain consistency between the rise in neoconservatives, the political influence of fundamentalist movements, the decline of environmental values, and the claim of an "American exceptionalism" that apparently encourages it to wrestle free from environmental constraints and discipline.

The Controversial Use of the Precautionary Principle

Europe's environmental policy has moved in a different direction. It has been considerably driven by the Scandinavian countries and Germany. Europe's reappropriation of the precautionary principle owes much to Germany's influence, which during the 1970s developed the concept of *Vorsorge* (precaution) and whose entire environmental policy hinges on this principle. To protect German forests against acid rain, the authorities were prompted to make drastic reductions in sulfur emissions well before scientific knowledge had clearly decided on the causes of deforestation.[63] In 1990, the ministerial declaration on the North Sea was a major step toward international recognition of the precautionary principle. This principle is defined as a recourse to preventive measures designed to avoid damage even in the absence of scientific evidence of a link between the emission of certain toxic substances and their supposed effects on the environment.[64] But even if Germany was always in the lead, it was not the only one to defend a very active environmental policy. Denmark and the Netherlands were also very involved in this area. This green troika within the European Community in turn benefited from the accession of countries with a strong environmental culture such as Sweden, Finland, and Austria. All these countries had either a strong environmental tradition or relatively powerful or influential green parties.[65]

This said, the remarkable fact in Europe is not so much the influence of green countries as the extension of this green culture to a whole swathe of Europe that was not sensitive to it until then. How did this contagion occur? This is where the question of political experience plays its full role. Indeed, most European countries were, beginning in the 1980s, either confronted with environmental or health crises, or strengthened by the existence of a European political framework able to take charge of their concerns.

Great Britain for instance never appeared to be a particularly green country. But the existence of a European environmental policy enabled it to promote its own agenda, dominated by a strong sensitivity to animal protection. Great Britain thus naturally formed alliances with the green countries of northern

Europe to put forward a series of provisions that were favorable to animal protection.[66] France did not have the image of a country with a particularly developed green culture either, especially because of its nuclear program. But through food safety issues this awareness was heightened, thus feeding the development of a particularly vigorous European policy in this area. France, a country with a strong culinary tradition, was the first European country to be confronted with the issue of GMOs, because it was in France that in 1997 the first applications for a license to introduce GMOs were filed on the European continent. For reference, GMO technology involves isolating genes in an organism, handling them in a laboratory and injecting them into another organism to increase product yield and resistance to pests, thereby reducing the use of herbicides and pesticides. At first, France nevertheless approved the application and forwarded it to the Commission. The Commission in turn consulted the member states. But seven of them rejected the license, on the grounds that the health guarantees offered were insufficient. Due to the lack of agreement, the decision went up to the environment ministers, who refused to vote in favor of an authorization to introduce genetically modified corn on the market. But after a favorable scientific opinion, in February 1997 the Commission authorized the sale of GM corn. France went along with the Commission's recommendation before backtracking one week later under pressure from the environment minister. In February 1998, the Jospin government again authorized the planting of GM corn. This time it was NGOs, including the Confédération Paysanne, that filed an appeal with the Conseil d'Etat. In September 1998, this institution handed down its ruling. It revoked the decision to authorize the production of GM corn on the grounds that it took inadequate account of the precautionary principle. The Conseil d'Etat decision was in turn reinforced by a European Court of Justice (ECJ) decision, considering that the GMO issue came under the sphere of shared competences between the European Union and the member states and thus invalidating the Commission's position that had authorized putting GM corn on the market. In the case in point, the ECJ emphasized the right of each member state to use the precautionary principle and thus to restrict or prohibit the use or sale of a product presenting a risk to public health or the environment.[67] The ECJ decision would prove to be essential, because it would enable several member states to justify their opposition to the marketing of GMOs products.

As a result, the Commission in Brussels was prompted to back down and to declare in 1999 a moratorium on new applications to approve GMOs.[68]

What is interesting to note in the case of GMOs is both the power acquired by the precautionary principle in conducting European policy as well as the way in which the various European experiences combined to fashion—not without difficulty or contradiction—a relatively ambitious European environmental policy.

This "combination of experiences," however, would have not acquired the influence that it did on the definition of European policy if different countries had not been faced with very serious environmental or food crises, among which, the mad cow crisis was decisive. It broke out in 1995 when the British government announced that 10 people had been discovered to be infected with Creutzfeldt-Jakob disease. This crisis, which would lead to the death of about 100 people, was to have two consequences. It would prompt deep wariness in Europe with regard to health regulation authorities and by the same token a demand for the reinforcement of precautionary measures throughout Europe. It also gave rise to a very strong sensitivity to health and environmental questions, a sensitivity attested by the vigor of the debate on GMOs. European reticence toward GMOs or the use of hormones in beef is largely due to public concern regarding the development of an industrial-scale agriculture driven by a profit rationale and prepared to take considerable health risks in pursuit of this logic. This concern corresponds not to one but several converging reasons: the loss of trust in national health regulation bodies following certain regulation crises, European sensitivity to culinary art, the fear that crops would be contaminated by GMOs due to physical proximity, and the memory of genetic engineering in Germany. All these elements converge toward a collective anxiety that has no equivalent in the United States,[69] particularly because they have not had any serious environmental crisis in the past 20 years.

The idea of "shared risks" has thus become central in the construction of a European identity as regards the environment. This collective awareness of sharing the same risks naturally leads to a European demand in environmental matters expressed in the publication by the Commission in the year 2000 of a white paper on food safety. It is reflected by the very strong increase in the European regulatory mechanism starting in the mid-1980s (use of hormones in beef and milk, GMOs, biodiversity, ecolabeling, issues of waste, global warming, recycling of junked vehicles, animal feed, biosecurity, recycling of electronic components). Now on all these subjects, American legislation is either less stringent or nonexistent.[70]

Today, it is on the question of GMOs that the differences are most perceptible. In the United States, everything has been done to encourage the authorization of GMO crops, even sidelining the Environmental Protection Agency.[71] As a matter of fact, in 2002 the European Union had not granted any more than 18 licenses for biotechnology products, only nine of which involved GMOs, whereas the various American agencies had granted 58 such licenses, including 50 for GMO crops.[72] Three-quarters of the plantations of crops containing GMOs were thus concentrated in the United States, whereas they are practically nonexistent in Europe except for experimental purposes. Today over 60 percent of the foodstuffs sold in the United States contain GMOs, which shows to what extent this biotechnology is established in the United States and how strong the difference remains with Europe. Remember that Europe has just put an end to the moratorium on GMOs, while subjecting the marketing of any GMO product to stringent traceability requirements. The conflict with the United States thus remains far from settled, as attests Washington's decision to lodge a formal complaint regarding this issue with the WTO.

Thus, as for the environment, Europe would like to recognize the precautionary principle not only recognized in its case law but enshrined at the WTO. But it must face planet-wide skepticism on this issue. The United States believes that existing safeguards are entirely sufficient and harbors extreme wariness with respect to the precautionary principle. As for developing countries, they see it either as a luxury of the rich unthreatened by hunger, or as a new strategy designed to prevent them from entering the northern markets.[73] It must indeed be clearly understood that this preference for the environment is not a purely abstract one. For although it may reflect irrefutable social preferences, it also expresses interests that lead the European Union to have a much more ambivalent attitude than it might appear to have. As regards biosecurity, for example, Europe successfully demanded recognition of the precautionary principle in the Cartagena Protocol on Biosafety in order to restrict consumption of GMOs. But when certain developing countries demand broad-sweeping international controls on the subject, they come up against European opposition keen to regulate the use of GMOs in the agriculture industry, but not in the pharmaceutical industry, a distinction that seems highly debatable. In this case, restrictive norms are clearly intended to protect commercial interests.[74]

Defense of the Multifunctionality of Agriculture

The other collective preference the European Union clearly displays has to do with agriculture, or more precisely with the principle of multifunctionality of agriculture. Sketched out during the Uruguay Round under the term "integrated rural policy," multifunctionality was defined in 1999 prior to the Seattle Summit. The idea is simple. It claims that agriculture is not a type of production like any other, because farmers are not there merely to exploit the land like a miner exploits a mine. They live in the midst of an environment that they cultivate and preserve. Agriculture thus has noncommodity functions that prohibit viewing farmers as the miners of the twenty-first century.[75]

The European Union has naturally strived to formulate this position of principle in order to counter critiques coming from those who, especially at the WTO, are demanding that the Common Agricultural Policy (CAP) be dismantled in order to open markets.

This configuration of positions could lead one to believe that there is a zero-sum game between the multifunctionality of

European agriculture and the free trade of agricultural foodstuffs. But in reality, the equation is infinitely more complex than that, because the opponents involved are far from constituting unified or stable groups.

Actually, the European Commission understood a long time ago that the "original CAP model" was simply no longer adapted to the conditions of European and world agriculture. Its productivist logic, which was understandable in the 1960s, ended up increasing the distortions within the agricultural world (because bonuses were given to the most productive) with respect to the world market and destroying the environment (because overproduction was rewarded). Matters have reached a point where the CAP, once held up as a model of multifunctionality, has managed to destroy this so-called multifunctionality, the basis of which remains sustainable development. This explains the necessity to modify the CAP without, for all that, giving the impression that such amendments are being made on the impetus of external constraints.

Using the argument of opening up markets to justify CAP reform had a dual disadvantage: it became even more illegitimate in the eyes of farmers—due to its being imposed from the outside—and lost all margin for negotiation with net exporters of agricultural products. Reforming the CAP under external constraints in the long run boiled down to eroding the very idea of multifunctionality. And so the political message was reinforced that CAP reform above all meets internal considerations and that it is on the basis of such considerations that Europe's bargaining position on agriculture can be inferred.[76]

To depolarize the situation, Europe thus began breaking down the problem, distinguishing three aspects of what is called agricultural protection: (1) export subsidies, which harm exporting developing countries while aggravating imbalances within Europe to the benefit of certain privileged farmers; (2) border protection, which aims to protect the local production of certain products such as meat, wheat, and sugar; and (3) internal support measures that aimed to sustain farmers' incomes while encouraging them to convert to more multifunctional activities.

By breaking down the problems, Europe seeks to rebuild its defense. It is no longer a question of defending agriculture across the board, but of defending multifunctionality as long as it does not introduce strong distortions on the world markets. In the long run, it is thus bound to accept the disappearance of export subsidies and to modulate its border protection, but to also maintain support for its farmers.

The implementation of this new framework nevertheless comes up against considerable obstacles. The first arises from the main agricultural exporters in the South, such as Brazil, to accept this delinking of agricultural protection. Their goal is to conquer northern markets and they consider that Europe aims to delay this inevitable perspective by any and all means. The second problem comes from the fact that Europe as a mercantilist actor can advance toward deprotection of its agriculture only if it is controlled; only if other countries that strongly subsidize their agriculture follow suit, such as the United States and China; only if exporters of agricultural products too agree to open their markets; only if, lastly, the concessions made by Europe in agricultural matters are accompanied by an opening up of industrial markets in countries such as Brazil and India. If we add to that the extreme complexity of negotiations and the very large number of actors involved in them, the outcome is a deadlocked and confused situation. From patent failures (Seattle, Cancun) to semi-successes (Doha, the Geneva Accords of 2004), the world trade system is making no headway because the countries of the G-20 have managed to polarize negotiation around a simple principle: the South will make no industrial tariff concessions as long as the countries of the North, particularly Europe, have not made any more specific commitments regarding the reduction of their agricultural protection.[77] There is nothing surprising about these deadlocks and this slowdown in themselves. The fact that the U.S. government has had such difficulty getting the Congress to adopt a free trade agreement with Central America, whose exports do not exceed those of the state of New Jersey, demonstrates that the preference for free trade remains structurally weak throughout the world.[78]

In response to this situation, the European Union can assert that the agricultural protectionism it is criticized for in no way constitutes an operation of "development denial" to the countries of the South. In fact, none of the southern hemisphere countries share common interests on agricultural questions. Except for the large agricultural-exporting countries such as Brazil, Thailand, or Australia, all the other countries of the South will be penalized by, the opening up and deprotection of European markets particularly those nations that enjoy preferred access to European markets. Actually, there is a divide among the countries of the South between net importers of agricultural products, for whom opening markets and ending subsidies would increase their agricultural bill, and net exporters, who would benefit from the unlikely reduction in support.[79]

But however justified, this line of defense seems threatened by the logic of nondiscrimination that rules world trade. Intuitively, it may seem "useful" or "reasonable" to grant privileged access to the less advanced countries of the South. But besides the fact that it seems difficult to define the principle and conditions on which to exercise this discrimination, it is hard to see why it would apply more to agriculture them to other products. Reference to multifunctionality could then be made to justify such discrimination. But there is no broad consensus on its meaning. Moreover, if a decision is made to grant sugar from Mauritius privileged access to the European market, it would be less to protect the multifunctionality of Mauritian agriculture than to protect a source of guaranteed income that Mauritius would enjoy due to the privileged access. This income would then act as a disincentive for Mauritius to diversify its agriculture.

Collective Preferences as Doctrine?

All this brings us back to our point of departure: to know under what conditions Europe can assert recognition of nonmarket social preferences as a general means of regulating globalization and not only as a set of ad hoc provisions that can reduce the social impact of market liberalization in a given area.

This is precisely the task that European trade commissioner Pascal Lamy set out to accomplish toward the end of his term, by publishing a substantial document entitled "The Emergence of Collective Preferences in International Trade: Implications for Regulating Globalisation."[80] This essay, which did not receive the Commission's imprimatur, provoked considerable reaction in Great Britain. To a certain extent, this text tends to admit that the effect of norms stops where more fundamental political issues step in. When facing the social resistance that usually confronts the opening of markets, it is not so much norms that are needed (still, they are), but political choices, on which new norms can be grafted. Without analyzing it in depth, Pascal Lamy's argument can be summarized thus: The dynamics of international trade are increasingly interfering with nonmarket social preferences that traditional regulation as practiced by the WTO will have more and more difficulty handling because they will place the liberalization of trade at odds with strong social, cultural, and identity issues.[81] In other words, trade conflicts will become less and less classic trade disputes because they will conflict with different collective preferences. For the moment, there are no guidelines available in the international system that can be used to settle a dispute between trade preferences and environmental preferences, or between trade preferences and social preferences. Furthermore, even if there were aspects of governance capable of arbitrating some of these conflicts, the global institutions that would settle a hypothetical conflict between trade norms and health norms do not exist.

World governance thus has a structural deficit in the hierarchy of norms. To compensate for this deficiency, Pascal Lamy has outlined a sort of provisional honorable exit that would involve having the WTO recognize the existence of collective preferences that can be enforced on the market to create compensatory mechanisms for actors who suffer from the imposition of these preferences. In the case of agriculture, for instance, Europe would have the right to protect its agriculture and its farmers even if this protection put certain countries at a disadvantage, but in exchange, the exporters who lose out would benefit from financial compensation to make up for this loss of income. The right to protection would thus be acknowledged, but this preference would have a cost.

In any event, Pascal Lamy thus proposes a system unlike the traditional safeguard clauses recognized by the WTO, of compensations to be paid immediately to the "victims" (producers) of the safeguard clause. Defense of collective preferences would thus be paid for twice: by protecting a market from the entry of less expensive products and by compensating those whose access to the market, the European market in this case, would be blocked. Why should Europe accept such a system? One reason might be that Europe needs to protect its agriculture due to the wide-ranging social utility that agriculture fulfills. But there is more than that. For the past few years, the Commission—or in any case certain departments of the Commission involved in development issues—has begun to understand that the approach to liberalization through reciprocal trade concessions as practiced with *developed countries* cannot be extended to *developing countries.* That is because the key to development in these countries is not necessarily the opening of their markets but internal socioeconomic reforms. In other words, negotiations should not involve opening European agricultural markets in exchange for opening southern industrial markets, but opening northern markets in exchange for macroeconomic conditionality. But such an approach is notoriously complex to implement, all the more so as it introduces a hiatus between European concessions on agriculture and the economic and social reforms in the countries of the South. That explains the mixture of common sense and self-interest with which one might ask why Europe should really sacrifice protection of its agriculture, if the trade-off for this sacrifice is arbitrary access to uncertain or relatively uninteresting markets.[82]

This idea of resorting to social and identity safeguard clauses has already been discussed by John Jackson and Dan Rodrik.[83] But it encounters several difficulties, including knowing who validates the collective preferences in the nation or in an entity such as Europe. Who makes sure that these preferences really reflect the people's mandate and not the dictates of certain interest groups?[84]

For neoliberal economists, the assertion of collective preferences is based on doubtful reasoning that causes one to lose sight of the one and only arbitrator of preferences: the consumer. Consumers are the ones who should decide if they wish to eat beef with hormones or not. It is also their responsibility to decide on the potential harmfulness of a product for which the risks are not formally established. Along these lines, making an issue out of collective preferences would thus merely be a new form of protectionism that Europe is trying to establish to protect its agriculture.[85]

Obviously, gaining recognition for collective preferences runs up against considerable obstacles, and converting sectional interests to collective preferences is not self-evident. But at the same time, the reduction of all preference conflicts to conflicts of individual preferences is hardly convincing. Consumer freedom is purely academic when it is reduced to a choice between a potentially harmful but inexpensive product and an expensive product free of all risk. In other words, if beef with hormones is considerably less expensive than traditional beef, consumer choice will be dictated not by preference but by income. It cannot be denied, then, that with regard to certain risks, the assessment and the means of assessing these risks vary from one country to another, from one society to another, and that, very often, the appreciable difference that results is more cultural than strictly scientific. It would for instance be difficult to explain the strong aversion German public opinion has to GMOs without taking into account the trauma caused by genetic engineering during the Nazi era. It would also be groundless to analyze French support for agricultural protection solely in terms of political clientelism; it may be an essential factor, but it does not explain everything. The French relationship to food and the rural world also has a historical dimension. It is not entirely ossified, but it cannot be disregarded either.

This is why, although the notion of collective preference may be debatable, it cannot be rejected out of hand merely on the grounds that it purportedly contravenes the rules and principles of free trade. And in fact, the WTO has already outlined a substantial number of measures that can be opposed to the unconditional opening of markets.[86] Steve Charnowitz proposes taking the issue of collective preferences seriously, but he suggests that a distinction should be made between preferences that reflect a strictly internal preference and those that have to do with a preference likely to obligate other actors to adopt one's own preferences.[87]

In the case of beef with hormones, one can perfectly accept the idea that Europeans want to guard themselves against this type of food rather than compel others to give it up (internal preference). On the other hand, when the United States declares an embargo on cat and dog fur, it naturally calls up an internal social preference (animal protection), but the goal is more ambitious because it aims to make China abandon certain practices. Thus there can be collective preferences that hardly clash with other's interests and collective preferences more universal in scope (core labor standards) that aim precisely to modify the collective preferences of other societies. This distinction, although methodologically interesting, does not necessarily seem convincing from an operational standpoint.

Actually, the real discriminating variable in this issue resides in the economic stakes a given collective preference represents. As long as the stakes of the preference remain relatively limited (beef with hormones), arrangements can always be found.[88] If, on the other hand, the precautionary principle is one day used by Europe to prevent the sales of Boeing aircraft, the stakes would be of an entirely different dimension. How then is it possible at the same time to accept the legitimacy of a concept, admit its fragility, and acknowledge the heterogeneity of collective preferences in the world? At first glance, Pascal Lamy's proposal for a broad safeguard clause based on the principle of financial compensation may seem credible and operational. But it runs up against two obstacles. The first is that the compensation mechanism can be seriously implemented only by rich countries. It is indeed hard to see how even an emerging country could compensate the European Union in the name of national collective preferences. Furthermore, the idea of directly compensating producers confronted with enforceable collective preferences is not necessarily always a good idea. It is easy to understand that the United States would compensate cotton producers in Burkina Faso who suffer from the overproduction of American cotton growers. But is it reasonable to compensate Brazilian latifundium whose colossal fortunes overshadow Brazil's criticism of European protectionism?

This is why, given these different constraints, two paths can be envisaged. The first involves integrating collective preferences into the system of waivers that three-quarters of the WTO members can ratify for fairly long periods of time. The second would involve persuading WTO panels to more boldly take into account the various sources of international law, and not only trade law, when they are called upon to settle disputes involving collective preferences.[89]

CHAPTER 4

European Governance and American Sovereignism

As discussed earlier, Europe's social preferences affect the rest of the world in highly variable conditions and proportions. To prohibit importation of beef with hormones from the United States reflects a relationship with food that Europeans can maintain without seeking to impose it on other societies. In the latter can reasonably make do with this. Such preferences shall thus be called *defensive social preferences*.

The ban on GMOs is already a more serious issue. For even if Europe manages to limit the use of them at home, it has every interest in ensuring that third world countries also restrict their consumption, or else it may find itself at risk of being "besieged" by them and inevitably obliged to accept GMO products in the long run. This explains its attempt to convince certain southern hemisphere countries to refuse American food aid that contains GMOs. In this case I will speak of *semidefensive collective preferences*.

Lastly, there are social preferences that Europeans can defend only if others also share them (*offensive collective preferences*). Let us take three examples: abolition of the death penalty, environmental protection, and the determination to bring war criminals to trial. In these three cases, however different, it is extremely difficult to think within a strictly European framework, for the content of these preferences is necessarily universal in scope. When one manages to abolish the death penalty at home, one is irremediably tempted to seek to have it abolished elsewhere; the issue calls up universal and not national categories. And this is, in fact, the order in which things occurred. The spread throughout Europe of the movement to abolish the death penalty eventually prompted Europeans to fight for the abolition of the death penalty in the United States.[1]

In environmental matters, it is even more difficult to maintain the discontinuity between the European and world framework because, by definition, greenhouse gas emissions are not confined within national borders. If Europe wants to advance the environmental cause, it must then clearly integrate into world regulation the states most directly involved. This is what it managed to do in strongly encouraging Moscow to ratify the Kyoto Protocol, thus enabling it to come into effect.

The issue is identical regarding questions of international criminal justice. The system's effectiveness depends on the adhesion of the greatest possible number of actors and, in particular, the greatest number of actors likely to be involved in this type of situation.[2]

This is why Europe's advocacy of the Kyoto Protocol and the International Criminal Court can be said to express a mild form of cosmopolitanism based on universal norms applicable to all individuals regardless of their community affiliations, whether ethnic, religious or national.[3] Europe likes to show that its international commitments express "an allegiance to a worldwide community of human beings."[4] The defense of a certain European preference is thus filtered through a temperate but undeniable cosmopolitanism. Naturally, the theoretical and practical conditions in which this can be exercised are extremely varied and often contradictory. But notwithstanding the content one invests in the European cosmopolitical commitment to deal with questions of global public goods such as the environment world peace; and justice, the question arises also as to whether there is not a conflict between cosmopolitanism and what Alasdair MacIntyre calls "the morality of patriotism."[5] MacIntyre, speaking from a philosophical standpoint, sees a contradiction between the interests in one's community (the morality of patriotism) and what he calls "the morality of impartiality," a legacy of the Enlightenment.[6] The morality of patriotism does not exclude reference to universal values or the desire to serve them. MacIntyre simply believes that the best way to do so is to start by taking care of the community that one has the closest ties with. The morality of patriotism necessarily draws on a certain wariness vis-à-vis abstract universalism.

It would, of course, be too simplistic to see an opposition between the Europeans' moderate cosmopolitanism and MacIntyre's "morality of patriotism" that can be said to characterize the United States. But the parallel is not absurd for all that. The Europeans, who invented modern sovereignty, are induced to take stock of its limits as if they had exhausted its resources. Naturally, the sharing of sovereignty is far from linear and the more or less hidden forms of sovereignism in Europe have hardly been defeated. Nonetheless, since 1957 there has been a basis in Europe on which to share sovereignty that is strongly rooted in the powerful effect of European jurisprudence. This is naturally not the case in other regimes, particularly in the United States. This can explain the conflict in worldviews that may pit Americans against Europeans. The former are attached to national sovereignty, the latter to a preference for governance based on shared sovereignty.

Europe's Normative Achievements

The fact is obvious. The European preference for norms is not necessarily shared by all the other world actors. When these norms concern "world governance," the fact that they are shared or not is decisive. It is, of course, always useful for Europe to be the great champion of basic social norms, because one can always wager that norms will undergo the often slow and necessarily uncertain process of interiorization, which differs precisely from the sovereign, swift, immediate, and binding form of decision making. But banking on the long term also presents considerable risks. It is indeed possible that in the long run, the United States will adhere to the Kyoto Protocol. But this cannot be taken for a strong probability. That is why one cannot study norms without examining the question of their effectiveness. I will thus proceed to assess Europe's normative achievements by comparing them with those of other world actors.

Table 4.1 provides a coherent view. It lists 32 basic documents of world governance considered as such by the United Nations, as well as 8 ILO framework conventions on rights at work.

Table 4.1 The normative achievements of the major world actors

	EU	*USA*	*Japan*	*Brazil*	*Russia*	*China*	*India*
RIGHTS AT WORK	8	2	6	7	8	3	4
1. Freedom of Association and Protection of the Right to Organize Convention	25	no	yes	no	yes	no	no
2. Right to Organize and Collective Bargaining	25	no	yes	yes	yes	no	no
3. Forced Labor	24	no	yes	yes	yes	no	yes
4. Abolition of Forced Labor	25	yes	no	yes	yes	no	yes
5. Equal Remuneration	25	no	yes	yes	yes	yes	yes
6. Discrimination (Employment and Occupation) Convention	24	no	no	yes	yes	no	yes
7. Minimum Age Convention	23	No	yes	yes	yes	yes	no
8. Worst Forms of Child Labor Convention	24	yes	yes	yes	yes	yes	no
HUMAN RIGHTS	7	4	4	5	5	4	3
1. International Covenant on Economic, Social, and Cultural Rights (New York, December 16, 1966)	25	Not ratified	yes	yes	yes	yes	yes
2. International Covenant on Civil and Political Rights (New York, December 16, 1966)	25	yes	yes	yes	yes	yes	yes
3. Optional Protocol to the International Covenant on Civil and Political Rights (New York, December 16, 1966)	24	no	no	no	yes	no	No
4. Convention on the Prevention and Punishment of the Crime of Genocide (New York, December 9, 1948)	24	yes	no	yes	yes	yes	yes
5. Convention against Torture and Other Cruel, Inhuman or Degrading Treatment or Punishment (New York, December 10, 1984)	25	yes	yes	yes	yes	yes	SpasR

	EU	*USA*	*Japan*	*Brazil*	*Russia*	*China*	*India*
6. Optional Protocol to the Convention against Torture and Other Cruel, Inhuman or Degrading Treatment or Punishment (New York, December 18, 2002)	3 + 10 not ratified	no	no	Not ratified	no	no	no
7. International Convention on the Protection of the Rights of All Migrant Workers and Members of their Families (New York, December 18, 1990)	no	no	no	no	no	no	no
8. Optional Protocol to the Convention on the Rights of the Child on the involvement of children in armed conflict (New York, May 25, 2000)	24 + 1 not ratified	yes	yes	yes	Not ratified	Not ratified	Not ratified
9. Optional Protocol to the Convention on the Rights of the Child on the sale of children, child prostitution and child pornography (New York, May 25, 2000)	21 + 4 not ratified	yes	yes	yes	no	Yes	
REFUGEES	2	1	2	2	2	2	0
10. Convention relating to the Status of Refugees (Geneva, July 28, 1951)	25	no	yes	yes	yes	Yes	no
11. Protocol relating to the Status of Refugees (New York, January 31, 1967)	25	yes	yes	yes	yes	Yes	no
PENAL MATTERS	3	0	0	2	1	1	0
12. Rome Statute of the International Criminal Court (Rome, July 17, 1998)	24	Not ratified	no	yes	Not ratified	no	no
13. Agreement on the Privileges and Immunities of the International Criminal Court (New York, September 9, 2002)	10 + 14 not ratified	no	no	Not ratified	no	no	No
14. Convention on the Safety of United Nations and Associated Personnel (New York, December 9, 1994)	25	Not ratified	yes	yes	yes	Yes	no

Continued

Table 4.1 Continued

	EU	*USA*	*Japan*	*Brazil*	*Russia*	*China*	*India*
TERRORISM	3	3	2	2	3	1	3
15. International Convention for the Suppression of Terrorist Bombings (New York, December 15, 1997)	24 + 1 not ratified	yes	yes	yes	yes	Yes	yes
16. International Convention for the Suppression of the Financing of Terrorism (New York, December 9, 1999)	25	yes	yes	not ratified	yes	not ratified	yes
17. International Convention for the Suppression of Acts of Nuclear Terrorism (New York, April 13, 2005)	25	yes	no	yes	yes	no	yes
ORGANIZED CRIME AND CORRUPTION	4	0	0	3	3	1	0
18. United Nations Convention against Transnational Organized Crime (New York, November 15, 2000)	25	not ratified	not ratified	yes	yes	yes	not ratified
19. Protocol to Prevent, Suppress and Punish Trafficking in Persons, Especially Women and Children, supplementing the United Nations Convention against Transnational Organized Crime (New York, November 15, 2000)	25	not ratified	not ratified	yes	yes	no	not ratified
20. Protocol against the Smuggling of Migrants by Land, Sea and Air, supplementing the United Nations Convention against Transnational Organized Crime (New York, November 15, 2000)	18 + 6 not ratified	not ratified	not ratified	yes	yes	no	not ratified
21. Protocol against the Illicit Manufacturing of and Trafficking in Firearms, Their Parts and Components and Ammunition, supplementing the United Nations Convention against Transnational Organized Crime (New York, May 31, 2001)		no	not ratified	not ratified	no	not ratified	not ratified
22. United Nations Convention against Corruption (New York, October 31, 2003)	24 not ratified	not ratified	not ratified	not ratified	not ratified	not ratified	no

	EU	*USA*	*Japan*	*Brazil*	*Russia*	*China*	*India*
ENVIRONMENT	3,56	0	4	4	1	2	
23. Kyoto Protocol to the United Nations Framework Convention on Climate Change (Kyoto, December 11, 1997)	23	not ratified	yes	yes	yes	yes	yes
24. Rotterdam Convention on the Prior Informed Consent Procedure for Certain Hazardous Chemicals and Pesticides in International Trade (Rotterdam, September 10, 1998)	25	not ratified	yes	yes	no	not ratified	no
25. Stockholm Convention on Persistent Organic Pollutants (Stockholm, May 22, 2001)	22 + 3 not ratified	not ratified	yes	yes	not ratified	yes	not ratified
26. Cartagena Protocol on Biosafety to the Convention on Biological Diversity (Montreal, January 29, 2000)	19	no	yes	yes	no	SpasR	yes
LAW OF THE SEA	2	1	1	1	2	1	2
27. United Nations Convention on the Law of the Sea (Montego Bay, December 10, 1982); Agreement relating to the implementation of Part XI of the United Nations Convention on the Law of the Sea of December 10, 1982 (New York, July 28, 1994)	25	no	yes	not ratified	yes	yes	yes
28. Agreement for the Implementation of the Provisions of the United Nations Convention on the Law of the Sea of December 10, 1982 relating to the Conservation and Management of Straddling Fish Stocks and Highly Migratory Fish Stocks (New York, August 4, 1995)	25	yes	not ratified	yes	yes	not ratified	yes

Continued

Table 4.1 Continued

	EU	*USA*	*Japan*	*Brazil*	*Russia*	*China*	*India*
DISARMAMENT	2	0	2	2	1	0	0
29. Comprehensive Nuclear-Test-Ban Treaty (New York, September 10, 1996)	25	not ratified	yes	yes	yes	not ratified	no
30. Convention on the Prohibition of the Use, Stockpiling, Production and Transfer of Anti-Personnel Mines and on their destruction (Oslo, September 18, 1997)	25	no	yes	yes	no	no	no
HEALTH	1	0	1	0	0	0	1
31. WHO Framework Convention on Tobacco Control (Geneva, May 21, 2003)	25	not ratified	yes	not ratified	no	not ratified	yes
LAW OF TREATIES	1	0	1	0	1	1	1
32. Vienna Convention on the Law of Treaties (Vienna, May 23, 1969)	24	not ratified	yes	not ratified	yes	yes	yes
TOTAL	37	11	23	28	27	16	16

Source: Data from the United Nations Treaty Collections (available at http://untreaty.un.org) and the International Labor Organization, Ratifications of ILO's Eight Core Conventions (http://www.ilo.org/).

The totals take into account only ratified treaties. The table shows, however, cases where treaties have been signed but not ratified. For European ratifications, the figures have been rounded off to show an average of the 25 member states, which does not always produce a square figure. "Yes" means "ratified"; "no" means "not signed." Between these two poles can be found cases in which the documents have been signed but not ratified.

The area covered by these texts is thus fairly broad: human rights (nine documents), legal issues (three, including the Rome Statute founding the International Criminal Court), environmental issues (four, including the Kyoto Protocol), maritime law (two), disarmament (two), health (1 document), refugees (two), terrorism (three), the fight against organized crime and corruption (five), and treaty law (the Vienna Convention).

Why Europe Does Better

Three observations emerge from this table:

The first is that there exists a very strong intra-European normative dynamic, even among new members of the EU. This fairly strong cohesion can be found not only in these documents but also more generally in the votes at the UN—with some very palpable differences nevertheless, depending on whether the convention is voted in the Security Council or the General Assembly.[7] This means that by joining the European Union, one adheres to a certain "worldview," a vision based on a preference for norms. But this dynamic of adhesion to a rationale of normative power does not pertain only to the new members. Some founding members have also submitted to it. This is precisely the case in which France found itself in negotiations for the Treaty of Rome regarding the creation of the International Criminal Court.

It is worth briefly reviewing the origins of this project and the stakes involved. There has long been an ambition to establish an international criminal justice system. The first reference to international justice appeared in article 227 of the Treaty of Versailles in 1919, which expressly provided for the prosecution of Emperor Wilhelm II by a special court "for supreme offence against international morality." But the trial was never to take place. Wilhelm

II was granted exile by the Netherlands, which refused to extradite him on the grounds that political reasons were not valid grounds for extradition.[8] In 1920, the League of Nations discussed the idea of creating a high court of criminal justice, but it was never really followed through. And yet, there is remarkable continuity in the thinking of legal experts on the subject. In 1922, the International Law Association argued in favor of establishing an international criminal court. In 1935, the Romanian jurist Vespasien Pella published an international penal code. In 1934, the French government submitted to the League of Nations a proposal to create an international criminal court that would prosecute terrorist acts such as those committed in Marseilles in October 1934 against the king of Yugoslavia and the French foreign affairs minister. The dawn of international criminal justice would not come, however, until the aftermath of the Second World War with the creation of the Nuremberg and Tokyo war crimes tribunals. On the legal level, the foundational value of the Nuremberg trials resides in the definition of international criminal offenses: crimes against peace, war crimes, and crimes against humanity. The statute of the International Criminal Court (ICC) is very close to these definitions. Article 5 recognizes four crimes: the crime of genocide, crimes against humanity, war crimes, and the crime of aggression.[9]

The first three of these crimes are defined in detail in articles 6, 7, and 8 of the statute, as opposed to the crime of aggression. But unlike the two existing international criminal tribunals, the International Criminal Tribunal (for the former Yugoslavia) established in 1993 and the International Criminal Tribunal for Rwanda established in 1994, the ICC is a permanent body formed on the basis of an international treaty and not a simple UN resolution. It thus immediately enjoys greater legitimacy because it is out of the grip of the Security Council's political control and any sort of geopolitical tropism in that its jurisdiction is universal. Moreover, and unlike ad hoc tribunals designed to punish, the ICC intends not only to punish but also to dissuade. That said, as soon as it displayed broader ambitions and greater independence, the ICC project inevitably collided with state sovereignty. For even when states remained favorable to the establishment of a permanent court, they could not accept a pure and simple abdication of their political sovereignty. This resulted in setting up a complex system based on the principle of complementarity between national jurisdictions and international criminal justice. Articles 12 and 17 guarantee the primacy of national jurisdictions to try their own citizens, the ICC acting only as a last resort against a state that refrains from initiating criminal proceedings against perpetrators of serious crimes.[10]

In theory, the ICC thus has no reason to act against constitutional states. And yet, some such states have expressed reservations with regard to this mechanism, particularly when they are engaged in peacekeeping operations. Their fear has been to see the ICC stand in for the Security Council in the name of a judicialization (even criminalization) of international politics, which could possibly lead soldiers in countries that are heavily involved in UN operations to be in a position to be prosecuted by the ICC.[11] The French and the Americans held similar positions on this point. This is why these two countries (unsuccessfully) defended the triple consent requirement to activate jurisdiction of the ICC: consent of the state in which the acts were committed, consent of the state of which the victims were nationals, and consent of the state from which the alleged perpetrators originated.[12] If such a proposal had been accepted, it would have led to paralyzing the ICC.[13] At this stage, France was closer to the United States than to Germany, for instance. The distance between the United States and France came at a later time, when the question arose as to whether these positions should be defended at all costs, including that of refusing to sign the document, or whether they should go as far as possible on the path to a compromise. France chose the second option. It decided to bend because it managed to display a certain legal creativeness. But the compromise can also be considered to have been dictated by the constraint of Europe. It was difficult for France to reject a document of such symbolic scope when negotiations had taken place in a European country, nearly all the states of the EU were in favor of it, there were strong pressures from NGOs, and French diplomacy has always wanted to associate its behavior with the pursuit of the ideals enshrined in the Declaration of Human Rights.

In areas where it was able to make itself heard, France clearly managed to influence the Rome Statute, particularly in suggesting the establishment of a Pre-Trial Chamber—which decides whether a case is admissible—as a framework within which states can dispute the court's jurisdiction or the admissibility of a complaint.[14] It also managed to introduce into the statute an article—article 124—that allows any state that has become party to the statute to decline the Court's jurisdiction for war crimes when such a crime has allegedly been committed on its territory or by its nationals. France is, in fact, the only country in the world to have announced its intention to use article 124, supposedly on the grounds of wanting to guard against any idea of universal jurisdiction of the ICC. But this protection remains relative because the principle of universal jurisdiction was already admitted by France when it adhered to the Geneva Conventions.[15] This is why several legal experts, even in France, strongly criticized such reservations.[16] Despite these qualms, France signed and ratified the ICC statute. As a member of the European Union collectively involved in the issue, France could not take the risk of going it alone and eluding such a symbolically strong collective discipline. The United States were not in the same situation, even if the Clinton administration, which had invested considerable energy in prosecuting war criminals from former Yugoslavia, nevertheless saw itself as a party to the ICC and hence signed the Treaty. But the Bush administration reneged on this commitment.

The second point to note about this table is the gap between Europe's normative achievements and those of other states. Japan, another great soft power, displays the narrowest gap with respect to Europe except, oddly enough, in the field of organized crime and the fight against corruption. But the slimness of this gap should not be overinterpreted. Since 1945, Japan as a state has naturally been seeking to fit its action and its international behavior to a normative rationale. Though it rarely initiates norms, it almost always strives to be part of them except when the normative dynamic, particularly in the field of human rights, enters into conflict with certain discriminatory practices in effect in Japan: harsh treatment of the mentally ill, discrimination against Koreans and certain castes (the Burakumin), reluctance to recognize its historical responsibility in Asia.[17]

This normative follow-my-leader attitude does not, for all that, mean that these international norms are interiorized. Iwasawa has for instance convincingly demonstrated that Japanese courts almost systematically reject arguments for the defense of human rights based on international principles, referring to international courts only nominally, very rarely invoking international jurisprudence and basically believing that international norms produce no additional protection with regard to Japanese constitutional provisions. In this way, no political claims to legal sovereignism are made, but it is openly practiced.[18]

Contrary to what might be expected, the gap with Russia is also fairly slim and there are, three complementary reasons for this: a legalistic Soviet legacy as regards form (even if norms were, of course, twisted or flouted); a desire to catch up and adhere to international norms starting in the 1990s; a neo-Sovietism that prompts politicians to express their multilateral good-faith (ratification of the Kyoto Protocol), even if that means integrating the idea of a discrepancy between acceptance (or even ratification of a document) and its implementation. It should be noted, however, that Russia has not yet ratified the treaty founding the ICC, it has not signed the accord on ICC privileges and immunities, and it has not signed two of the four most important conventions on the environment. In other words, the gap with Europe remains significant in sensitive areas.

There remain the cases of China, India, and the United States. With China, there is a very wide gap in the area of rights at work (low rate of ratification of ILO conventions), public freedoms (low rate of ratification of human rights conventions), military power (disarmament), and international criminal issues and organized crime. Despite their very different political systems, India's record is quite similar to China's, as India's reservations pertain to documents likely to conflict with its political sovereignty.

There is nothing about this worldwide normative landscape to reassure Europe, even if it is not set in stone. For Europe must deal with three world actors who do not share its preference for norms. These three states happen to be the powers of today (the United States) and tomorrow (China and India). The assumption can naturally be made that as they develop and integrate world political checkerboard, India and China will come around to sharing this European preference. But the American counterexample, which will be explored in greater depth, shows that it is not necessarily reasonable to assume this normative teleology will function. The idea that more globalization calls for more interdependence and so more governance is a European hypothesis. But nothing indicates that it is shared by all the other actors.

It is thus essential to show here at once how the preference for international norms took root in Europe, and why, almost symmetrically, there has been a very strong decline of this preference in the United States, a decline that cannot be ascribed to the neoconservative project alone.

The Preference for Shared Sovereignty

The preceding chapters reviewed the historical factors that would rather naturally explain Europe's preference for norms. But this preference derives its full originality from the fact that it is based on an essential principle of European integration: shared sovereignty. It is a principle that serves to harmonize European national positions with respect to the rest of the world.

The preference for shared sovereignty is not simply an act of faith or a political proclamation. It is so legally entrenched that, as Joseph Weiler says, the European Union's operational mechanism is no longer governed by general principles of international public law—which traditionally governs relations between states—but by an interstate structure specific to the European states.[19]

What characterizes the European legal system is the fact that it is essentially based on all whole series of mechanisms that place national legal systems under the authority of European law. The most crucial of them has to do with what is called the direct effect principle. It came about in 1963 and established the presumption that community norms should be considered as national norms.[20] It is extremely broad in scope, because it no longer makes European states the necessary intermediaries of international law. A European citizen can enforce the rule of European law on his or her own state if the latter happens to violate it.[21] The revolutionary principle of direct effect was strengthened by a second principle that was just as decisive: that of *primacy*. Established in 1964, it comes down to saying that within the community space, any community norm, whatever its status, wins over any contrary national norm, irrespective of whether it came before or after.[22] These two principles combined underscore to what extent Europe has, on the legal level, interiorized the submission of national laws to European law. This historical event makes it naturally predisposed to accept implementation of rules that, on a global scale, will take primacy over the law of various states.[23] In other words, the EU attitude is, "What we have done amongst ourselves, the world can try to do as well." Europe does not officially present itself this way. But such discourse is part of its relationship to the world, an unprecedented way of relating to the world and the law that in today's globalized context clashes with a form of sovereignism that is taking the form of a real counterrevolution in the United States.

The American Counterrevolution

At first glance, the United States—the epitome of the constitutional state—has an impressive track record as a normative power, even in recent years. Between 1993 and 2000—a period that corresponds to the Clinton presidency—the president of the United States submitted 184 treaties to Congress for ratification, 170 of which were approved at the end of 2002.[24] But this raw data warrants a closer look. In fact, out of these 184 treaties, 126 were bilateral treaties and 40 of them multilateral treaties. Although the Senate approved 126 of the 130 bilateral treaties, it ratified only 31 of the 40 multilateral treaties. Moreover, out of these 31 approved treaties, 24 approvals were conditional, which means that unconditional ratification is no longer at all the norm in the United States.[25] The conditional nature of these ratifications is symbolized by the extremely long time it takes from the moment these treaties are submitted to Congress to the time a decision is made. For the 31 above-mentioned international treaties, this timeframe was on the average just over six years.[26] Leaving the quantitative dimension aside to consider the qualitative nature of the treaties, American reluctance seems even greater. Out of the 32 international documents the United Nations considers as being central to world governance, the United States had ratified only nine of them in 2005. Nine of the treaties have not yet been sent to Congress, twelve of them were ratified after an average of eleven years, and nine of the treaties ratified have conditions attached to them. Thus, out of the 40 major international treaties (see table), the United States has ratified only 11 of them compared to 34 for the European Union. There is obviously an increasing political reluctance on the part of the United States to endorse global choices made by the international community in areas that pertain to the management of global public goods such as the environment, health, criminal justice, the fight against pandemics, and other such areas. From the American perspective, the preferences generally challenged have to do with the model of energy consumption, capital punishment, abortion, arms control, or the status of religion in public life.[27] How can such reluctance be explained?

The first reason has to do with the fact that the new regulatory instruments of globalization finalized by treaties or conventions differ from the major traditional treaties in both form and content. Treaties supposed to regulate globalization no longer have the strictly interstate nature of major traditional treaties. They are instead intersocietal treaties that precisely establish a relationship between national collective preferences.[28]

Let us take the example of the environment. The United States was for a long time world leader in this area as much from the standpoint of initiating accords as from the position of signing and ratifying them.[29] But since the Rio Earth Summit in 1992, which still serves as a reference for global environmental governance, American reluctance has increased, particularly because the United States has no longer been the initiator of these new treaties. It just so happens that these new treaties are based on the 1992 Rio Declaration that lays down two principles that the United States energetically opposes: the precautionary principle and the principle of differentiated responsibility of states depending on their level of development.[30] They do not systematically oppose these two principles in and of themselves, but they want to prevent them at all costs from becoming principles of customary international law that would impose on them de facto responsibilities and obligations they would not be able to depart from.[31] The United States wants to avoid being caught up in a legal maze of which they do not control all the ins and outs.

A second explanation for American reluctance to sign international treaties applies both to the environment and global public goods on the whole: It pertains to the transformation of the instruments of world governance. In the classic international legal schema that has dominated so far, states negotiate, sign, and ratify treaties that then come into force. Today, the dynamics of world agreements is slightly different. Given that right from the start the idea is to involve the greatest number of actors, the documents outline framework provisions and it is the job of the conference of the parties to specify the details of them. The result is that framework treaties on global governance are looking more and more like international organizations that carry out actions according to a collective process in which no actor taken individually controls the game.

Symmetrically, these documents generate models of normative conduct there again produced by the dynamic nature of the negotiations and the protocols implemented.[32] This dynamic, which encourages the existence of pivotal actors, does not necessarily work in favor of large states. The ICC statute for instance stipulates that its area of jurisdiction may be extended by a two-thirds majority.

What the United States fears is that sovereign states will lose their control in the face of an emerging global legal corpus where commitments made by states would be administered, interpreted, and implemented by multilateral institutions, thus transforming international cooperation into international law.[33] Tthe United States refusal to ratify the Kyoto Protocol or the ICC statute clearly expresses these fears.[34] The body of law created by courts such as the ICC is argued to have the major disadvantage of being based on a principle of authority that leaves no room for the power of representative democracy.[35] But it is interesting to note the coincidence in the timings of the rise of legal revisionism in the United States that is increasingly hostile to the interiorization of international law by American law and the emergence of a political, ideological, and militant sovereignism training its sights on "world governance."

American Legal Revisionism

American legal revisionism was spawned by two American legal scholars, Curtis Bradley and Jack Goldsmith. In an article published in 1997,[36] these two authors criticized the increasing and direct intrusion of international law in American law with no control or mediation from representatives of the American people. More precisely, they dispute the idea that customary international law (CIL)[37] is self-executory by American courts without having first been ratified or implemented by the U.S. Congress itself.[38] They deem this position, which they call "modernist," contrary to the principles of separation of powers, federalism, and representative democracy. To them, assimilating CIL with federal law is nothing short of illegitimate.[39] The internal order remains fundamentally distinct from the international order and, under such conditions, the federal authorities alone are entitled to enforce and interpret CIL.

This legal sovereignism aims to reverse a trend that was set by the famous *Restatement of the Foreign Relations Law of the United States*, which is widely taken as a reference for legal specialists, whether they are professors, lawyers, or judges.[40] This *Restatement*, produced by internationalist legal scholars, confirms the idea that international law is clearly part of federal American law, which is precisely what Bradley and Goldsmith dispute. In support of their thesis, the two authors refer to a highly substantial body of Supreme Court jurisprudence in a degree of detail that will not be repeated here.[41] On the other hand, what is worth remembering about this revisionist movement is its political significance and the contrast it offers with regard to the European position. In a complementary article, Curtis Bradley carries his reasoning further. He disputes the self-executory inclusion of customary international law in federal American law by restating the preceding arguments, but this time he adds more political than legal arguments: Unlike the customary international law that prevailed in the nineteenth century and up until the Second World War, the new customary international law is highly focused on human rights, being based on political declarations rather than practices established by states; instead of seeking to regulate relations between states, it attempts to control the way a state treats its own fellow citizens, particularly as regards human rights, thus creating a conflict between domestic law and international law.[42]

Actually, American legal revisionism boils down to challenging two principles that the European states have all approved: the principle of direct effect and that of the primacy of Community law. In addition, there is another evolution that Europeans deem positive but that American revisionists fear above anything else: the constitutionalization of international law in the sense of a body of law granting primacy of individual rights over those of states.[43]

Recognizing citizens' rights over and above their state amounts to admitting that an authority other than the American state can have control over American citizens. This fundamental postulate reflects the confidence Americans place in their own institutions—and the implicit wariness they have for systems other than their own—thus refusing to unbind the exercise of law from its national framework, deemed to be the only legitimate framework in a democracy, as well as to accept changes in the domestic order imposed from the outside.[44]

The Attack on Global Governance

Actually, and over and above its strictly legal aspects, this form of "revisionism" is interesting especially in its political implications. Empirically, the intrusion of international law in American law hardly seems established. Even when, at the end of the 1980s, at the behest of the executive, the U.S. Congress decided to ratify four major human rights treaties (Convention on the Prevention and Punishment of the Crime of Genocide, International Covenant on Civil and Political Rights, Convention against Torture, International Convention on the Elimination of All Forms of Racial Discrimination), each time it expressed reservations that removed any self-executory character from these documents such that, without explicit and specific legislation passed by Congress, the treaties could have no legal value on American soil.[45]

Moreover, in reaction to any attempt to use international treaties as arguments, in particular to stay executions, the United

States courts have systematically refused to accept their enforceability on federal or state law.[46] The International Protocol on Civil and Political Rights held up by American plaintiffs was deemed not admissible by the American courts precisely because, among the reservations made by the Senate when the document was ratified, there figured the refusal to accept this protocol as a source of national law.[47]

The screening of international law through national lenses thus remains substantial in the United States, with perhaps the exception of the Alien Tort Claims Act (ATCA) that Andrea Bianchi rightly considers an American "anomaly" and that the "revisionists" have, in fact, used as a starting point for their offensive.[48] The ATCA, which actually goes back to the eighteenth century, installed before its time a sort of universal jurisdiction that allows a foreigner residing in the United States to sue a person or a state outside of the United States as long as the offenses invoked were against the law of nations or a treaty signed by the United States.[49] On the shelf for nearly two centuries, this act was reactualized when in 1980 an American court handed down a now famous decision (Filartiga v. Peña-Irala) that authorized a Paraguayan citizen to bring a lawsuit against a Paraguayan police officer accused of torture.[50] It should be noted here that the acceptance by an American court of the principle of universal jurisdiction came at a time when the Carter administration had made human rights a political crusade after the debacles of Vietnam and Watergate. There is hence nothing surprising about the fact that legal revisionism coincides with the reassertion of American national power. Seen from a European perspective, this relation between case law and politics may seem shocking. But in the United States there is nothing shocking about it, because, as Rubenfeld points out, "if the law is to be democratic, the law and the courts that interpret it must retain strong connections to the nation's democratic political system."[51] In other words, when the American legal authorities change their viewpoint, the law has to adapt to this change in the name of the primacy of politics over law. Naturally, this interpretation is not shared by the entire American legal community. There is a whole "internationalist" current among those who argue in favor of an increased inclusion of international documents and norms in domestic law.[52] But that has hardly prevented American legal revisionism from radicalizing. Eric Posner for instance goes much farther than Bradley and Goldsmith. In answer to the question "Should a state obey international law?" he very clearly replies "no," even if that state is already bound by an international treaty. According to him, consenting to a document is more like a promise than a legal obligation. For a promise to become a legal obligation, it must meet certain criteria that do not meet with international consensus. International law thus can be binding only if it is rational for the states to comply with it.[53] Of course, he does not describe the content of this rationality. But he does underscore to what extent the idea of norm can be disputed, even rejected. The idea that an international norm can lead to a change in American legislation is massively rejected by the American legislator for whom no international law can override American law.[54]

The interest of this debate is that it is powerfully conveyed by the American neoconservatives working first within the framework of foundations, and then within the Bush administration. Its figurehead is John Bolton, the U.S. ambassador to the United Nations, who was appointed in August 2005 by President Bush despite U.S. Senate reservations and resigned in December 2006.

His thesis, however unconvincing, has the merit of being clear. According to him, globalization has given rise to a sort of "globalist ideology," the benchmark for which remains the Bruntland Report on global governance, and the dynamics of which threaten the United States' political sovereignty, its political system, and the international flexibility it needs to act in the world.[55]

Bolton identifies four areas in which globalism is a threat: the conditions for recourse to force, human rights, NGOs in the development of formal and informal world regulation.

As regards recourse to force, it is the ICC, the Convention on Anti-Personnel Mines, and the Comprehensive Nuclear-Test-Ban Treaty (CTBT) that are identified as sources of global governance nibbling away at American sovereignty. And, in fact, the United States has ratified none of these three treaties, thereby contradicting Bolton's claim that "globalists" have won the game.[56] Moreover, the Bush administration undertook an offensive to limit the effects of international treaties that might undermine its sovereignty. In May 2002, it announced its withdrawal from the Rome Statute. Three months later, the U.S. Congress passed a law allowing the United States to sign immunity agreements with foreign states. Since that day, the United States has managed to sign 75 immunity agreements, 32 of which are with signatory states of the Rome Statute.[57] The extradition agreement signed with Great Britain in March 2004 seems to include a nonextradition clause.[58] In fact, the United States has managed to protect itself against any utilization of the ICC against its own citizens.

Fire on Europe!

The Americanist and antiglobalist line of argument is a familiar one. It essentially says that world governance aims to keep American political sovereignty in check and place it under the authority of nondemocratic institutions.[59] This feeling has naturally been reinforced since September 11, 2001, to the extent that the sovereignist logic has been extended to the rules of war. Eric Posner, who in a 2003 article expressed the belief that states had no moral obligation to obey international law, repeated the offense in 2005 by stating that the fight against terrorism exempted the United States from feeling bound by the rules of war and even called on the United states to devise implicit norms in this area to serve its own interests.[60]

But beyond its criticism of global governance, what is interesting to note about American revisionism is the role it gives Europe as a vehicle of global governance and thus as a potential adversary of the United States. Bolton writes, for instance, that in many respects Europe has replaced the Third World in globalist rhetoric. "Not content alone with transferring their own national sovereignty to Brussels, they have also decided, in effect, to transfer some of ours to worldwide institutions and norms, thus making the European Union a miniature precursor to global governance."[61] Such ideas lead Jeremy Rabkin to believe that the most fundamental source of conflict likely to oppose the United States and Europe will not be any subject in particular but the very concept of sovereignty. For Rabkin, Europe constitutes a model of shared sovereignty that, if it were to spread, would erode the sovereignty of nation-states.[62] In support of his argument, he takes the example of the environment where, as I have pointed out elsewhere in this chapter, green states have pulled in tow those that were less so. The fact is proven and undebatable. But more important than the fact itself is the way it is interpreted. Rabkin believes that from a sovereignist standpoint, encouraging other states to align their position along that of a group of states—in this case proenvironmental states—is an infringement on state sovereignty and that from a legal standpoint, this process is reprehensible.[63] In his opinion, European member states have a tendency not only to influence one another, but also to be overly influenced by NGOs, particularly environmentalist ones.[64]

In its radicalism, American legal revisionism takes into account the entire body of global regulation, including trade regulation through the WTO,[65] the only international agency the Bush administration has not attacked. In the archipelago of global governance, the WTO remains a preserved oasis for reasons that have to do with Republican free trade ideals and the many lines of cleavage within this institution. In many cases, the United States are, for instance, less isolated than the Europeans precisely because their demands in terms of environmental preservation, health, food, and social norms are not as strong as those of the Europeans.

In any event, and over and above the ideological activism of the neoconservatives who are also sovereignists, looms a deeper issue, there again related to what I have called the Euro-American *chassé-croisé*.

As I wrote in *The Great Disruption*, the Euro-American conflict is primarily a conflict of experience. By that I mean that the trajectories of the United States and Europe diverge because the two entities find themselves at difference historical moments. They do not experience these moments in the same manner. I have demonstrated this as regards environmental questions. Twenty years ago American standards were higher than European standards. Since then, the relationship to risk has been inverted. The same holds true for the relationship to law. According to Robert Pildes, who wrote some enlightening pages on the topic, Euro-American differences over international law also have to do with this conflict of experience. Europeans, according to him, are caught in a logic of constitutionalization of the law, a logic that even the British can no longer escape and that they would like to extend to the international sphere; whereas the Americans express increasing disenchantment with regard to the judicialization of their social and political system: "It is quite intriguing—and enormously significant in this context—that the attachment to legalism and judicial institutions outside the United States is reaching this peak in the same period in which within the United States there has been general and increasing skepticism about judicial institutions."[66] Thus, at a time when Europe sees in law, and thus in norms, a resource for expressing its identity and organizing the world, the United States sees in it a potential means of stifling its autonomy at a time when it no longer has the power to be the initiator of everything.

CHAPTER 5

Is Constitutionalizing the World Order the Answer?

At that point, the question for Europe becomes: How should it use its preference for norms? Should it wave them like a flag in international forums even if Europe does not have the means to plant them firmly on the international scene? Or on the contrary, should Europe more boldly assert its preference for norms so that it becomes shared by the entire world system? In that case, the issue would seem to be to standardize norms, codify them, make them consistent, and rank them, in other words, to constitutionalize the world order. The outcome of global governance would logically be the constitutionalization of the world order.

Constitutionalizing the world order means providing it with normative coherence by

- devising norms for all areas of global activity, creating a legal continuity between internal order and international order;
- giving citizens rights that are guaranteed to be enforceable on their own states;
- ranking norms in such a way that they enter into contradiction with one another as little as possible;
- setting up bodies to arbitrate the inevitable conflicts between norms;
- codifying in as much detail as possible the procedures for implementing these norms;

- prescribing legitimate conduct that flows from the choice of these norms.

Constitutionalizing the world order thus means changing the structuring principle of the international system. It would no longer be a matter of guaranteeing sovereign equality of states but rather state compliance with the world constitutional order.

The order of factors would thus be inverted. Recognition of state sovereignty would be subject to a certification process based on compliance with the world constitutional norm, held to be superior.

Is it to Europe's benefit to embark on this path, assuming it is in a position to do so?

Before answering this question, I should first undertake to sketch out a normative picture of the world in the age of globalization. This picture is fundamentally baroque in that it blends contradictory forms.

The Baroque World Picture

From the European viewpoint, the picture of the world is made up of forms that without a doubt reflect its preferences, even its institutional model.[1]

The first element in this picture has to do with the undeniable interweaving of national order and international order, particularly between national law and international law. Many legal principles born and applied within the internal order itself are increasingly extended internationally to the point of becoming standards of international life. This is particularly the case of human rights and democracy.[2]

Alongside such internationalization of internal standards, there is an equally powerful process of internalization of international norms. More and more world standards are being integrated into national legislation, including constitutions. Swiss law has constitutionalized the principal of non-refoulement laid out in the UN convention relating to the status of refugees and is about to do the same for the protection of children, this being in compliance with the principles of the International Convention on the Rights of the Child.[3] And France has enshrined the precautionary principle in its constitution.

The second element of the picture has to do with the emergence of documents aiming to frame the regulation of global public goods and not only the regulation of relations between states. Underlying the ICC and the Kyoto Protocol is the idea that there are global public goods that warrant preservation over and above national prerogatives. Their protection requires the adhesion of the entire world community.[4] One might certainly object that nearly all the international treaties and conventions are universal in scope. But there will always be a difference between treaties whose effectiveness requires the endorsement of the greatest number of actors and those whose effectiveness requires the endorsement of the most powerful actors.

The third element of the picture has to do with the increasing pluralization of the international system, which is less and less state-centric. Naturally, the role of states remains decisive at every stage of the process of "normalization." But the role of market actors or NGOs cannot be neglected in the success of certain treaties (Kyoto, ICC) or in the failure of others (MAI for instance). Even more fundamentally, it can be said that the sovereign state is no longer the exclusive source of legitimacy for international norms.[5]

The last element of the picture has to do with the appearance of regulatory systems that are binding for states, as can be seen in the judicialization of dispute settlement procedures at the WTO. Such judicialization, far from being on the wane, is on the rise to the benefit of developing countries who use it more and more to break down the barriers of European agricultural protection, particularly in certain areas such as sugar and cotton.

We are thus a far cry from the commonsense perception that would like to accredit the idea of a totally deregulated world. All the more since alongside the international or global regulation of states is the powerful process of self-regulation initiated by market actors.

But because the picture of the world is baroque, it is naturally threatened by conflicting forces and processes. The first has to do with the fragmentation of global governance processes, a fragmentation that results both from legal activism in various domains and from the impossibility of linking them and even less of ranking them. One of the major difficulties that global governance encounters flows precisely from the lack of regulation of regulations, whereas the interpenetration of globalized fields of action is intensifying. The whole difficulty of reconciling trade and the environment, state sovereignty and respect for human rights, free movement of capital and obstacles to the free movement of people results precisely from the difficulty of arbitrating between these different preferences.

The second problem results from differences in the degree of elaborateness of global governance processes. In some areas (trade), normativity is advanced or relatively advanced, whereas in others (economic and social rights), it has not made very much progress. Such that the rights of globalization often appear ahead of the globalization of rights.[6]

The third problem is to be found in the heterogeneity of actual mechanisms for implementing the fragments of global governance. The only area in which an obligatory regime of sanctions exists is trade, through the WTO dispute settling mechanism. In all other areas, the power to sanction is very weak (social measures) or discretionary (recourse to force).

The fourth problem, which is perhaps the most serious of all, has to do with the resistance or "exit" mechanisms from the world game, mechanisms that can be seen very clearly at work in the United States. As I have shown, such conduct draws on legal arguments—there is no international legitimacy that can be enforced on the national legitimacy born of representative democracy—as well as on more classic political arguments referring to states' freedom of choice in a "anarchic world." The U.S. government's decision to agree to deliver civilian nuclear equipment to India—not a signatory to the Treaty on the Nonproliferation of Nuclear Weapons—while denying Iran—a signatory of the NPT—the right to acquire civilian nuclear power is indicative of this freedom of choice exacted by the United States. The fact that this country is at the crux of the system of opposition to the logic of global governance is, of course, a major political fact. But the problem is likely to amplify if the emerging major powers join the United States in their argument against global governance. In a substantial critique of global governance, Indian legal scholar B.S. Chimni discusses seven objections that he summarizes by what he calls the emergence of a global state working for transnational capital and the dominant states and against the interests of peoples and states of the Third World.[7] Naturally, in these critiques there is a very strong ideological dimension that in a way is poles apart from American criticisms. But where these recriminations meet is in the undermining of state sovereignty to the benefit of multilateral institutions or NGOs and in the erosion of national control mechanisms that alone have any real legitimacy.[8]

How then, from such a contradictory global context, can a line of thought and action be drawn that takes charge of globalization without yielding to a mechanical globalism based on a simple transposition of national mechanisms to a global level, with all the implied inherent risks of political and identity dispossession? How can sovereignism and the attendant regime of exceptions to the rule be refuted without neglecting the reality of processes and national identities?

As I have said before, Europe does not have to choose between governance and sovereignism. However, it does have to choose between two highly different modalities of governance through norms. These two modalities are *ethic governance*, the ambition of which would be to constitutionalize the world order, and *political governance*, which would seek to seal the cracks in global governance without ever yielding to the temptation of acting as a great architect. The first form should be discouraged. The second should be prescribed.

The Dangers of Constitutionalizing the World Order

Indeed, given the contradictory dynamics of the world system and the extreme complexity of the processes underlying it, Europe's temptation might be to want to overstandardize norms by using a method that actually is not so very remote from that of the European Convention: since the processes are complex, since citizens fail to understand the rationality behind them, since the mechanisms of legitimation seem to be disputed or blocked, since individual states can no longer handle the European dynamic on their own, it is time to undertake a task of clarification, simplification, and relegitimation of the treaties that would lend the European project coherence. It would be entirely exaggerated to interpret this exercise, today reduced to naught by the failure of the French and Dutch referendums, retrospectively as an excessively voluntaristic and senseless exercise. But the determination it expressed cannot be denied: that of constitutionalizing Europe and its political future based on the idea that, by the magic of a text reputed to be simpler, major contradictions would have been overcome, historic ambiguities lifted, and resistance defused. Naturally one might point out, and rightly so, that in taking over negotiation of the Constitutional Treaty, states obliterated the "constitutionalist" advances of the text. But this explanation—accurate in itself—is hardly enough to explain the failure of the referendum method. It can instead be ascribed basically to the ambition, even the pretension, of wanting to constitutionalize European political life in the absence of a real European *demos*. This created the impression of an attempt to "force the document through," even if, in fact, the final treaty contained very few advances. This also explains the campaigning at cross purposes in which those in favor of the "yes" vote minimized the advantages of the text whereas its adversaries overstated them better to combat them.

If I discuss the Constitutional Treaty in connection with global governance, it is precisely because there is a very comparable ambition at the world level, particularly in Europe, that aims to constitutionalize the international order through law.[9] This idea of constitutionalizing the world order is particularly strong in Germany. It draws on three hypotheses: the deepening ethical dimension of international relations, the increasing demand to make these norms effective, and the partial emancipation of these dynamics from state will.[10] However appealing it may seem on the surface, this approach presents considerable dangers.

For a political ensemble such as Europe to have ethical preferences is not only praiseworthy but indispensable. Believing in law rather than force, believing in deliberation rather than authority, believing in a plurality of actors rather than their conscription under the state banner are all social preferences that have an indisputable ethical content Europe should promote. But there is a fundamental difference between conceiving political action on the basis of ethical principles or strong normative preferences and seeing political action as the remote-controlled arm of these ethical preferences.

Reducing politics and political action to a mere ethical implementation amounts to denying the plurality of determinants of political action and to de facto exempting these ethical preferences from any democratic political control on the pretense that they have undergone public and democratic deliberation. To embark on this path would be to embark on a path that Kant called despotism, which he defined in particular as the intention of making men virtuous citizens:

> Woe to the legislator who wishes to bring about through coercion a constitution directed to ethical ends, for he would thereby not only achieve the very opposite of ethical ends, but also undermine his political ends and render them insecure.[11]

Morality, according to Kant, is the common test of the common law and not the experience of the exercise of freedoms. To constitutionalize the world order is precisely to seek to transform a community of values into a political community, to the point of taking one for the other, no longer distinguishing between common trials and public experience. This is why Europe should remain Kantian not in the sense that Kantian orthodoxy might mean, but in the sense that Kant gave to politics and the mortal danger of confusing ethics, morality, and politics.

Let us take an example. Suppose that the environmental preference is constitutionalized on a global scale. That would mean that violating the Kyoto Protocol would be likened to destroying a global public good and that, moreover, the Security Council would consider the destruction of a global public good as a threat to peace. It is easy to imagine that violating the Kyoto Protocol would legalize the Security Council's recourse to force against a recalcitrant state. We would resort to war to protect the environment.

The move from environmental protection to recourse to force would be not only entirely legal but also perfectly coherent, because respect for the norm would have been placed legally above all political judgment. With this example it is obvious that constitutionalizing the environmental world order, with all the sanction mechanisms it implies, would erode the capacity of politics to assess the balance of risks induced by a possible recourse to force before acting. On the other hand, if political reason recommended not resorting to force, it is politics that would then be in breach of the ethical principles it is supposed to enforce.

Naturally, constitutionalization of the world order would not necessarily lead to war. But the aim here is to point out that the clarifying and simplifying virtue implicitly expected of the constitutionalization of the world order is both illusory and dangerous. Illusory, because the law in general and norms in particular provide a means of governing and codifying only what people are prepared to codify and not what we would like to force them to accept as a common rule. Dangerous, because all "major clarifications," or those that supposedly are, lead to rejections if the norm is too strong and strictly binding. In Europe, it is already plain to see to what extent community norms, however rational, very often provoke forms of rejection. The fact that these rejections are irrational, incoherent, or groundless makes no difference. Norms have a regulatory but not salvational function. To constitutionalize the world order would be to succumb to a salvational vision that believes that by carrying a process to its logical conclusion, we can settle the world's problems. That would be giving in to an ideal of perpetual equilibrium—but an ideal that has absolutely nothing to do with Kantian philosophy. Kant harbored profound hostility toward dogmatism, a belief that consisted in confusing the idea with the result.[12] Constitutionalizing the world order is precisely believing that principles founded and constructed on the demand for justice can lead only to "just" choices. Confusing an idea with the result is thus to demonstrate an inability to imagine that a just principle can lead to a morally unjust or politically disastrous result. Kant, moreover, never thought that perpetual philosophical peace implied the emergence of a constitutional state or a rational consensus about rules that allowed free discussion in a controlled and peaceful manner.[13] It is on the contrary the condition in which ideas can assert their force, hone their powers, and increase their strength.[14] In other words, a normative order must always be founded on the tensions that clear a space for political action and the indetermination that it involves. There again, the French debate on the Constitutional Treaty turns out to be instructive. The controversy that raged over Part Three, the part of the treaty that constitutionalized EU policies, is very indicative of the problem. Adversaries to the treaty pointed out that constructing European policies would end up rigidifying them, carving them in stone, and devitalizing them to the point of making them intangible. Whether this argument is grounded or not matters little here. The main thing is simply to see and to measure how much overconstitutionalization of a political order can be experienced as the negation of political autonomy as long as the political body does not spontaneously appear in favor of approving such constitutionalization. Kant warned against hollow and inapplicable principles. Closer to us, Robert Schuman contrasted "single plans" and "concrete achievements."

If the constitutionalization of the European political order seems extremely risky, it is hardly difficult to imagine that the constitutionalization of the world order would be explosive. Why? For at least three fundamental reasons.[15]

The first is that aside from the principal of equal sovereignty among states, there are few principles on which the actors of the world system agree.

The second reason is that the constitutionalization of the world order would not automatically offer superior guarantees to the most vulnerable actors of the world system. Even where there already exist fragments of constitutionalization of the world order, as is the case with the WTO, it is plain to see that the formal equality among states with respect to trade cannot overcome the real inequality among states. All states have the right to apply sanctions, for instance. But the way their effects are distributed is totally unequal depending on whether they are declared by a rich country against a less rich country or by a less rich country against a rich country. If the European Union declared sanctions against Peru, Peru's loss of the European market would be incommensurable.

On the other hand, if Peru were to sanction the European Union, the cost to the latter would be insignificant. To that should be added the fact that constitutionalization necessarily implies proceduralization and that its costs are, there again, always higher for the weaker countries than for the stronger countries.

Lastly, formal equality with respect to norms is often eroded by the fact that the reciprocal right to inspection it carries is rarely operative. Let us take the example of the environment. Through their state governments or NGOs, rich developed societies will always have the means to verify a given country's compliance with a given norm. But do poorer countries really have the means to verify that rich countries are not causing harm to the environment? Can we imagine an Indian NGO coming to France to criticize environmental damage caused by farmers in Brittany, whereas the reverse seems an already secured possibility? Certainly, we can imagine that the world community deems that the preservation of certain global public goods must be defended unconditionally. But that boils down to saying that there are "global processes" whose implementation can be enforced based on choices made democratically by a political ensemble.

Many arguments militate in favor of this, particularly when a process produces externalities that overreach the national framework. But however justified they may be, such arguments cannot be taken for granted and especially cannot be imposed in the name of a "superior human reason" that all people have not accepted.

This entire line of argument may seem to be a charge against the primacy of norms, an encouragement toward unilateralism, even recourse to force. But that is not the case.

Respect for freely agreed upon norms remains the most effective bastion against violence and force and the least evil means of protecting the weak against the unilateralism of the most powerful. From this perspective, Europe does not have to choose between norms and force.

But the resistance that excessive normativity provokes—rightly or wrongly—within Europe should motivate it to use greater self-restraint and introspection when it considers constitutionalizing the world order. Europe must remain Kantian in that it must keep in mind that the will to combat despotic behavior in the world, particularly that of the most powerful, should not lead to a global despotism adorned with the best of intentions. Between refusing to settle the world's problems by simply and selfishly invoking one's own preferences and disregarding those of others, and believing that the world's problems can be solved once they are brought under the wing of a stable and overarching norm, there is a considerable margin of appreciation that is precisely that of politics. On the global scale, like on the European scale, only "concrete achievements" will enable governance to make progress.

CHAPTER 6

Norms and Geopolitics

For 15 years now, Europe has been facing, as I have recalled, the realities of a multifarious world that it could not simply ignore. Its normative ambition is thus now more than ever subject to the reality principle. This is because the more norms are applied to situations remote from the context in which they were conceived, the more they run the risk of noncompliance. Europe thus has three choices: it can either be proactively more demanding as regards respect for the norms it propagates, take liberties with the norms that it formally prescribes, or enter into a more or less muffled clash with its partners.

The first possibility would involve spelling out, clarifying or toughening norms that it exports whenever it meets situations in which the dissemination of norms can no longer be taken for granted.[1] This is the scenario that prevailed during enlargement toward the Central and Eastern European countries (CEEC) after the end of the cold war. In 1993, at the Copenhagen Summit, the European Union agreed to CEEC membership in principle. But it attached the start of membership talks to an unprecedented formalization of the accession criteria for joining the European Union. These accession criteria are those well-known conditions that were to become the Copenhagen criteria, laid down as follows:

- *Membership requires that the candidate country has achieved stability of institutions guaranteeing democracy, the rule of the law, human rights, and respect for and protection of minorities.*

- *Membership requires the existence of a functioning market economy to cope with competitive pressure and market forces within the Union.*
- *Membership presupposes the candidate ability to take on the obligations of membership including adherence to the aims of political economy and monetary Union.*[2]

But in addition to these three formal conditions, there is an additional, more informal condition that states that "*the Union's capacity to absorb new members while maintaining the momentum of European integration is also an important consideration in the general interest of both the Union and the candidate countries.*"[3]

At the time, this criterion was not perceived as such and most conditionality studies do not recognize it as a criterion in and of itself. But with the opening of accession talks with Turkey, it was clearly "reactivated," particularly by those member states hostile to Turkey's membership.[4] This latter criterion is interesting in the perspective examined here, because it shows to what extent a conditionality that is also a norm can give rise to extensive uses that are at odds with the European discourse claiming that norms are a codification of relations between equals. Accession talks with Turkey are no longer even a case of conditionality in which the norm-maker imposes its norm on the norm-taker. Rather, the European Union is using a rationale in which it alone estimates its capacity to welcome a new member state, a decision that is not open to dispute.

Europe has thus embarked on a totally different logic in that it leaves itself a discretionary margin of appreciation that is totally disconnected with the partner's performances. The criterion relative to its absorption capacity thus boils down to saying that, even assuming the applicant country fulfills all the accession criteria, membership could still be denied.

The first three Copenhagen criteria do not go that far. For even if many dispute the clarity and precision of these criteria, which are also too vague not to be open to interpretations of pure political contingency, they nevertheless fit within a contractual normative framework. If an applicant country fulfills its obligations, it is qualified to join the EU.

For all that, the relative clarity in which this conditionality is exercised should not make us lose sight of its profoundly asymmetrical nature. To become a member, a country must satisfy the Copenhagen criteria and adopt the 80,000-page long *acquis communautaire* in its entirety. This is a take-it-or-leave-it condition. What is commonly referred to as "talks" is actually a process by which the European Union verifies that the applicants have indeed incorporated the *acquis communautaire* into their domestic legislation, chapter by chapter, page by page.[5] In practice, the reality has turned out to be more complex. In fact, the broader and more massive the conditionalities, the more they leave room for arbitration between the various priorities, thereby creating a degree of leeway for the applicants.[6] However, neither the rigor of European conditionality nor, on the other hand, the interstices left open to the local actors by such conditionality suffice to explain the success of European enlargement to Central and Eastern Europe. It has to do with the fact that right from the start the perspective of membership exerted a considerable power of attraction over societies in which the system they were leaving—communism—had not only failed but, what's more, also restricted state sovereignty. So even before European conditionality was exercised, the elites had interiorized it, so to speak, as soon as they were assured locally of a consensus to join the European Union.[7] Thus, through electoral competition, the political forces in favor of membership won the game on the domestic checkerboard even before the opportunity to engage in accession talks was put to debate.

This was thus a far cry from the zero-sum game in which an external actor attempts to impose a norm on an actor that wants nothing to do with it. This still did not make it a game between equals, because the conditionality was defined by the norm-maker. The context was instead one in which asymmetry was interiorized due to the tangible rewards involved in complying with it.[8]

Norms and Asymmetry

Reproducing this pattern becomes problematic when Europe can no longer commit to offering a reward as substantial as accession. Its entire neighborhood policy, the famous European Neighborhood Policy (ENP), is designed to solve this problem, which can be summarized thus: Europe is no longer able to or no longer wants to offer membership as a perspective to its neighbors, while leading them to believe that this fundamental change will not make a big difference to them. But the distinction makes a big difference. It first makes a difference to Europe, which can no longer use the perspective of membership as a disciplinary mechanism first to discipline its neighbors. It also makes a big difference for its partners, for which the cost of compliance with European standards from both economic and political standpoints is not apparently offset by decisive advantages. Now if membership policies have succeeded despite the initially asymmetrical nature of the relations between the EU and its candidates, it is because the trade-off in terms of costs and benefits was established from the start.[9]

From the standpoint of perceptions, we must first take into account states that refuse from the start to accept the ENP framework as an overall contractual framework for their relations with Europe. This is the case of Russia, which was initially part of the system and later withdrew from the initiative. Now consider those who do not accept this framework but have no choice for lack of anything better. This is the case of Ukraine, for which the only serious political perspective with Europe is membership and which sees the ENP as a mechanism to delay its accession.[10] We must take into account also the case of countries that have no problem formerly entering this framework, but do not seem for all that to have made up their mind to accept all the modalities, especially if they contain new obligations. Take, for instance, Algeria: because it constitutes a precious source of energy supply for Europe, it knows perfectly well that Europe will not risk imposing on it political conditionalities or economic reforms it does not want to implement. The only potential interest Algeria has in the ENP framework is the free circulation of people. But it knows that Europe is not prepared to grant this.[11] That leaves most others—countries for which there is no chance of joining the European Union in the next 10 to 15 years and for which the principle advantage is to attract European resources in an attempt to build viable states. The remainder is a particular set of countries that have specific expectations with regard to Europe and for which the formal framework governing relations with Europe is of little importance or even signification. All this makes it legitimate to wonder whether ENP is not mainly a political-institutional system that holds meaning first and foremost for the EU itself.

Indeed, the ENP was fundamentally designed as a policy of nonmembership, even if it was bureaucratically conceived by those who are responsible for enlargement.[12]

Initially entitled *Wider Europe* in 2003, it was pared down to the European Neighborhood Policy the following year, precisely to underscore the fact that being a European neighbor in no way implies being a member of Europe.[13] In this perspective, the major political fact resides in the discarding of any political right to joining European Union even for states whose Europeanity is not disputed.[14] Like any policy, it rests on explicits and implicits. What has been made explicit is that Europe has an interest in being surrounded by a "ring of friends" that have the characteristic of being economically prosperous, politically stable, and well governed.[15] What has been left unsaid is a desire to avoid unintentionally importing security risks into the EU from unstable or little-developed countries in the form of uncontrolled migration, Mafia-like conduct, or terrorist action. This point is the most fundamental one, because deep down it is the only characteristic shared by countries as different as Moldavia, Lebanon, and Tunisia. The ENP actually constitutes a very classic semiperiphery control policy that aims to set up a virtuous circle encompassing development, democracy, and good governance so as not to jeopardize Europe's security and stability. It is the very example of a *milieu goal policy*.[16] Europe thus does geopolitics with norms.

Europe does not claim to be creating this circle. But it hopes to encourage it while believing that it has neither the power nor the will to impose its own norms.[17] The question should then be posed in the following terms: What can the partners find that is new or attractive enough to embark on the path offered by Europe through its ENP? The answer is probably "not much," except for some of them to whom the ENP is a necessary step on the road to accession.

On the economic and trade level, for instance, the ENP offers "deep trade and economic integration with the EU" that one imagines might take the route of what is again called "deep and comprehensive free trade agreements."[18] But what is really meant by "deep and comprehensive free trade agreements"? The European Commission's answer is the following: "a deep and comprehensive FTA should cover substantially all trade in goods and services between the EU and ENP partners including those products of particular importance for our partners and should include strong legally-binding provisions on trade and regulatory issues."[19] In exchange for greater access to its market, Europe demands that its partners comply with its constraints in terms of technical norms and standards, industrial policy, intellectual property, rules of origin, taxation, public procurement, and the like.[20] In other words, Europe is striving to wrest bilateral recognition for norms that it is unable to impose on a global scale. "Adopt our norms and in exchange, we'll open our markets." But this apparently fair deal is actually deeply imbalanced and not always attractive. Imbalanced because the concessions made by the two parties are not equal in nature. When Europe, through a bilateral treaty, offers a country greater access to its market, it is apparently granting a favor with respect to other partners. But this preference is fragile: on one hand, because nothing prevents Europe from granting it to a country in competition with another, on the other, because nothing proves that in the event of a multilateral agreement, the preferences granted to the two countries will not eventually diminish, or even disappear. Moreover, the existence of a free-trade agreement does not prohibit maintaining limitations on sensitive agricultural or industrial products, not to mention the movement of people.[21]

Europe will have nothing to lose. On the contrary it stands to gain. For in exchange for granting tenuous and relative preferences, it will have wrested from its partners lasting concessions in the regulatory areas that interest it, as we have seen, to the utmost.[22] Indeed, that the ultimate objective of Europe is to "*share a common regulatory basis and similar degree of market access*" confirms the potential imbalance of such agreements. Moreover, there is no evidence to show that a free-trade agreement presents truly new opportunities in terms of access to the European market. Europe's partners are usually fettered in their export policy to Europe either by internal difficulties preventing them from increasing their exports, or by drastic EU regulatory obstacles that Europe forces them to accept precisely in the framework of free-trade agreements or preferential accords. Certainly, Europe's partners are not required to adopt the full spectrum of the *acquis communautaire*. But this freedom has a price: not being allowed to fully integrate into the single market, thus making the idea of access to "everything but the institutions" entirely theoretical. Incidentally, this offer is ambiguous. For although, for Europe, it means "don't get discouraged, because finally you can have almost everything," this may well be interpreted by its partners as "even if we do everything the way they do, they'll never accept us." Misunderstandings notwithstanding, this approach poses a real political problem: "everything but the institutions" means that these countries will never be able to take part in defining the European policies that they will have nevertheless adopted. They are thus bound to remain forever norm-takers. From that standpoint, the ENP constitutes a mechanism aimed at normalizing the asymmetry between Europe and its noncommunity partners. Actually, in many cases, already fairly extensive and usually underutilized access to the European market is much less valuable than some form of regional integration, for instance. The ENP is built on a foundation that exacerbates bilateralism. It naturally claims to foster development of regional integration. But in actual fact, it does not give itself the means to realize it, especially when obstacles to this integration are highly political in nature. We know, for instance, that regional integration in the Maghreb is hindered by the Algeria-Morocco rivalry and that the European Union obviously does not have the means to settle it. In fact, the ENP has given rise to no new trade initiative moving toward "*deep integration*." The Balkans are covered by the famous Stabilization and Association Agreement (SAA), the Mediterranean countries by the Euro-Med agreements. The only two free-trade agreements offered have been to countries that are not covered by the ENP: South Korea and India. Talks with Ukraine in view of an "enhanced agreement" are underway. But this is primarily a formula aimed to mollify the Ukrainians who seem disappointed by the lack of a membership calendar.

These difficulties are multiplied when shifting from the economic sphere to more sensitive areas such as those pertaining to good governance or human rights. In theory, the ENP is meant as a comprehensive policy in the sense that it intends to tie in the various dimensions of its cooperation with its neighbors. But in practice, this ambition is seriously belittled as soon as political questions are touched on.

For the same question arises once again: What benefits do authoritarian political regimes derive from complying with the rules of good governance and democracy if the incentives to change are weak? Incentives can be understood either as possible sanctions the European Union would apply to recalcitrant countries, or on the contrary rewards it would offer in exchange for compliance with these norms. In view of the results obtained so far, ENP achievements are modest.

To realize this, it is methodologically interesting to compare three European instruments: the 2004 *Strategy Paper*, the *Country Reports* and the *ENP Actions Plans*. The *Strategy Paper* defines a general framework of the ENP, the *Country Reports* its specific application, the *Action Plans* their implementation by both parties.[23] In these three documents, the common policy reference point is that of *shared values*. The 2004 *Strategy Paper* claims to link the level of ambition of relations with its neighbors "to the extent to which those values are effectively shared."[24] But this principle is ignored in practice since the ENP does not constitute a new legal instrument able to enforce commitments taken in a framework of partnership or association agreements. Moreover, the European Commission seems to interpret article 2 (pertaining to respect for human rights) of these agreements in the Euro-Mediterranean framework in a very minimalist sense.[25] Lastly, the financial instruments, such as the MEDA program, that Europe has made available with respect to the Mediterranean countries make very little reference to respect for human rights.[26]

One first notes that no *Country Report* or *Action Plan* has been drafted for four countries integrated into the ENP. These countries are Belarus, Algeria, Libya, and Syria. Although the absence of Belarus can be explained by this country's very slim political achievements, explicitly acknowledged by the EU, the other three cases are different. These are sensitive countries with which the EU and its member states have important political or economic relations but with respect to which it hesitates to take a confrontational position, particularly as regards democracy and human rights. The lack of an *Action Plan* with these countries thus reflects either the European preference for stability of these three regimes, where Islamism represents a threat, or the lack of a basis for agreement between the EU and these countries, or possibly both. Even in countries that have managed to reach an agreement with the EU about *Action Plans*, there is a total lack of EU discussion with local NGOs dealing with human rights issues.[27]

Structurally, the ENP seems extremely poorly equipped to come to the aid of civil society NGOs.[28] Although it may deny this, Europe actually practices a very classic double standard. In human rights matters, the EU is much more intrusive with European countries such as Moldavia or Ukraine, which are likely to join someday in the future, than with Arab countries.[29] Moreover, even when critiques are directed at the same Arab countries in the *Country Reports*, which engage the EU alone, they tend to disappear in the *Action Plans* drafted in conjunction with the local governments. The *Action Plan* with Egypt for instance states that the two parties pledge to "*strengthen the culture of respect for human rights and fundamental freedoms in Egypt and the EU.*" This is a very vague commitment, but it has a powerful political meaning, for the Egyptians in any case. The commitment to strengthen "the culture of respect for human rights" is perfectly acceptable, for who could claim that it has no improvements to be made in this regard? It is all the more acceptable since it is followed by the phrase "in Egypt and in the EU," which for the Egyptians means that even the Europeans could make improvements in their human rights record.

As we can see, the normative nature of the European power raises many more questions than one might have thought. And if these issues are worth examining in order to understand Europe in the world, such analysis, in order to make sense, must now make reference to questions of reception. The next step is an in-depth reflection on the theory of reception in international relations that, applied to Europe, would enable us to consider it as a living, complex, and contradictory actor, and not as an idealized actor whose preference for norms is seen as a guarantee of its good faith and disinterestedness.

CONCLUSION

The crucial question for the international system is and will remain that of order. What should be done so that the political entities that compose it can ensure their survival without doing so at others' expense or, more precisely, in such a way that the conditions posed by a political community for its own survival do not accentuate the disorder of the entire world system?

In an attempt to answer this focal question, I formed the hypothesis at the beginning of this book that there were two possible visions: governance and sovereignism. Between these two conceptions, Europe has made clear its choice for governance. This choice is made necessary by the historical conditions of its political refoundation since 1957 as a political ensemble that is not a state: it is not the ultimate guarantor of its own security and it wants to protect itself through norms to avoid having to face the trial of confrontation.

There is little chance that this reality will change very much in the course of the coming decades. This is why, even if Europe were to provide itself with a military force, that would not make it a hard power. For Europe to become a hard power, it would take some form of federalization of its foreign policy. This is hardly possible without federalizing the European political system, if security and defense are admitted to constitute the hard core of state sovereignty. The only likely possibility is that Europe's foreign policies will be harmonized according to a logic of socialization among European political actors, interdependence among societies, rationalization of military spending, and convergence of interests. This process is and will remain uncertain. It has every chance of remaining ambiguous. If we look at what has happened in Europe since 1989, the major event has been Germany's keeping a political distance from the United States. But this distantiation has not really created any strong European dynamic. The Franco-German couple so talked about has produced nothing tangible since Maastricht, except perhaps a reinforcement of classic interstate rationales. Europe is not at risk of imploding, but it is highly likely to operate on the basis of a baroque compromise between shared norms (rule of law, respect for freedoms, market regulation, environmental protection) and competition between states (diplomacy and economics). European power remains enigmatic. Under such circumstances, political distantiation with the United States will always remain relative. Certainly, in order to assert itself, Europe will always have to react by stressing its difference from the United States. But the end of classic Atlanticism does not for all that automatically trigger a fundamental distantiation. All the more so since China's rise in power is highly likely to prompt Europe to move closer to the United States.

This is why, and without indulging in futurology, it is reasonable to believe that five stable and distinctive features will continue to characterize European power.

The first is the declared and fully assumed refusal of any notion of European supremacy over the rest of the world. This refusal of any idea supremacy ipso facto goes along with a refusal to think of the world from the Schmittian perspective of friend versus foe. Europe is and will remain Kantian. There is little chance of its becoming Schmittian. That is what sets it apart most from the United States and what its preference for norms is based on. Naturally, neither China nor India nor Russia spontaneously shares this vision. But it is not by mimicking the major powers that Europe will promote its interests and values. Europeans in any event have no inclination to embark on this path. The race between global governance via norms and "realist" governance by states has clearly begun, and its outcome is uncertain. This is all the more true since realism can be taken to mean different things. In its chemically pure form, realism does not let ideological considerations get in its way. It reasons in terms of power struggles but respects state sovereignty. The U.S. policy under the Bush administration is neorealist in nature. It starts from a balance of power overwhelmingly in favor the United States but uses it to promote an ideological vision that refuses to sanctify the sovereignty of other states. The theory of regime change used in Iraq is well and truly an expression of this neorealism. But the more time goes by, the more the limits of this new paradigm will come to light. Barring an always possible headlong flight into madness, regime change theory is highly likely to stop in Baghdad. But reverting to a more classical realist position will not necessarily make the United States more accommodating as regards issues of global governance.

The second feature of European identity is that of a necessarily more self-centered power than other state powers, precisely because its very structure forces it to undertake many internal arbitrations that national power does not need to do or less so. Consequently, its political reactivity will always be slower and weaker. But it can turn this weakness into an asset, considering that the game of power rests not only on reactivity but also on a capacity to modify the game by relying on the long-term effects of the choices made rather than on their immediate consequences. After all, the business in Iraq shows that "change through force" has turned out to be ambiguous to say the least, even with respect to the objectives that it had assigned itself. Europe can rightly believe that international norms may have greater power to transform the world order in the long run than a strategy of destruction or confrontation that may prove to be spectacular in the short run but totally unsuccessful in the long haul. It is even perfectly possible to think that Europe's political ambition should involve not shifting from soft power to hard power, but acting in such a way that today's issues of soft power do not become tomorrow's conflicts of hard power, precisely because they were not settled in time. If no concerted policy action takes responsibility for climate change, for example, it is highly likely that environmental wars will break out in the future when the most powerful feel threatened. It nevertheless remains true that all issues are not conceivable in terms of soft power, some of them being hybrids between hard and soft power. Nuclear proliferation is a good example of this overlapping. That said, should the possibility of a transformative power be accepted without seeking to idealize it?

As regards the rest of the world, Europe will always appear as a power that is both more attractive and less convincing. More attractive because, not being a hard power, it seems a more reasonable power, more sensitive to other people's arguments, more willing to compromise than to enter into confrontation. But at the same time, it will prove to be less convincing, and even less credible, precisely because it is not a coercive power. This is the viewpoint of China, India, and Russia. It points up the ambivalence of European power as well as the disadvantages of what is commonly called multipolarity. For it all depends on what is meant by multipolarity. If advocating multipolarity means promoting a sort of world pluralism to counterbalance the unilateral hegemony of the United States, there is no reason to harbor reservations about this idea. All the more so since the multiplication of sources of wealth and power is a process underway that American unilateralism can mask or curb but not prevent. On the other hand, if multipolarity means a sort of organized pluralization of the world around power clusters that revive the tradition of power politics, Europe has no advantage in embarking on this path. This is so for a simple reason: China, India, and Russia are seeking the construction of a multipolar order, not necessarily to build a multilateral world but to acquire a privileged status that will enable them to negotiate on equal footing with the United States. Multipolarity in their eyes is merely a means of gaining recognition as a major power by the United States, even if it means acting on the international stage—once this recognition is obtained—in a largely similar way to the United States. In that case, it is not at all certain that norms can triumph over force.

Europe will always have a decisive comparative advantage over the rest of the world each time that shared sovereignty seems more beneficial than sovereignism. The development of this advantage will depend not only on the context in which it can be used (the environment rather than defense) but also on the nature and the state of the world cycles. Since the end of the cold war, we have been in a strong multilateral cycle symbolized by the Rio Earth Summit in 1992 and the powerful sovereignist cycle that appeared with September 11, 2001. Naturally, cyclical effects always ripple out beyond the boundaries that are supposed to contain them, such that environmental multilateralism, for instance, did not end with September 11. But on the other hand, no one yet knows how much longer the world political cycle born on September 11 will last. The world cycle is definitely unfavorable to Europe, but that of course does not mean that it should abandon its principles. On the contrary, the countercyclical influence that Europe could have in a world once again caught up in sovereignism may turn out to be beneficial. All the more so since signs of disenchantment with the meager results of the neoconservative counterrevolution are beginning to appear even in the United States.

Norms are and will remain not only Europe's best shield but also its finest banner. The collective capacity to resort to force will never constitute a political goal in itself for Europe. Even if the pursuit of norms seems less rewarding or spectacular than taking the route of force, they cannot be abandoned and even less underestimated. The sizeable and inevitable qualitative mutations of the world undergo long, chaotic, and reversible maturation phases. It is not because human rights violations are abundant, constant, and sometimes increasing that the defense of these rights should not be pursued. It is not because great harm is being done to the environment that one should give up promoting the idea that protecting it involves protection of global common goods and that it is not a national responsibility one can shirk.

Europe has no other choice and no other aim than to defend norms on the world scale. But as it intensifies this attitude, it will have to defend itself against any attempt to constitutionalize the world order. Such an approach would inevitably lead to a cemetery of good intentions. It would also be a negation of its Kantian heritage.

NOTES

1 Why Europe Cannot Be a Superpower

1. Michael E. Smith's book, *Europe's Foreign and Security Policy. The Institutionalization of Cooperation*, Cambridge, Cambridge University Press, 2004, is typical of this approach. His meticulous analysis of the procedures, regulations, and declarations is totally dissociated from any attempt to analyze their effectiveness or content.
2. Jean Monnet, *Mémoires*, Paris, Fayard, 2004, p. 371.
3. Russia's case is a clear example of this. In the early years following the collapse of the Soviet Union, it seemed to turn its back on its past in an attempt to "Westernize" and even renounce its role as a superpower. Since Vladimir Putin has taken office, the ambition is obvious to reappropriate the Soviet legacy to attempt to position Russia in the sphere of superpowers.
4. Out of the six major geographical spaces, only India, with 3.2 million square km, is slightly smaller in area than the European Union (3.9 million square km. But the configuration of the two spaces is very different. The surface areas of the other spaces are Russia, 17 million square km; the United States, 9.6 million; China, 9.5; and Brazil, 8.5 million.
5. The Americans ended up turning down China's offer on national security grounds, which indeed confirms the hypothesis of an apparently purely economical representation of geopolitical stakes.
6. *Financial Times*, June 27, 2005.
7. National Intelligence Council, *2020 Project. Mapping the Global Future*, GPO Washington, 2004, p. 63.
8. *Le Monde*, July 3–4, 2005.
9. This perception in fact does not entirely exclude more traditional reasoning put forth by certain European member states that see Russia as a world "power center" that must be treated tactfully, also on certain occasions it may counterbalance American power. That is very likely France's viewpoint, as well as Germany's and England's.

10. Cited in *EU Energy Policy: Internal Developments and External Challenges*, The Economist Intelligence Unit, 2006.
11. Ibid., p. 43.
12. Marie Mendras, "Back to Besieged Fortress?" (mimeo), March 2007.
13. This point is remarkably shown in the study by A. Correljé and C. van der Linde, "Energy Supply Security and Geopolitics: A European Perspective," *Energy Policy* 34 (5), March 2006, pp. 532–543.
14. As reported by Ron Suskind in the *New York Times Magazine*, October 17, 2004.
15. It should be obvious that in this author's eyes, such distinction does not carry any normative judgment. A new reality can be created for the worse and be subjected to this same reality for the better.
16. Javier Solana, *A Secure Europe in a Better World. European Security Strategy*. Brussels, December 12, 2003. Available at http://ue.eu.int/ueDocs/cms_Data/docs/pressdata/FR/reports/76256.pdf
17. *Financial Times*, July 1, 2005.
18. H. Kissinger and L. Summers, *Renewing the Atlantic Partnership*, New York, Council on Foreign Relations, 2004.
19. This demand is backed by London, which, on the other hand, is fiercely opposed to changing the voting system to a qualified majority for matters of external policy and European defense.
20. According to François Heisbourg, 90% of the American troops no longer come under NATO or European command. *Le grand schisme d'Occident*, Paris, Odile Jacob, 2005, p. 127.
21. On the details of the Europe-United States confrontation over Galileo, see the essay *Bruxelles-Washington. La relation atlantique sur le métier. La République des Idées,* by Florence Autret. Available at the Fondation Jean Jaurès Web site http://www.jean-jaures.org/.
22. World Public Opinion, *Views of European Union's Influence*. Available at http://www.worldpublicopinion.org/pipa/articles/.
23. Peter Mandelson, "The Global Economic Agenda: Europe and India's Challenge," EU Commission, January 13, 2005. Available at http://ec.europa-eu/commission_barroso/mandelson/speeches.
24. Arvind Virmani, *A Tripolar Century: USA, China and India*, New Delhi, Indian Council for Research on International Economic Relations, March 2005. Available at www.icrier.org.
25. "The United States is in the process of deciding a strategic transformation for the 21st century that hinges on a trio composed of the United States, China and India," *Le Figaro*, May 31, 2007.
26. Virmani, *Tripolar Century*.
27. The Indian report, drafted in response to a European document, "An EU-India Strategic Partnership" states significantly that this partnership expresses "a level of relationship higher than that maintained by either side with non strategic partners, and immune from the vicissitudes of either side's

relationship with a third party." The sense of the message is clear: we are not a partner like the others.

28. I refer to the presentations given by Indian colleagues during the symposium "Are European Preferences Shared by Others?" Paris, CERI/Centre d'Etudes Européennes de Sciences Po, June 2006.
29. Joseph Nye, *Soft Power. The Means to Success in World Politics*, New York, Public Affairs, 2004.
30. Actually, Nye seems divided between the practical *binary* distinction between hard and soft power and his effort to conduct a *ternary* analysis of the international system in which he sees three dimensions: the diplomatic-strategic, economic interdependence, and cultural interdependence. This is why in his more recent book, he talks less about the distinction between hard and soft power than about soft power, economic power, and military power. He also acknowledges that economic power has a coercive dimension.
31. It should nevertheless be remembered that for the millions of people anxious to flee poverty to survive, that Europe remains an exceptionally attractive geographical space that the Europeans are seeking precisely to render less attractive. The attraction differential between the United States and Europe enters into play with regard to very narrow but very decisive population segments—researchers, for instance.
32. "Hard Power, Soft Power and the Goals of Diplomacy," in David Held and Mathias Koenig-Archibugi (eds.), *American Power in the XXI Century*, Oxford, Polity Press, 2004, 299 p.
33. See Zaki Laïdi, "Les métaphores du Titanic," *Tribune de Genève*, June 13–14, 1998.
34. Regarding these debates, see Philippe Crouzet and Nicolas Véron, "La mondialisation en partie double. La bataille des normes comptables," *Cahiers d'En Temps Réel* (3), April 2002. Available at www.entempsreel.org.
35. R. Daniel Kelemen and Eric C. Sibbitt, "The Globalization of American Law," *International Organization*, Winter 2004, pp. 103–136.
36. Joseph Nye writes that "Power in the global information age is becoming less tangible and less coercive." *The Paradox of the American Power*, p. 11. It is likely, however, that Nye's naivety is calculated. Nye is a multilateralist democrat. His analysis has a specific political function: it aims to make the American political elites understand that the United States has so many trump cards to play in the world that it stands nothing to gain in resorting too hastily to the use of armed force.
37. The states of the European Union produce an average of 764 films per year, behind India (877) but ahead of the United States (611). *European Audiovisual Observatory*, 2004. Available at http://www.obs.coe.int/medium/prod.html.fr.
38. Jean Michel Baer, "L'exception culturelle. Une règle en quête de contenu," *Cahiers d'En Temps Réel* 11, October 2003. Available at www.entempsreel.org.

39. American films occupy 75% of the movie screens and 73% of the television screens in Spain. In France, the proportions are 56% and 28% respectively. (Source: European Audiovisual Observatory. 2002 figures).
40. This indubitable reality carries no value judgment as to the legitimacy of such a regime. Tyler Cowen, for instance, believes that cultural trade fosters diversity within societies and reduces it between societies. Conversely, French-style cultural protectionism supposedly maintains a diversity between France and the United States, for example, but such protection translates into a reduction in the diversity within the national sphere (Tyler Cowen, *Creative Destruction. How Globalization Is Changing World's Cultures*, Princeton, Princeton University Press, 2002). Françoise Benhamou confirms this last argument in showing that the increase in the proportion of French songs in musical programming—subject to quotas—leads to an unexpected reduction in the offer on the radio: fewer than 3% of titles make up 70% of the programming. Cultural exceptionalism thus does not coincide with cultural diversity. Needless to say that such an assertion virtually passes for blasphemy in France. (Françoise Benhamou, "L'exception culturelle. L'exploration d'une impasse," *Esprit* 5, May 2004, pp. 85–113.)
41. See Tony Judt and Denis Lacorne (eds.), *With US or against US, Studies in Global Anti-Americanism*, London, Palgrave Macmillan, 2005.
42. *Financial Times*, June 30, 2005.
43. Charles Kupchan, *The End of American Era*, New York, Knopf, 2003, p. 149.
44. Idem.
45. Ibid., p. 143.
46. Some authors did not wait for the demise of the Constitutional Treaty to sing the praises of the political achievements of the European Union as an international actor. Hazel Smith, for instance, wrote unabashedly that "In practice, the Union can now intervene in almost any area of the world in almost any aspect of foreign policy." Hazel Smith, *European Union Foreign Policy. What It Is and What It Does*, London, Pluto Press, 2002, p. 267. Such optimism is baffling.
47. Cited in Jean-Louis Quermonne, *Le système politique de l'Union européenne*, Paris, Montchrestien, 2005, 6th edition.
48. Jeremy Rifkin, *The European Dream*, Cambridge, MA, Polity Press, 2004, p. 209.
49. Ibid., p. 208.
50. Ibid., p. 83.
51. Ibid., p. 213.
52. Robert Kagan, "Power and Weakness," *Policy Review* 113, June–July 2002, http://www.mtholyoke.edu/acad/intrel/bush/kagan.htm.
53. This obviously does not mean that the reality of the world can be compared exclusively to a billiard game between states, which is the principal error of "realist" analyses.

54. For Christopher Hill, power involves the concentration of decision-making authority, such that it is hard to imagine the emergence of a Super European power without a Super State. *Super State or Superpower? The Future of the European Union in World Politics*, London, LSE, July 2002, p. 14.
55. Joseph Weiler, "Fédéralisme et institutionnalisme: Le *Sonderweig* européen," in Renaud Dehousse (ed.), *Une constitution pour Europe?* Paris, Presses de Sciences Po, 2002, p. 156.
56. Idem.
57. Miguel Maduro, cited by Weiler, in "Fédéralisme et institutionnalisme," p. 166.
58. Renaud Dehousse and Olivier Duhamel, "Beaucoup de bruit pour presque rien? Deux lectures contradictoires de la constitution européenne," Paris, *Cahiers d'En Temps Réel* 19. Available at www.entempsreel.org.
59. See Arjun Nijebver, *The First Dutch Referendum*. Pre-ballot Assessment, May 2005.
60. Interview with Joseph Borell, president of the European Parliament, *Libération*, July 12, 2005.
61. Jacques Lacan, *Le Seminaire*, Livre III, *Les Psychoses,* cited in Slavoy Zizek, *Que veut l'Europe? Réflexions sur une nécessaire réappropriation*, Paris, Climats, 2005, p. 81.
62. It should be pointed out that in France the 2005 referendum campaign crystallized actually around "the social question" and not around the question of sovereignty, as was the case during the Maastricht Treaty referendum campaign.
63. I draw here on Zizek's comments in *Que veut l'Europe?* p. 58.
64. Jacques Rupnik, "Europe. Les malentendus de l'élargissement," Paris, *Cahiers d'En Temps Réel*, April 8, 2003. Available at www.entempsreel.org.
65. Robert Cooper, "The New Liberal Imperialism," *The Guardian*, April 7, 2002.
66. 78% of Europeans say they are in favor of a European defense and security policy. Eurobarometer 62, May 2005. www.europa.eu.int/comm/public_opinion/standard.
67. This was very aptly demonstrated by Hubert Védrine, "Single foreign policy cannot be defined by decree. You can replace one currency with another.... You cannot decree that next March 1, we will all think the same thing about the Middle East." *Face à l'Hyper-puissance*, Paris, Fayard, 2003, p. 330.
68. *Le Monde*, July 1, 2005.
69. The German Court of Justice in Karlsruhe, for instance, blocked the implementation of a European arrest warrant following a request to extradite a German citizen from Spain.
70. *The Economist*, July 23, 2005.
71. "Questions terroristes," En Temps Réel/ENS seminar, May 2005.

2 Norms over Power

1. Johan Galtung, *The European Community: Superpower in the Making*, London, George Allen & Unwin, 1973.

2. François Duchêne, "Europe's Role in World Peace," in R. Mayne (ed.), *Europe Tomorrow: Sixteen Europeans Look Ahead*, London, Fontana, 1972; "The European Community and the Uncertainties of Interdependence," in M. Kohnstamen and W. Hager, *A Nation Writ Large? Foreign Policy Problems before the European Community*, Basingstoke, Macmillan, 1973; John Galtung, *The European Community. A Superpower in the Making*, London, Allen & Unwin, 1973 and Andrew Shonfield, *Europe: Journey to an Unknown Destination*, London, Allen Lane, 1973.
3. On interdependence, the starting point is Joseph Nye and Robert Keohane's book, *Transnational Relations and World Politics*, 1972; on the decline of war, Alastair Buchan, *Change without War: The Shifting Structures of World Power*, London, Chatto & Windus, 1973.
4. F. Duchêne, "The European Community," in M. Kohnstamen and W. Hager, *A Nation Writ Large?* p. 20.
5. Edwar Carr, *The Twenty Years' Crisis, 1919–1939: An Introduction to the Study of International Relations*, London, Macmillan, 1962.
6. Hedley Bull, "Civilian Power Europe: A Contradiction in Terms?" *Journal of Common Market Studies* 21 (2), 1982, pp. 149–164.
7. Ibid., p. 157.
8. In the internationalist literature a whole series of essays have appeared on the emergence of international regimes inspired by institutionalism. See Stephen Krasner (ed.), *International Regimes*, Ithaca, Cornell University Press, 1991.
9. H. Maull, "Germany and Japan. The New Civilian Powers," *Foreign Affairs* 69 (5), 1990, pp. 91–106.
10. K. Twichett (ed.), *Europe and the World: The External Relations of the Common Market,* St. Martin's Press, 1976.
11. Bull, "Civilian Power Europe," p. 151 and Christopher Hill, "The Capability-Expectations Gap, or Conceptualizing Europe's International Role," *Journal of Common Market Studies* 31 (3), September 1993, p. 309.
12. Hill sees Europe as a regional peacemaker, mediator of conflicts, global actor, bridge between the rich and poor, and co-supervisor of the world economy.
13. Ibid., p. 315.
14. Ibid., p. 322.
15. See, for example, Smith, *Europe Foreign and Security Policy.*
16. Ian Manners, "Normative Power Europe: A Contradiction in Terms?" *Journal of Common Market Studies* 40 (2), 2002.
17. R. Rosencrance, "The European Union: A New Type of International Action," in Jan Zielonka (ed.), *Paradoxes of European Foreign Policy*, The Hague, Kluwer Law International, 1998, pp. 15–23.
18. Manners, "Normative Power Europe," p. 239.
19. Idem.
20. Thomas Christiansen, "Legitimacy Dilemmas of Supranational Governance: The European Commission between Accountability and Independence," in M. Nentwich and A. Weale (eds.), *Political Theory and the European Union,*

London, Routledge, 1997; J.H.H. Weiler, *The Constitution of Europe*, Cambridge, Cambridge University Press, 1999; Brigid Laffan, "The European Union Polity: A Union of Regulative, Normative and Cognitive Pillars," *Journal of European Public Policy* 8 (5), 2001, pp. 709–727.

21. Manners, "Normative Power Europe," art. cit.
22. My analysis of constructivism owes much to John Ruggie's article, "What Makes the World Hang Together? Neo-utilitarianism and the Social Constructivism Challenge," *International Organization* 52 (4), Autumn 1988. See also Jeffrey T. Checkel, "Social Constructivism in Global and European Politics" (A Review Essay) in ARENA, working papers WP/15/03.
23. Stefano Guzzini, *Constructivism and the Role of Institutions in International Relations*, Copenhagen, CPRI. Available at http://www.ciaonet.org/wps/gus06/.
24. Joseph Nye, "Neorealism and Neoliberalism," *World Politics* 40 (2), 1988, p. 240.
25. Ibid., p. 241.
26. Kenneth Waltz, *Theory of International Politics*, Reading, MA, Addison-Wesley, 1979.
27. Martha Finnemore and Katheryn Sikkink, "International Norm Dynamics and Political Change," *International Organization* 52 (4), Autumn 1998, p. 891.
28. Martha Finnemore, "Norms, Culture and World Politics: Insights from Sociology's Institutionalism," *International Organization* 325, 1996.
29. Manners, "Normative Power Europe."
30. Robert Rosencrance, *The Rise of the Trading State: Commerce and Conquest in the Modern World*, New York, Basic Books, 1986.
31. Manners, "Normative Power Europe," p. 241.
32. Ibid., p. 243
33. Romano Prodi, "2000–2005: Shaping the New Europe," speech before the European Parliament in Strasbourg, February 15, 2000.
34. Manners, "Normative Power Europe," p. 245 and 248.
35. "The European Union... is tending to impose on national actors a convergence of national public policies by means of norms laid down." Christian Lequesne, "The European Union: How to Deal with a Strange Animal," in Marie-Claude Smouts, *The New International Relations. Theory and Practice*, London, Hurst, 2001, p. 126.
36. Patrick Artus and Charles Wyplosz, *La Banque Centrale Européenne*, Paris, Conseil d'Analyse économique, La Documentation Française, 2002, 181 p.
37. Jean Pisani-Ferry and Elie Cohen, "Les paradoxes de l'Europe-puissance," *Esprit*, August–September 2002.
38. For the details of the normative system of "exceptional circumstances," see Richard Baldwin and Charles Wyplosz, "The Economics of European Integration," Chapter 14. Available at www.unige.ch/wyplosz/, p. 11.
39. Quermonne, *Le système politique de l'Union européenne*, p. 70.

40. "Setting development as a goal means instituting new rules.... These rules must be adapted to the situations experienced in developing countries. For if they are expected play on an equal footing with developed countries such as the US or the EU, they are likely to be swept aside." Pascal Lamy, "L'Europe: Le développement pour objectif, le commerce pour instrument," International Conference on Globalization, November 26, 2002.
41. "Europe has developed an innovative technique for governance that goes radically beyond the nation-state paradigm by inaugurating elements of transnational governance." Pascal Lamy, *La démocratie-monde. Pour une autre gouvernance globale*, Paris, Le Seuil, 2004, p. 56.
42. Kalypso Nicolaïdis and Robert Howse, "This is my EUtopia...Narrative as Power," *Journal of Common Market Studies* 40 (4), 2002, p. 771. Regarding the importance of the discourse on power in general, see Karoline Postel-Vinay, *L'Occident et sa bonne parole. Nos représentations du monde de l'Europe coloniale à l'Amérique hégémonique*, Paris, Flammarion, 2005.
43. There is nothing automatic, however, about this reality. In the case of GMOs, 22 states out of the Union's 25 recently refused to lift the safeguard clauses against introducing GM rapeseed and corn, contrary to the EU Commission's opinion recommending states to condemn recourse to safeguard clauses. Finding itself at odds not only with European member states but also with European public opinion on such a sensitive subject, the EU Commission is taking the risk of seeing its legitimacy weakened. *Le Monde*, June 26–27, 2005.

3 Norms for What Preferences?

1. Friedrich Kratochwil, "How Do Norms Matter?" in Michael Byers (ed.), *The Role of Law in International Politics*, Oxford, Oxford University Press, 2000, p. 60.
2. Interviews. This very personal speech by Fischer did not reflect the views of the German chancellor, as could be seen a few months later at the Nice Summit in the pugnacity with which he defended strictly German interests. It would appear, however, that Joschka Fischer's speech had to do more with domestic political considerations than with a truly well-developed European ambition. I owe this interpretation to Renaud Dehousse.
3. Thierry Le Roy, "L'union européenne et la souveraineté à la française: Le point de vue d'un juriste," *La Revue Tocqueville* 19 (2), 1998, p. 41.
4. See Andrew Moravsik, "Taking Preferences Seriously: Liberal Theory of International Politics," *International Organization*, Fall 1997.
5. Kenneth Waltz, "Reflections on Theory of International Politics: A Response to My Critics," in Robert Keohane (ed.), *Neorealism and Its Critics*, New York, Columbia University Press, 1986, p. 331.
6. *The National Security Strategy of the USA*, September 2002, p. 1.

7. The five threats identified are terrorism, nuclear proliferation, regional conflicts, failed states, and organized crime.
8. Carl Schmitt, *Le* nomos *de la Terre*, Paris, PUF, 1998, p. 35.
9. Ibid.
10. Solana, *Secure Europe.*
11. EDA. *An Initial Long-Term Vision for European Defence Capability and Capacity Needs.* http://www.operationspaix.net/An-initial-long-term-vision-for
12. Ibid., p. 9.
13. Immanuel Kant, *Perpetual Peace and Other Essays on Politics, History and Morals*, Indianapolis, Hackett Publishing Inc., 1983 (new edition).
14. See Clara Portela "Community Policies with a Security Agenda: The Worldview of Benita Ferrero-Waldner," EUI working papers. RSCAS 2007/10. Available at http://cadmus.iue.it/dspace/handle/1814/6752.
15. EDA, *Initial Long-Term Vision*, ibid., p. 13.
16. William Wallace, "Is There a European Approach to War?" *European Foreign Policy Unit*, working paper 2005/2, March 2005. Available at www.lse.ac.uk/Depts/intrel/pdfs/EFPU%20Working%20Paper%202005%202%20WW.pdf
17. Solana, *Secure Europe.*
18. Raymond Aron, *Paix et Guerre entre les nations*, 8th edition, Paris, Calmann-Lévy, 2004.
19. Robert Kagan, "Power and Weakness," *Policy Review* 113, June–July 2002, art. cit.
20. Thomas Hobbes, *Leviathan*, London, Oxford University Press, 1996, p. 508.
21. Kant, *Perpetual Peace.*
22. Jürgen Habermas, *La Paix perpétuelle. Le bicentenaire d'une idée kantienne*, Paris, Le Cerf, 1996, p. 56.
23. Ibid.
24. Aron, *Paix et Guerre entre les nations*, p. 5.
25. Carl Schmitt, *La notion de politique; Théorie du Partisan*, Paris, Flammarion, (Champs) 1992, p. 80.
26. Ibid., p. 73.
27. Etienne Balibar, "Le Hobbes de Schmitt, le Schmitt de Hobbes," in Carl Schmitt (ed.), *Le Leviathan dans la doctrine de l'Etat de Thomas Hobbes. Sens et échec d'un symbole politique*, Paris, Seuil, 2002, p. 38.
28. See Zaki Laïdi and Pascal Lamy, "A European Approach to Global Governance," in *Progressive Politics* 1 (1), September 2002.
29. Balibar, "Le Hobbes de Schmitt," p. 36.
30. *Trade Policy in the Prodi Commission. 1999–2004. An Assessment.* Available at http://trade.ec.europa.eu/doclib/docs/2006/september/tradoc_120087.pdf.
31. Out of the 26 trade conflicts brought before the WTO in which the European Union is implicated, in 13 of them the dispute is with the United States. In 10 of these 13 conflicts, Europe is the complainant. The other three conflicts, in which the United States is the complainant, have to do with issues with a

strong societal and identitarian dimension (GMOs, hormones, designations of origin).

32. European Commission. *General Overview of Active WTO Dispute Settlement Cases with the EC as Complainant or Defendant.* Brussels, June 30, 2004 (mimeo).
33. Lionel Fontagné, Michel Fouquin, Guillaume Gaulier, Colette Herzog, and Soledad Zignago, *European Industry's Place in the International Division of Labor: Situation and Prospects*, Brussels, CEPII-CIREM 2004.
34. Vincent Aussilloux and Edouard Bourcieu, *L'émergence de la Chine dans l'économie mondiale: Quels enjeux pour l'industrie européenne?* (mimeo).
35. *Trade Policy in the Prodi Commission. An Assessment*, p. 54.
36. Ibid., p. 10.
37. It is, however, far from certain that in the case of CAFTA (Central America Free Trade Agreement), environmental or social concerns were discussed. The United States imposes a low level of conditionality. The aim of the project seems fairly political. CAFTA overcomes the hurdles encountered in setting up the free trade area of the Americas and also counters the regional activism of Hugo Chavez's administration in Venezuela.
38. This is one of the reasons that led to listing the "Singapore questions" on the agenda of the last WTO negotiations. The multilateral framework thus prevents it from suffering too much from the competition distortions due to corruption without having to wonder if European economic actors do not share partial responsibility in this game.
39. Kari Tapiola, "Core Labor Standards and Globalization," July 2002. Available at www.adb.org/SocialProtection/tapiola.pdf.
40. Interviews, Brussels, December 2001.
41. See John Chenoy and Anuradha Chenoy, "The Social Clause as an Ideology," *The Third World Network.* Available at http://www.aidc.org.za/?q=book/view/64
42. James Galbraith, *"Why Populists Need to Re-think Trade," The American Prospect,* May 10, 2007.
43. Sandra Polaski, "Protecting Labor Rights Through Trade Agreements: An Analytical Guide." Available at http://www.carnegieendowment.org/publications/index.cfm?fa= view&id=15796
44. It would seem that regulatory obstacles to trade directed by Europe penalize more the developing countries among the OECD members. Anne-Célia Disdier, Lionel Fontagné, and Mondher Mimouni, "The Impact of Regulations on Agricultural Trade: Evidence from SPS and TBT Agreements." CEPII, February 2007. Available at www.cepii.fr/anglaisgraph/workpap/summaries/2007/wp0704–.htm.
45. Lionel Fontagné, "Quelle spécialisation optimale pour la France?" *Esprit*, June 2007, p. 23.
46. H. Selin and S. Vandeveer, *Raising Global Standards, Hazardous Substances and E-waste Management in the EU.* Available at http://www.encyclopedia.com/doc/1G1157196839–.html
47. Ibid.

48. Ibid.
49. Ibid.
50. F. Ackerman, E. Stanton, and R. Massey, *European Chemical Policy and the United States: The Impacts of REACH.* Available at http://ase.tufts.edu/gdea/Pubs/wp/0606–USREACH.pdf
51. Zaki Laïdi, *The Normative Empire. The Unintended Consequences of European Power.* Garnet Policy Briefs Number 6, February 2008, p. v.
51. S. Gstöhl (2007) *Political Dimensions of an Externalization of the EU Internal Market*, Bruges: Collège de Bruges, EU Diplomacy Papers 3.
52. In the *shrimp* conflict, the United States was criticized for not having first tried to negotiate an agreement with Asian states before applying sanctions. In the *gasoline* conflict, the United States was charged with discriminating against Latin American imports. But in both cases, enforcing environmental norms was recognized as legitimate by the United States.
53. The WTO decision in the appeal on the shrimp-sea turtle dispute in November 2001, in fact, overturned the preceding jurisprudence in that it more clearly recognized the precedence of environmental rules over trade. Regarding the interpretation of this panel, see Peter Singer's remarks, *One World*, New Haven, Yale University Press, 2002, p. 67 and 70.
54. This demand, which was answered in a climate of deep wariness of developing countries and the United States toward any linking of trade and the environment, had little effect, all the more so as it can prove to be even counterproductive. The Doha declaration limited application of the relationship between MEAs and the WTO to those that are party to the MEAs in question, whereas the WTO environmental panels have developed a jurisprudence that does not take into account whether a state is party to an MEA (*La politique commerciale de la Commission Prodi*, p. 38).
55. David Vogel, "The WTO, International Trade and Environmental Protection: Europe and America Perspectives," p. 19. Available at the author's Web site http://faculty.haas.berkeley.edu/vogel/greengiantfeb.pdf.
56. W. Grant, D. Matthews, and P. Newell, *The Effectiveness of European Environmental Policy*, London, McMillan Press, 2000, p. 35.
57. David Vogel, "The Politics of Risk Regulation in Europe and the United States," *Yearbook of European Environmental Law* 3, p. 39.
58. Natalie McNellis, "EU Communication on the Precautionary Principle," *Journal of International Economic Law*, 2000, pp. 545–551.
59. Commission of the European Communities, *Communication on the Precautionary Principle*, COM (2000) 1, Brussels, CEC.
60. Alasdair Young, "The Incidental Fortress: The Single Europe Market and World Trade," *Journal of Common Market Studies* 42 (2), 2004, p. 410.
61. See Tim Flannery, "Endgame," *New-York Review of Books*, August 11, 2005.
62. Regarding this point see the inspired viewpoint of Adam Werbach, president of the Sierra Club, "Is Environmentalism Dead?" Available at http://www.grist.org/news/maindish/2005/01/13/werbach-reprint/.

63. Andrew Jordan and Timothy O'Riordan, "The Precautionary Principle in Contemporary Environmental Policy and Politics," in C. Raffensparger and J. Trickner (eds.), *Protecting Public Health and the Environment*, Washington DC, Island Press, 1999, p. 21.
64. E. Soule, "Assessing the Precautionary Principle," *Public Affairs Quarterly* 14 (4), 2000, p. 318.
65. David Vogel, "The Protestant Ethic and the Spirit of Environmentalism: The Cultural Roots of Green Politics and Policies," September 2001, Haas School of Business, p. 11. Available at htpp://faculty.hass.berkeley.edu/vogel/.
66. See Albert Weale, "Environmental Rules and Rules-Making in the European Union," *Journal of European Public Policy*, 1996.
67. Alexis Roy and Pierre-Benoît Joly, "France: Broadening Precaution Expertise," *Journal of Risk Research* 3 (3), 2000, pp. 247–254.
68. Vogel, "Politics of Risk Regulation," p. 67.
69. Marsha Echols, "Food Safety Regulation in the European Union and the United States: Different Cultures, Different Laws," *Columbia Journal of European Law* 4 (4), 1987, pp. 525–543.
70. Vogel, "Politics of Risk Regulation," p. 18.
71. Ibid., p. 19.
72. David Vogel, "'The Hare and the Tortoise,' Revisited. The New Politics Consumer and Environmental Regulation in Europe." Available at htpp://faculty.hass.bakely.edu/vogel/uk%20oct.pdf.p5.
73. See Olivier Godard, "Environnement et commerce international. Le principe de précaution sur la ligne de fracture," *Futuribles*, March 2001, pp. 37–62.
74. Robert Falkner, "The European Union as a Green Normative Power. EU Leadership in International Biotechnology Regulation," Center for European Studies, working paper series n° 140 (2006), p. 8. Available at www.ces.fas.harvard.edu/publications/docs/pdfs/Falkner.pdf.
75. Franz Fischler, "Rural Development and Fisheries. European Agricultural Model in the Global Economy," speech to the Second International Conference on Globalization, Université de Louvain, November 26, 2002. See also Pascal Lamy, Conférence-Débat *The Economist*, October 3, 2002. On the European discourse on multifunctionality as regards free trade, See Eve Fouilleux, "CAP Reforms and Multilateral Trade Negotiations: Another View on Discourse Efficiency," *West European Politics* 27 (2), March 2004, pp. 235–255. This special issue, coedited by Vivien Schmidt, is one of the most valuable sources for analysis of European discourse.
76. *La politique commerciale de la Commission Prodi*, p. 30.
77. *Financial Times*, July 29, 2005.
78. On CAFTA, see *International Herald Tribune*, July 28, 2005. On the slim preference for free trade, see Zaki Laïdi, *The Great Disruption*, Cambridge, MA, Polity Press, 2007.
79. See Joseph Stiglitz and Andrew Charlton, "A Development Round of Trade Negotiations?" Available at www2.gsb.columbia.edu/faculty/stiglitz.

80. Available at http://trade.ec.europa.eu/doclib/html/118925.htm.
81. "Collective preferences in international trade are by no means new... It is only recently that the issue has risen to prominence, as the world economy has become more integrated, the range of traded goods and services has increased and the level of public awareness has risen, resulting in more and more disputes (the turtle-shrimp case, hormones, asbestos etc.), perceived as disputes about collective preferences," pp. 5–6.
82. "The specific problem of integrating developing countries calls for questioning the approach of trade liberalization through reciprocal trade concessions," Commission memo, December 1999 (mimeo).
83. John Jackson, *The World Trading System*, Cambridge, MA, MIT, 1992 and Dani Rodrik, "Labor Standards in International Trade," in Robert Z. Lawrence, Dani Rodrik, and John Whalley (eds.), *Emerging Agenda for Global Trade*, Baltimore, Johns Hopkins University Press, 1996.
84. See Charles Wyplosz's remarks, "Comment on Pascal Lamy. From Social to World Preferences" (mimeo).
85. See the opinions in the *Financial Times*, February 6 and 10, 2004, and those of European business, "UNICE Slams Lamy over 'Collectives Preferences,'" *European Report*, May 2004.
86. Steve Charnowitz, "An Analysis of Pascal Lamy's Proposal on Collective Preferences," *Journal of International Economic Law* 8 (2), 2005, pp. 453–454.
87. Ibid., p. 463.
88. Ibid., p. 464.
89. These two proposals were formulated by Marco Bronkers, "Exceptions to Liberal Trade in Foodstuffs," in *EEA, EU and WTO Law: The Precautionary Approach and Collective Preferences*, December 10, 2004 (mimeo).

4 European Governance and American Sovereignism

1. Manners, "Normative Power Europe," art. cit.
2. Naturally, no country is targeted in terms of international criminal justice, but some countries may feel more vulnerable to such legal action because, by political will or by tradition, they are highly engaged in international military operations in which some of their soldiers may end up implicated.
3. Europe has in fact very clearly understood the full political benefit it could draw from an international stance that would allow it to appear as the world champion of "global public goods" and, by virtue of this very fact, as the promoter of values transcending the sovereignty of nation-states.
4. See Samuel Scheffler, *Boundaries and Allegiances. Problems of Justice and Responsibility in Liberal Thought,* Oxford, Oxford University Press, 2001. Also see David Held's essential work, *Global Covenant, The Social Democratic Alternative to the Washington Consensus*, Cambridge, MA, Polity Press, 2004.

5. Alasdair MacIntyre, "Is Patriotism a Virtue?" in R. Beiner (ed.), *Theorizing Citizenship*, 1995, New York, State University of New York Press, pp. 209–228.
6. Ibid.
7. See Bardo Fassbender, "The Better People of the United Nations? Europe's Practice and the United Nations," *EJIL* 15 (5), (2004), pp. 857–884.
8. Pierre Brana, *Rapport 2141*, French National Assembly, February 15, 2000, p. 7. *Rapport fait au nom de la Commission des Affaires Etrangères sur le projet de loi autorisant la ratification de la Convention portant Statut de la CPI* (cited hereafter as *Brana Report*).
9. Statute of the International Criminal Court. Available at www. icc.cpi.cut/ docs/baisdocs/rome-statute(f).html.
10. Brana, *Brana Report*.
11. This fear appears groundless today. Since the war in Iraq, British soldiers accused of abuses have been brought before British courts and tried by them. No one mentioned the idea of bringing these soldiers before the ICC, which proves that the principle of complementarity can indeed function. See Philippe Sands, *Lawless World. America and the Making and Breaking of Global Rules*, London, Penguin, 2005, p. 59.
12. Brana, *Brana Report*, p. 4.
13. Article 12 of the Statute allows ICC jurisdiction only if the country on whose territory the crimes were committed (or the country of which the accused is a citizen) is party to the treaty. The ICC's universal jurisdiction is, in fact, recognized only by the UN Security Council. Cf FIDH. *Rapport Cour Pénale Internationale: "La route ne s'arrête pas à Rome,"* November 1998 (266). Available at www.fidh.imaginet.fr/rapports/r266.htm.
14. Brana, *Brana Report*, p. 42.
15. Ibid., p. 28.
16. Ibid.
17. Philip Altson, "Review Essay. Transplanting Foreign Norms: Human Rights and Other International Legal Norms in Japan," *EJIL* 10 (3), 1999. Available at www.ejil.org/journal/vol10/n°3/rev.html.
18. See Y. Iwasawa, *International Law, Human Rights Law and Japanese Law: The Impact of International Law on Japanese Law*, Oxford, Clarendon Press, 1998.
19. Joseph Weiler, "The Transformation of Europe," *Yale Law Journal*, June 1991, p. 2407.
20. Joseph Weiler, "Une révolution tranquille. La CJCE et ses interlocuteurs," *Politix* 32 (3), (1995), p. 121.
21. Weiler, "Transformation of Europe," p. 2412.
22. Weiler, "Une révolution tranquille," p. 122.
23. Regarding the articulation of the European legal order and world legal order, see the volume edited by Vincent Kronenberg (ed.), *The European Union and the International Legal Order: Discord or Harmony?* La Haye, TMC Asser Press, 2001.

24. David Sloss, "International Agreements and the Political Safeguards of Federalism," *Stanford Law Review* 55 (May 2003), p. 1984.
25. Ibid., p. 1985.
26. Ibid.
27. This said, even if this new situation must be taken into account, it does not entirely explain the U.S. wariness toward world norms that, moreover, the United States has often contributed to forging, particularly in matters of security: the ABM Treaty in 1972, rejection of the Convention on Biological and Toxic Weapons, definition of a new nuclear strategy in violation of art. VI of the NPT (See Jonathan Greenberg, "Does Power Trump Law?" *Stanford Law Review*, May 2003, p. 1814.
28. John Ruggie, "American Exceptionalism, Exemptionalism and Global Governance," p. 5 in Michael Ignatieff (ed.), *American Exceptionalism and Human Rights,* Princeton, Princeton University Press (available at the Kennedy School of Government Web site, *Faculty Research Working Papers Series.* February 2004. Page references are to the working paper).
29. Glennon and Steewart, "The United States: Taking Environmental Treaties Seriously," in Weiss E. Brown and H.K. Jacobsen (eds.), *Engaging Countries: Strengthening Compliance with International Environmental Agreements*, 1998, Cambridge, MA: MIT Press, pp. 174–175.
30. Jutta Brunnée, "The United States and International Environmental Law," *EJIL* 15 (4), 2004, p. 629
31. Ibid., p. 630.
32. Ibid., p. 637.
33. Jed Rubenfeld, "The Two World Orders," *Wilson Quarterly*, Autumn 2003, p. 34.
34. See Paul Stephan, "International Governance and American Democracy," *Chicago Journal of International Law*, Autumn 2000.
35. Ibid., p. 38.
36. Curtis Bradley and Jack Goldsmith, "Customary International Law as Federal Common Law: A Critique of the Modern Position," *Harvard Law Review* 110 (4), 1997, p. 815.
37. Customary international law is defined as "the set of unwritten norms resulting from a general and consistent practice of states that they follow from a sense of legal obligation." *Restatement (Third) of Foreign Relations Law of the United States*, § 701, Philadelphia, American Law Institute, 1987.
38. Ibid.
39. Ibid.
40. John Ruggie, "American Exceptionalism," p. 23.
41. Andrea Bianchi, "International Law and US Courts: The Myth of Lohengrin Revisited," *EJIL* 15 (4), 2004, pp. 773 and 775.
42. See Curtis Bradley, "International Delegations, the Structural Constitution and Non-self Execution," 2000, *Stanford Law Review* 55, May 2003.

43. Peter Spiro, "Treaties, International Law and Constitutional Rights," *Stanford Law Review*, May 2003, p. 2.
44. Andrea Bianchi, "International Law and US Courts," p. 780.
45. Christian Vergaris, "The Federalism Implications of International Human Rights Law," *The Federalist Society for Law and Public Policy Studies*, p. 9. Available at www.fed-soc.org.
46. Ibid.
47. Jack Goldsmith, "Should International Human Rights Law Trump US Domestic Law?" *Chicago Journal of International Law*, Autumn 2000, p. 328.
48. Andrea Bianchi, "International Law and US Courts," p. 777. In fact, the new point of departure for American legal sovereignism came in 1985 with Washington's decision to withdraw from the compulsory jurisdiction of the International Court of Justice.
49. Judiciary Act of 1789, chapter 20, § 9 (6), 1 Stat. 73, 77.
50. "The Federalism Implication," p. 5.
51. Jed Rubenfeld, "The Two World Orders," pp. 22–36.
52. See inter alia, Peter Spiro, "The New Sovereignists: American Exceptionalism and Its False Prophets," *Foreign Affairs,* November–December 2000 as well as Anne-Marie Slaughter, "Building Global Democracy," *Chicago Journal of International Law*, Autumn 2000.
53. Eric Posner, "Do States Have a Moral Obligation to Obey International Law?" *Stanford Law Review*, May 2003, p. 1918.
54. Kenneth Roth, "The Charade of US Ratification of International Human Rights Treaties," *Chicago Journal of International Law*, Autumn 2000, p. 138.
55. John Bolton, "Should We Take Global Governance Seriously?" *Chicago Journal of International Law*, Autumn 2000, p. 220.
56. Ibid., p. 205.
57. Sands, *Lawless World,* p. 64.
58. Ibid., p. 67.
59. Paul Stephan, "International Governance and American Democracy," *Chicago Journal of International Law*, Autumn 2000, p. 249.
60. Eric A. Posner, "Terrorism and the Law of War," *Chicago Journal of International Law*, Winter 2005, p. 433.
61. Bolton, "Should We Take Global Governance Seriously?" p. 220.
62. Jeremy Rabkin, "Is EU Policy Eroding the Sovereignty of Non-members States?" *Chicago Journal of International Law*, Autumn 2000, p. 273.
63. Ibid., p. 279 and 280.
64. Ibid., p. 72.
65. See Jeremy Rabkin, *The Case for Sovereignty. Why the World Should Welcome American Independence*, Washington, AEI Press, 2004.
66. Richard Pildes, "Conflicts between American and European Views of Law: The Dark Side of Legalism," *Virginia Journal of International Law*, Autumn 2003, p. 147.

5 Is Constitutionalizing the World Order the Answer?

1. Anne-Marie Slaughter, "The Real New World Order," *Foreign Affairs* 76, September–October 1997.
2. Anne Peters, "Global Constitutionalism Revisited," p. 3. Available at http://law.ubalt.edu/asil/peters/html.
3. Ibid.
4. The notion of global public goods applies to the set of problems for which the most relevant community of reference is the global community and not the national community. See Mattias Kumm, "The Legitimacy of International Law: A Constitutionalist Framework of Analysis," *EJIL* 15 (5), 2004, p. 923.
5. Ibid.
6. See the works of Mireille Delmas-Marty, particularly *Trois défis pour un droit mondial*, Paris, Seuil, 1998.
7. B.S. Chimni, "International Institutions Today: An Imperial Global State in the Making," *EJIL* 15 (1), 2004, p. 2.
8. Ibid.
9. Armin von Bogdandy, "Globalization and Europe: Law to Square Democracy, Globalization and International Law," *EJIL* 15 (5), 2004, p. 894.
10. See among other sources of this German school, Christian Tomuschat, "International Law as the Constitution of Mankind," in United Nations, *International Law on the Eve of the Twenty-First Century*, 1997.
11. Kant, *Perpetual Peace*.
12. Ibid., p. 33.
13. Ibid.
14. Ibid.
15. On the dangers of European ethnocentrism, see Matti Koskenniemi, "International Law in Europe: Between Tradition and Renewal," *EJIL* 16 (1), 2005, pp. 113–124. The author's relativism is excessive, but his appeals for caution are not entirely groundless.

6 Norms and Geopolitics

1. It is, for instance, revealing to note that the Netherlands, in discussions about a simplified treaty, have requested that the Copenhagen criteria be incorporated into the treaties.
2. European Council in Copenhagen. Presidency conclusions June 21–22, 1993. Available at ue.eu.int/ueDocs/cms_Data/docs/pressdate/en/ec/72921.pdf
3. Michel Emerson, Senem Aydin, Julia De Clerck-Sachsse, and Gergana Noutcheva, "Just What Is the 'Absorption Capacity' of the European Union?" CEPS policy brief. September 2006. Available at shop.ceps.be/BookDetail.php?item_id=1381]

4. Ibid., p. 3.
5. Andrew Moravsick and Milada Anna Vachudova, "National Interests, State, Power and EU Enlargement," *East-European Studies and Societies* 17 (1), 2003, p. 7. Available at www.ces.fas.harvard.edu/publications/docs/pdfs/Moravcsik_Vachudova.pdf.
6. James Hugues, Gwendolyn Sasse, and Claire Gordon, *Europeanization and Regionalization in the EU's Enlargement to Central and Eastern Europe: The Myth of Conditionality*, New York, Palgrave Macmillan, 2004, 231 p.
7. Geoffrey Pridham, "European Union Accession Dynamics and Democratization in Central and Eastern Europe: Past and Future Perspectives," *Government and Opposition* 41 (3), 2006, p. 386.
8. "The rewards of membership were so substantial that eventually all plausible candidates in the region come around to electing a pro-EU government and get to work on fulfilling the membership requirements." Milada Ana Vachudova, *The Leverage of International Institutions on Democratizing States: Eastern Europe and the European Union.* EUI working papers. Available at www.iue.it/RSCAS/WP-Texts01_33.pdf
9. "A state adopts EU rules if the benefits of EU rewards exceed the domestic adoption costs," Franck Schimellfennig and Ulrich Sedelmeier, "Governance by Conditionality: EU Transfer to the Candidate Countries of Central and Eastern Europe," *Journal of European Public Policy*, August 2004, p. 664.
10. "*We do not accept any substitute for European policy like the one proposed by the concept of Europe Neighborhood Policy.*" Ukrainian ambassador's statement before the Parliamentary Cooperation Committee. February 15, 2007.
11. See the Algerian ambassador's remarks to the EU. "The most important market liberty for Algeria, the free circulation of people, has been withdrawn from the EU's offer and cannot be found in the Action Plan," in *The Greening of the European Neighborhood Policy.* Available at atassets.panda.org/downloads/enpandtheenvironment.pdf.
12. Judith Kelley, "New Wine in Old Wineskins: Promoting Political Reforms through the New European Neighborhood Policy," *Journal of Common Market Studies* 44, March 1, 2006, p. 30.
13. The March 13, 2003 document was entitled *Wider Europe: Neighborhood: A New Framework for Relations with Our Eastern and Southern Neighbors.* A year later, *Wider Europe* vanished behind the *European Neighborhood Policy* in the *Strategy Paper.* The *Strategy Paper* talks about offering a different perspective from membership, whereas the 2003 edition confines itself to saying this new policy "would not in the mid term include a perspective of membership," p. 5.
14. "For European ENP partners, the ENP does not in any way prejudge the possible future development of their relationship with the EU," *European Neighborhood Policy, Strategy Paper.* 2004. Available at ec.europa.eu/world/enp/pdf/com06_726_en.pdf. p. 13.

15. "The premise of ENP is that the EU has a vital interest in seeing greater economic development and stability and better governance in its neighborhood." EU Communication for the Commission to the Council and the European Parliament on strengthening the European Neighborhood Policy. December 4, 2006. Available at atec.europa.eu/world/enp/pdf/com06_726_en.pdf
16. Arnold Wolfers contrasts *milieu goals* and *possession goals.*

    Milieu goals are out not to defend or increase possessions they hold to the exclusion of others, but aim instead at shaping conditions beyond their national boundaries.... It is one thing to be in good physical of financial condition within an orderly and prosperous community, but quite another thing to be privileged by the wealth of one's possessions in surroundings of misery, ill health, lack of public order and widespread resentment. *Discord and Collaboration. Essays on International Politics.*

    Available at www.mtholyoke.edu/acad/intrel/pol116/wolfers.htm.
17. *European Neighborhood Policy, Strategy Paper.*
18. Ibid., p. 4.
19. Ibid., p. 4, author's emphasis.
20. Ibid., p. 4.
21. Stephen Woolcock, "European Union Policy towards Free Trade Agreements," EUPE, Working Brussels Papers—3/2007. Available at www.ecipe.org/pdf/EWP-32007–.pdf
22. Often European discourse on reciprocity is belied by European practices. For instance, certain agreements mention mutual recognition of rules and standards but in practice the European Union expects its partners to conform to European standards. Stephen Woolcock, p. 8.
23. But the essential point is that the *Country Reports* come out of the EU Commission alone, whereas the *Actions Plans* express an agreement between the EU Commission and the partner countries. Pinpointing the differences between the two documents is thus a means of measuring the gaps between European expectations and what the EU can really wrest from the countries involved in the ENP.
24. *European Neighborhood Policy. Strategy Paper,* May 15, 2004, p. 3.
25. Michelle Pace, "The EU Surrounded by a 'Ring of Friends': The Impact of the ENP on Europe's South." Available at www.bisa.ac.uk/2006/pps/pace.pdf.
26. E. Emerson and G. Noutcheva, "From Barcelona Process to Neighborhood Policy: Assessments and Open Issues," CEPS, Working Document (220), Brussels, 2005, p. 6. Available at shop.ceps.be/BookDetail.php?item_id=1209-10k
27. "*It is unfortunate that the actions plans agreed between the EU are negotiated behind closed doors without consultation of NGO's, especially those involved in the question of human rights.*" Euro-Mediterranean Human Rights Network. Available at http://ec.europe.eu/world/enp/pdf/com06_726_en.pdf

28. See Kristi Raik, "Promoting Democracy through Civil Society," Brussels, CEPS Working Document 237, February 2006. Available at shop.ceps.be/downfree.php?item_id=1298
29. Giselle Bosse, "Values in the EU's Neighborhood Policy: Political Rhetoric or Reflections of a Coherent Policy?" *European Political Economic Review* Summer 2007, p. 49. This hypothesis is confirmed by the fact that the *Actions Plans* for countries such as Ukraine are, from the standpoint of political conditionality, very close to the Accession Partnerships signed with the applicant countries. See Elena Baracani, "ENP Political Conditionality. A Comparison between Morroco and Ukraine," CEPS, April 21–22, 2006 (mimeo), p. 12. The Commission has already admitted as much in a document put out in 2006 on the ENP that indicates "*Moldova and Ukraine have already undertaken more substantial commitments in the human rights and governance field than have other ENP partners*," p. 2. Commission Staff Working Document. Accompanying the communication from the EU Commission to the EU Council and the European Parliament on strengthening the ENP. Overall assessment—December 4, 2006. Available at http://euromedrights.net/usr/00000026/00000027/00000029/00000844.pdf

Conclusion

1. This is unfortunately the trap Mark Leonard falls right into in Why Europe Will Run the 21st Century, London, Fourth Estate, 2005.
2. Richard Haas, "Regime Change and Its Limits," Foreign Affairs, July–August 2005.

BIBLIOGRAPHY

Adler, Emanuel, and Beverly Crawford. 2004. "Normative Power: The European Practice of Region Building and the Case of Euro-Mediterranean Partnership." Institute of European Studies, Paper 040400 (April). Available at: http://repositories.cdlib.org/ies/040400

Ancelovici, Marcos. 2002. "Organizing against Globalization: The Case of ATTAC in France." *Politics and Society* 30 (3): 427–463. Available at: http://web.mit.edu/polisci/students/mancelovici/Ancelovici.pdf

———. 2004. "ATTAC et le renouveau de l'antilibéralisme." *Raisons politiques* 16: 5–61.

Andreosso-O'Callaghan, Bernadette, and Françoise Nicolas. 2007. "Complementary and Rivalry in EU. China Economic Relations in the 21st Century." *European Foreign Affairs Review* 12: 32.

Appleton, Arthur. 1999. "Shrimps/Turtle: Untangling the Nets." *Journal of International Economic Law* 2 (3): 477–496.

Aussilloux, Vincent, and Edouard Bourcieu. 2005. "L'émergence de la Chine dans l'économie mondiale: Quels enjeux pour l'industrie européenne." Brussels: Mimeo.

Autret, Florence. 2005. *Bruxelles-Washington. La relation atlantique sur le métier.* La République des Idées. Available at: http://www.repid.com/IMG/pdf/Bruxelles-Washington.pdf.

Baer, Jean Michel. 2003. "L'exception culturelle. Une règle en quête de contenu." *Cahiers d'En Temps Réel* 11 (October). Available at: http://en.temps.reel.free.fr/accueil.htm

Baker, Susan. 2002. "European Union Biodiversity Policy." *EUI Working Paper.* Florence: EUI European University Institute.

Baracani, Elena. 2004. "The EU and Democracy Promotion: A Strategy of Democratization in the Framework of Neighbourhood Policy?" In Fulvio Attina and Rosa Rossi (eds.). *European Neighbourhood Policy: Political, Economic and Social Issue.* Catania: 37–57. Available at: http://www.fscpo.unict.it/EuroMed/ENPCataniabook.pdf. A publication of the European Union Neighbourhood Policy of the Faculty of Political Sciences, University of

Catania, a project cofinanced by the European Commission Jean Monnet Project—Heading A-3022 Catania.

Baracani, Elena. 2005. "From the EMP to the ENP: A New European Pressure for Democratization in the Southern Mediterranean? The Case of Morocco." In Roberto Di Quirico (ed.). *Europeanization and Democratization. Institutional Adaptation, Conditionality and Democratisation in European Union's Neighbour Countries.* Florence: European Press Academic Publishing.

———. 2006. "ENP Political Conditionality. A Comparison between Morocco and Ukraine." Center for European Policy Studies (April 21–22). mimeo.

Barrieu, P., and B. Sinclair-Desgagné. 2003. "The Paradox of Precaution." *Ecole Polytechnique Cahier 2003–012.* Available at: http://ceco.polytechnique.fr/CAHIERS/index.html

Bodansky, Daniel. 2002. *US Climate Policy after Kyoto: Elements of Success Policy Brief.* Washington: Carnegie Endowment. Available at: http://www.carnegieendowment.org/files/Policybrief15.pdf

Bolton, John. 2000. "Should We Take Global Governance Seriously?" *Chicago Journal of International Law* 1 (2) (Autumn): 205–221.

Bosse, Giselle. 2007. "Values in the EU's Neighbourhood Policy: Political Rhetoric or Reflections of a Coherent Policy?" *European Political Economic Review* 7 (1) (Summer): 38–62.

Bouët, Antoine, Lionel Fontagné, and Sébastien Jean. 2005. *Is Erosion of Preferences a Serious Concern?* Paris: CEPII (September 14). Available at: www.cepii.fr/anglaisgraph/workpap/pdf/2005/wp05-14.pdf

Bouët, Antoine. *Telos.* December 12, 2005 and March 20, 2006. Available at: www.telos-eu.com.

Bradley, Curtis, and Jack Goldsmith. 1997. "Customary International Law as Federal Common Law: A Critique of the Modern Position." Harvard Law Review 110 (4): 815–876.

Brana, Pierre. 2000. *Rapport fait au nom de la Commission des Affaires Etrangères sur le projet de loi autorisant la ratification de la Convention portant Statut de la CPI.* Paris: French National Assembly (February 15): 7. Available at: http://www.assemblee-nationale.fr/legislatures/11/pdf/rapports/r2141.pdf

Brouns, B., H.E. Ott, W. Sterk, and B. Wittneben. 2004. "It Takes Two to Tango: US Stalls as EU Awaits Change of Heart at the Climate Conference in Buenos Aires." Buenos Aires: Wuppertal Institute for Climate, Environment and Energy (December).

Brown, Gordon. 2005. *Global Europe: Full Employment Europe* (October 13). Available at: http://www.hm-treasury.gov.uk/documents/international_issues/global_challenges/int_global_europe.cfm

Brunnée, Jutta. 2004. "The United States and International Environmental Law." *EJIL* 15 (4). Bull, H. 1982. "Civil Power Europe: A Contradiction in Terms?" *Journal of Common Market Studies* 21 (2).

Bureau, Jean-Christophe, and Sébastien Jean. *Telos* (December 12, 2005). Available at: www.telos-eu.com

Cameron, James. 1999. "The Precautionary Principle." In Sampson G. and Chambers W.-B. (eds.). *Trade, Environment and the Millennium*. New York: United Nations University Press.

Chandler, David. 2003. "Governance the Unequal Partnership." In Wim van Meurs (ed.). *Prospect and Risks beyond EU Enlargement. Southeastern Europe: Weak State and Strong International Support* (Vol. II). Opladen: Leske & Budrich.

———. 2004. "The State-Building Dilemma: Good Governance or Democratic Government?" Roundtable on "Development, Under-Development and Armed Conflict." Rome: Military Centre for Strategic Studies (October 25). Available at: http://www.wmin.ac.uk/sshl/page-939-smhp=1.

Charnovitz, Steve. 2005. "An Analysis of Pascal Lamy's Proposal on Collective Preferences." *Journal of International Economic Law* 8 (2).

———. 2000. "The Supervision of Health and Biosafety Regulations by World Trade Rules." Available at: http://www.geocities.com/charnovitz/Tulane.htm.

Checkel, Jeffrey T. 2003. "Social Constructivism in Global and European Politics" (A Review Essay). Working Papers WP/15/03. Oslo: ARENA. Available at: http://www.arena.uio.no/publications/wp03_15.pdf

Chenoy, John, and Anuradha Chenoy. "The Social Clause as an Ideology." *The Third World Network*. Available at: http://www.aidc.org.za/?q=book/view/64

Commission of the European Communities. 2000. *Communication on the Precautionary Principle*, COM 1. Brussels: CEC. Available at: http://ec.europa.eu/environment/docum/20001_en.htm

Cowen, Tyler. 2002. *Creative Destruction. How Globalization Is Changing the World's Cultures*. Princeton: Princeton University Press.

Cowles, Maria G., and Michael Smith (eds.). 2000. *The State of the European Union, Risks, Reforms, Resistance and Revival* 5. Oxford: Oxford University Press.

Cremona, Marie Louise. 2005. "EU Enlargement: Solidarity and Conditionality." *European Law Review* 30 (1).

Crouzet, Philippe, and Nicolas Véron. 2002. "La mondialisation en partie double. La bataille des normes comptables." *Cahiers d'En Temps Réel* 3. Available at: http://en.temps.reel.free.fr/accueil.htm

De Buréa, Gráinne, and Joanne Scott. 2000. "The Impact of the WTO on EU Decisions-Making." Harvard Jean Monet Working Paper 6/00. Available at: http://www.jeanmonnetprogram.org/papers/00/000601.html.

Dehousse, Renaud. 1999. "L'Europe par le Droit." *Critique Internationale* 2 (Winter). Available at: http://www.ceri-sciencespo.com/cerifr/publica/critique/criti.htm#

della Porta, Donatella, and Hanspeter Kriesi. 1999. *Social Movements in a Globalizing World*. New York: St Martin's Press.

Delmas Marty, Mireille. 1998. *Trois défis pour un droit mondial*. Paris: Seuil.

Denis, Cecile, Kieran McMorrow, and Röger Werner. 2006. *Globalisation: Trends, Issues and Macro-implications for the EU*. European Economy. European

Commission. Economic Papers 254 (July). Available at: http://ec.europa.eu/economy_finance/publications/economic_papers/2006/ecp254en.pdf

Diamantopoulou, Anna. "The European Social Model: Past Its Sell-By Date?" Speech to the Institute for European Affairs. Dublin. Available at: http://ec.europa.eu/employment_social/speeches/2000/000720ad.pdf

———. 2000. "The European Identity in a Global Economy." Speech at the Europe Horizons Conference. Sintra (February 18). Available at: http://ec.europa.eu/archives/commission_1999_2004/diamantopoulou/past_speeches_en.html

Disdier, Anne-Célia, Lionel Fontagné, and Mimouni Mondher. 2007. "The Impact of Regulations on Agricultural Trade: Evidence from SPS and TBT agreements." CEPII (February). Available at: www.cepii.fr/anglaisgraph/workpap/summaries/2007/wp07-04.htm

Drodziac, William, Geoffrey Kemp, Flynt L. Leverett, Christopher J. Makins, and Bruce Stokes. 2004. "Partners in Frustration: Europe, the United States and the Broader Middle East." *Policy Paper.* Washington DC: The Atlantic Council (September). Available at: www.acus.org/docs/0409-Partners_Frustration_Europe_United_States_Broader_Middle_East.pdf

Duchêne, François. 1973. "The European Community and the Uncertainties of Interdependence." In Max Kohnstamm and Wolfgang Hager (eds.). *A Nation Writ Large? Foreign Policy Problems before the European Community.* New York: John Wiley & Sons.

Echols, Marsha. 1998. "Food Safety Regulation in the European Union and the United States: Different Cultures, Different Laws." *Columbia Journal of European Law* (4).

Eckerseley, Robyn. 2004. "The Big Chill: The WTO and Multilateral Environmental Agreements." *Global Environmental Politics* 4 (2).

Elbasani, Arolda. 2004. *Democratisation Process in Albania: Manipulation or Appropriation of International Norms?* Florence: EUI. Available at: www.ksg.harvard.edu/kokkalis/GSW7/GSW%206/elbasani.pdf

Emerson, Michael. 2004. "Has Turkey Fulfilled the Copenhagen Political Criteria?" *Policy Brief* 48. Center for European Policy Studies (April).

Emerson, Michael, Senem Aydin, Julia De Clerck-Sachsse, and Gergana Noutcheva. 2006. "Just What Is the 'Absorption Capacity' of the European Union?" CEPS Policy Brief. Brussels: CEPS (September).

Emerson, Michael, and Gergana Noutcheva. 2005. "From Barcelona Process to Neighbourhood Policy: Assessments and Open Issues." Brussels: CEPS Working Document (220).

EURACTIV. 2003. "EU Emissions Trading Will Be Tied to Kyoto Flexible Mechanisms." E-journal article.

———. 2005. "Heroes vs. Villains? EU and US Policies on Climate Change." E-journal article.

European Commission. 2001. *Eurobarometer: Public Opinion in the European Union*, Report 55 (October). Available at: http://europa.eu.int/comm/public_opinion/archives/eb/eb55/eb55_en.pdf

———. 2004. *European Neighbourhood Policy. Strategy Paper* (May 15): 3.

———. 2006. *Globalisation: Trends, Issues and Macro-implications for the EU.* Economic Publication (July).

———. 2001. *Eurobarometer: Public Opinion in the European Union.* Report 55 (October). Available at: http://europa.eu.int/comm/public_opinion/archives/eb/eb55/eb55_en.pdf

———. 2003. *Communication on Reinvigorating EU Actions on Human Rights and Democratisation with Mediterranean Partners.* COM 294 final. Brussels (May 21). Available at: http://www.eu-delegation.org.eg/en/more_about_eu/hr.pdf

———. 2005. *Climate Change: Commission Outlines Core Elements for Post-2012 Strategy.* Brussels. Available at: http://europa.eu/rapid/pressReleasesAction.do?reference=IP/05/155&format=PDF&aged=1&language=EN&guiLanguage=en

———. 2005. *Meeting the Climate Change Challenge.* Speech by Stavros Dimas (April 18). Available at: http://www.europa-eu-un.org/articles/en/article_4601_en.htm

———. 2005. "Communication de la Commission: Vaincre le changement climatique planétaire." COM (35). Available at: http://www.europa.eu.int/eur-lex/lex/LexUriServ/site/fr/com/2005/com2005_0035fr01.pdf

———. 2006. "The European Consensus on Development." Brussels (June).

European Defense Agency. *An Initial Long-Term Vision for European Defense Capability and Capacity Needs.* Available at: http://www.operationspaix.net/An-initial-long-term-vision-for

———. 2006. *An Initial Long-Term Vision for European Defense Capability and Capacity Needs* (October 3). Available at: http://www.euractiv.com/fr/securite/ministres-soutiennent-rapport-avenir-defense-europeenne/article-158484

European Opinion Research Group. *Eurobarometer* 2001—Special Edition: Survey Carried out for the European Commission's Representations in the Member States. National Highlights. Available at: http://europa.eu.int/comm/public_opinion/archives/eb/ebs_150_highlights_en.pdf

European Trade Union Confederation. 2005. *The Social Dimension of Globalisation.* Available at: http://www.etuc.org/a/365?var

———. 2001."Les Européens, la globalisation et la libéralisation." *Eurobarometer* 55 (1) (Spring). Available at: http://ec.europa.eu/public_opinion/archives/ebs/ebs_152_fr.pdf

———. 2006. "Les Européens et la PAC" (February). *Eurobarometer* 64 (3). Available at: http://ec.europa.eu/public_opinion/archives/ebs/ebs_242_fr.pdf

Evenett, Simon. 2007. "Global Europe: An Initial Assessment of the European Commission New Trade Policy" (January). Available at: www.evenett.com/articles/ECNewTradePol.pdf

Falkner, Robert. 2006. "The European Union as a Green Normative Power. EU Leadership in International Biotechnology Regulation." Harvard: Center for European Studies. *Working Paper Series* 140 (8). Available at: www.ces.fas.harvard.edu/publications/docs/pdfs/Falkner.pdf.

Fassbender, Bardo. 2004. "The Better People of the United Nations? Europe's Practice and the United Nations." *EJIL* 15 (5): 857–884. Available at: http://www.ejil.org/journal/Vol15/No5/1.pdf

Feho, Ernst, and Urs Fischbacher. 2002. "Why Social Preferences Matter. The Impact of Non-selfish Motives on Competition, Cooperation and Incentives." *The Economic Journal* 112 (March): C1–C33.

Ferrera, Maurizio, Anton Hemerijck, and Martin Rhodes. 2000. "La refonte des Etats-Providence européens." *Pouvoirs* 94.

Ferry, Jean-Marc. 2000. *La question de l'Etat européen*. Paris: Gallimard.

FIDH. 1998. *Rapport Cour Pénale Internationale: "La route ne s'arrête pas à Rome"* (266). Available at: http://www.fidh.org/rapports/r266.htm

Finnemore, Martha, and Katheryn Sikkink. 1998. "International Norm Dynamics and Political Change." *International Organization* 52 (4): 887–917.

Fischler, Franz. 2002. "Rural Development and Fisheries. European Agricultural Model in the Global Economy." Speech to the Second International Conference on Globalisation. Université de Louvain (November 26). Available at: http://europa.eu.int/rapid/pressReleasesAction.do?reference=SPEECH/02/590&format=HTML&aged=1&language=EN&guiLanguage=en

Fitoussi, Jean-Paul. 2002. *La règle et le choix. De la souveraineté économique en Europe*. Paris: Le Seuil.

Flannery, Tim. 2005. "Endgame." *New York Review of Books* (August 11).

Fligstein, Neil, and Frederic Merand. 2002. "Globalisation or Europeanisation? Evidence on the European Economy since 1980." *Acta Sociologica* 45 (1).

Fontagné, Lionel. 2007. "Quelle spécialisation optimale pour la France?" *Esprit* (June): 23.

Fouilleux, Eve. 2004. "CAP Reforms and Multilateral Trade Negotiations: Another View on Discourse Efficiency." *West European Politics* 27 (2) (March).

Galbraith, James. 2007. "Why Populists Need to Re-think Trade." The American Prospect (May 10).

Garapon, Antoine. 2002. "Désaccords euro-atlantiques. A propos de justice internationale et de lutte contre le terrorisme." *Esprit* (August–September).

Genschel, Philipp. 2004. "Globalization and the Welfare State: A Retrospective." *Journal of European Public Policy* 11 (4).

Gerstlé, Jacques. 2003. "La réactivité aux préférences collectives et l'imputabilité de l'action publique." *Revue Française de Science Politique* 53 (6): 859–885.

Gillespie, Richard. 2004. "A Political Agenda for Region-Building? The EMP and Democracy Promotion in North Africa." *Paper 040530*. Berkeley: Institute of European Studies (May 30). Available at: http://repositories.cdlib.org/cgi/viewcontent.cgi?article=1042&context=ies

Godard, Olivier. 2001. "Environnement et commerce international. Le principe de précaution sur la ligne de fracture." *Futuribles* (March).

Goldsmith, Jack. 2000. "Should International Human Rights Law Trump US Domestic Law?" *Chicago Journal of International Law* (Autumn).

Grabbe, Heather. 2002. "European Union Conditionality and the Acquis Communautaire" *International Political Science Review* 23 (3): 249–268.

———. 2006. *The EU's Transformative Power: Europeanization through Conditionality in Central and Eastern Europe.* London: Palgrave MacMillan.

Grant, Wyn, Duncan Matthews, and Peter Newell. 2002. *The Effectiveness of European Environmental Policy.* London. Palgrave Mcmillan.

Greenberg, Jonathan. 2003. "Does Power Trump Law?" *Stanford Law Review* (May).

Haas, Richard. 2005. "Regime Change and Its Limits." *Foreign Affairs* (July–August). Available at: http://www.foreignaffairs.org/20050701faessay84405/richard-n-haass/regime-change-and-its-limits.html

Haddadi, Said. 2004. "Political Securitisation and Democratisation in the Maghreb: Ambiguous Discourses and Fine-Tuning Practices for a Security Partnership." *Paper 040323.* Berkeley: Institute of European Studies (March 23). Available at: http://repositories.cdlib.org/ies/040323

Hamladji, Noura. 2002. *Do Political Dynamics Travel? Political Liberalization in the Arab World.* EUI Working Papers SPS 2002/11. Available at: http://cadmus.iue.it/dspace/bitstream/1814/331/1/sps200211.pdf

Harris, Paul. 2002. *Sharing the Burdens? The Euro-Atlantic Community and Global Environmental Change.* EUI Working Papers, RSC 2002/63. Available at: http://www.iue.it/RSCAS/WP-Texts/02_63.pdf

Hay, Colin, and Ben Rosamond. 2002. "Globalization, European Integration and the Discursive Construction of Economic Imperatives." *Journal of European Public Policy* 9 (2).

Hayden, Robert. 2005. "'Democracy' without a Demos?' The Bosnian Constitutional Experiment and the Intentional Construction of Nonfunctioning States." East European Politics and Societies 19 (2): 226–259. Available at: http://eep.sagepub.com/cgi/content/abstract/19/2/226

Hennis, Marjoleine. 2002. "New Transatlantic Conflicts. American and European Food Policies Compared." RSC 2002/01. Berkeley: European University Institute. Available at: http://www.iue.it/RSCAS/WP-Texts/02_01.pdf

Hill, Christopher. 2002. *Super State or Superpower? The Future of the European Union in World Politics.* London: LSE (July). Available at: http://www.lse.ac.uk/Depts/intrel/pdfs/EFPU-superpowerorsuperstate.pdf

Hoyt, Christopher, and Stephen G. Brooks. 2003–2004. "A Double-Edge Sword: Globalization and Biosecurity." *International Security* 28 (3) (Winter): 123–148.

Hugues, James, and Gwendolyn Sasse. 2003. "Monitoring the Monitors: EU Enlargement Conditionality and Minority Protection in the CEECs." Available at: www.ecmi.de/jemie/download/Focus1-2003_Hughes_Sasse.pdf

Hugues, James, Gwendolyn Sasse, and Claire Gordon. 2004. *Europeanization and Regionalization in the EU's Enlargement to Central and Eastern Europe: The Myth of Conditionality.* New York: Palgrave Macmillan.

Imig, Doug, and Sidney Tarrow. 1999. "Contentious Europeans: Is There a European Repertoire of Collective Action?" *Columbia International Affairs Online* 8 (99). Available at: http://ciaonet.org/wps/imd03

International Labour Organization. 2004. *The Report of the World Commission on the Social Dimension of Globalization*. Available at: http://www.ilo.org/public/english/fairglobalization/report/index.htm

Ismer, Roland, and Karsten Neuhoff. 2004. "Border Tax Adjustments: A Feasible Way to Address Non-participation in Emission Trading." DAE Working Paper Series. Cambridge: University of Cambridge Press.

Iwasawa, Yuji. 1998. *International Law, Human Rights Law and Japanese Law: The Impact of International Law on Japanese Law*. Oxford: Clarendon Press.

Jackson, John. 1992. *The World Trading System*, Cambridge, MA: MIT Press.

Jacquemin, Ode. 2006. "La conditionnalité démocratique de l'Union européenne. Une voie pour l'universalisation des droits de l'Homme? Mise en œuvre, critiques et bilan." Working Paper 3. CRIDHO.

Jordan, Andrew, and Timothy O'Riordan. 1999. "The Precautionary Principle in Contemporary Environmental Policy and Politics." In Carolyn Raffensparger and Joel Trickner (eds.). *Protecting Public Health and the Environment*. Washington DC: Island Press.

Judt, Tony, and Denis Lacorne (eds.). 2005. *With US or against US: Studies in Global Anti-Americanism*. New York: Palgrave Macmillan.

Kagan, Robert. 2002. "Puissance et faiblesse." *Commentaire* 25 (99): 517–535.

Kant, Immanuel. 1983. *Perpetual Peace and Other Essays on Politics, History and Morals* (new edition). Indianapolis: Hackett Publishing Inc.

Kelley, Judith. 2006. "New Wine in Old Wineskins: Promoting Political Reforms through the New European Neighbourhood Policy." *Journal of Common Market Studies* 44 (March): 29–55.

Kierzkowski, Henry (ed.). 2002. *From Europeanization of the Globe to Globalization of Europe*. London: Palgrave.

Kissinger, Henry, and Lawrence H. Summers. 2004. *Renewing the Atlantic Partnership*. New York: Council on Foreign Relations. Available at: http://www.cfr.org/content/publications/attachments/Europe_TF.pdf

Korpi, Walter. 2003. "Welfare State Regress in Western Europe: Politics, Institutions Globalization and Europeanization." *Annual Review of Sociology* 29.

Koskenniemi, Martti. 2005. "International Law in Europe: Between Tradition and Renewal." EJIL 16 (1).

Kratochwil, Friedrich. 2000. "How Do Norms Matter?" In Michael Byers (ed.). *The Role of Law in International Politics*. Oxford: Oxford University Press.

Kronenberg, Vincent (ed.). 2001. *The European Union and the International Legal Order: Discord or Harmony?* La Haye: TMC Asser Press.

Kumm, Mattias. 2004. "The Legitimacy of International Law: A Constitutionalist Framework of Analysis." *EJIL* 15 (5). Available at: http://www.ejil.org/journal/Vol15/No5/3.pdf

Kupchan, Charles. 2003. *The End of the American Era. US Foreign Policy and the Geopolitics of the Twenty-First Century*. New York: Knopf.

Laïdi, Zaki. 2007. *The Great Disruption*. Chapter 4. Cambridge, MA: Polity.

———. (ed.). 2008. *The Reception of Europe. EU Preferences in a Globalized World*. London: Routledge.

Laïdi, Zaki, and Pascal Lamy. 2002. "La gouvernance ou comment donner sens à la globalisation." *Gouvernance mondiale. Rapport du Centre d'Analyse Economique*. Paris: La Documentation française. Available at: www.laidi.com.

———. 2002."A European Approach to Global Governance." *Progressive Politics* 1 (1). Available at: www.laidi.com/papiers/progpol0902.pdf

Lamy, Pascal. 2002. "Après Doha. Les chemins de la gouvernance mondiale." *Cahiers d'En Temps Réel* (1) (February): 34. Available at: http://en.temps.reel.free.fr/accueil.htm

———. 2002. "L'Europe: le développement pour objectif, le commerce comme instrument." Conférence internationale sur la mondialisation. Louvain (November 26). Available at: http://www.globalisationdebate.be/2002/trades/speech/sp_lamy.htm

Leary, Virginia. 1997. "The WTO and the Social Clause: Post Singapore." *European Journal of International Law* 8.

Leonard, Marc. 2005. *Why Europe Will Run the 21st Century*. London: Fourth Estate.

Le Roy, Thierry. 1998. "L'union européenne et la souveraineté à la française: le point de vue d'un juriste." *La Revue Tocqueville* 19 (2).

Lightfoot, Simon, and Jon Burchell. 2005. "The EU and the World Summit on Sustainable Development: Normative Power Europe in Action?" *Journal of Common Market Studies* 43 (1): 75–95.

Majone, Giandomenico. 2003. "What Price Safety? The Precautionary Principle and Its Policy Implications." *Journal of Common Market Studies* 40 (1).

———. 1996. *La Communauté européenne, un Etat régulateur*. Paris: Montchrestien.

———. 2002. *International Economic Integration, National Authority, Transnational Democracy: An impossible Trinity. EUI Working Paper*, RSC 48. Florence: European University Institute. Available at: http://www.iue.it/RSCAS/WP-Texts/02_48.pdf

Mandelson, Peter. 2006. "Trade Policy and Decent Work Intervention." Speech at the EU Decent Work Conference. EU Commission (December 5). Available at: http://ec.europa.eu/commission_barroso/mandelson/speeches_articles/sppm134_en.htm

———. 2005. "The Global Economic Agenda: Europe and India's Challenge." Speech at the Confederation of Indian Industry Partnership Summit at Kolkata, India. EU Commission (January13). Available at: http://ec.europa.eu/commission_barroso/mandelson/speeches_ articles/sppm010_en.htm

Manners, Ian. 2002. "Normative Power Europe: A Contradiction in Terms." *Journal of Common Market Studies* 40 (2): 235–258.

Manners, Ian. 2004. "Normative Power Europe Reconsidered." Oslo: Cidel Workshop (October). Available at: http://www.arena.uio.no/cidel/WorkshopOsloSecurity Manners.pdf

Manning, Nick P., and Bruno Palier. 2003. "Globalization, Europeanization and the Welfare State." *Global Social Policy* 3 (2): 139–143.

Maull, Hanns. 1990. "Germany and Japan: The New Civilian Powers." *Foreign Affairs* 69 (5).

McFaul, Michael. 2002. "The Fourth Wave of Democracy and Dictatorship." *World Politics* 54 (2): 212–244.

McNellis, Natalie. 2000. "EU Communication on the Precautionary Principle." *Journal of International Economic Law* 3 (3): 545–551.

Meadcroft, James. 2002. *The Next Step: A Climate Change Briefing for European Decision-Makers*. Policy Paper RSC 2 (13). Florence: European University Institute. Available at: http://www.iue.it/RSCAS/WP-Texts/02_13p.pdf

Moravcsik, Andrew. 1997. "Taking Preferences Seriously: Liberal Theory of International Politics." *International Organization* 51 (4): 513–553. Available at: http://www.princeton.edu/~amoravcs/library/preferences.pdf

———. 2004. "One Year on: Lessons from Iraq." *Chaillot Paper* 68 (March): 172–173. Paris: Institute for Security Studies. Available at: http://www.princeton.edu/~amoravcs/library/lessons.pdf

———. 2002. "Liberal International Relations Theory." In Colin Elman and Miriam Fendius Elman (eds.). *Progress in International Relations Theory*. Cambridge, MA: MIT Press.

Moravcsik, Andrew, and Milada Anna Vachudova. 2003. "National Interests, State Power, and EU Enlargement." *East European Politics and Societies* 17 (1): 42–57. Available at: www.princeton.edu/~amoravcs/library/eeps.pdf

Morrisey, Wagner. 2000. "RL30522: Global Climate Change: A Survey of Scientific Research and Policy Report." *CRS Report for Congress*. Washington DC (April 13). Available at: http://ncseonline.org/nle/crsreports/climate/clim-24.cfm

Moschella, Manuela. 2004. "European Union's Regional Approach towards Its Neighbours: The European Neighbourhood Policy vis-à-vis Euro-Mediterranean Partnership." Jean Monnet Centre. Department of Political Studies. University of Catania. Available at: http://www.fscpo.unict.it/EuroMed/moschella.pdf

Narlikar, Amrita, and Diana Tussie. 2004. "The G-2O at the Cancun Ministerial Developing Countries and Their Evolving Coalitions in the WTO." *World Economy* 27 (7): 947–966.

Nicolaïdis, Kalypso, and Robert Howse. 2002. "This Is My EUtopia… Narrative as Power." *Journal of Common Market Studies* 40 (4): 767–792.

Nye, Joseph. 1988. "Neorealism and Neoliberalism." *World Politics* 40 (2): 235–269.

———. 2004. *Soft Power. The Means to Success in World Politics*. New York: Public Affairs.

Pace, Michelle. 2006. "The EU Surrounded by a Ring of Friends: The Impact of the ENP on Europe South." Presented at the British International Studies Association 31st Annual Conference. University College Cork (December 18–20). Available at: www.bisa.ac.uk/2006/pps/pace.pdf

Palier, Bruno, and Louis-Charles Viossat (eds.). 2001. *Politiques sociales et mondialisation*. Paris: Ed. Futuribles [Proceedings of the symposium organized by the World Bank Social Protection Unit and CEVIPOF. April 27, 2000. Paris].

Panebianco, Stefania. 2004. "The Constraints to EU Action as a 'Norm Exporter' in the Mediterranean." Unpublished article (July). Available at: www.democracy agenda.org.

Panebianco, Stefania, and Rosa Rossi. 2004. "EU Attempts to Export Norms of Good Governance to the Mediterranean and Western Balkan Countries." *Jean Monet Working Papers in Comparative and International Politics* (53) (October). Available at: http://www.fscpo.unict.it/EuroMed/jmwp53.pdf

Peters, Anne. "Global Constitutionalism Revisited." ASIL centennial discussion on "Just World Under Law: Why Obey International Law?" University of Baltimore School of Law. Available at: http://law.ubalt.edu/asil/peters.html

Pildes, Richard. 2003. "Conflicts between American and European Views of Law: The Dark Side of Legalism." *Virginia Journal of International Law* (Autumn).

Pippan, Christian. 2004. "The Rocky Road to Europe; The EU's Stabilisation and Association Process for the Western Balkans and the Principle of Conditionality." *European Foreign Affairs Review* 9: 219–245.

Pisani-Ferry, Jean, and Elie Cohen. 2002. "Les paradoxes de l'Europe-puissance." *Esprit* (August–September).

Plümper, Thomas, Schneider, Cristina, and Vera Troeger. 2004. "The Politics of EU Eastern Enlargement: Evidence from a Heckman Selection Model." Social Science Research Network (May). Available at: http://ssrn.com/abstract=561362

Polaski, Sandra. 2004. "Protecting Labor Rights through Trade Agreements: An Analytical Guide." *Journal of International Law and Policy* (July). Available at: http://www.carnegieendowment.org/publications/index.cfm?fa=view&id=15796

Pollack, Mark A., and Gregory Schaffer. 2000. "Transatlantic Conflict over GMO: Why the US Is Avoiding a Trade War." *The Washington Quarterly* 23 (Autumn).

Portela, Clara. 2007. "Community Policies with a Security Agenda: The Worldview of Benita Ferrero-Waldner." European University Institute. Working Papers RSCAS 10. Available at: http://cadmus.iue.it/dspace/handle/1814/6752

Pridham, Geoffrey. 2006. "European Union Accession Dynamics and Democratization in Central and Eastern Europe: Past and Future Perspectives." *Government and Opposition* 41 (3): 386.

Quermonne, Jean-Louis. 2005. *Le système politique de l'Union européenne*. Paris: Montchrestien (6th edition).

Rabkin, Jeremy. 2000. "Is EU Policy Eroding the Sovereignty of Non-member States?" *Chicago Journal of International Law* 1 (2): 273–290.

———. 2004. *The Case for Sovereignty. Why the World Should Welcome American Independence.* Washington, DC: AEI Press.

Raik, Kristi. 2006. "Promoting Democracy through Civil Society." Brussels: CEPS Working Document 237 (February).

Rifkin, Jeremy. 2004. *Le Rêve Européen.* Paris: Fayard.

Rodrik, Dani. 1996. "Labor Standards in International Trade." In Robert Z. Lawrence, Dani Rodrik, and John Whalley (eds.). *Emerging Agenda for Global Trade.* Washington, DC: Overseas Development Council.

Rosamond, Ben. 1999. "Globalisation and the Social Construction of European Identities." *Journal of European Public Policy* 6 (4): 652–668.

Rosamond, Ben, and Colin Hay. 2002. "Globalization, European integration and the Discursive Construction of Europe." *Journal of European Public Policy* 9 (2): 147–167.

Rosamond, Ben, and Knud Erik Jörgensen. 2002. "Europe: Regional Laboratory for a Global Polity." In Ougaard Morten and Richard Higgott (eds.). *Towards Global Polity.* London: Routledge.

Rosencrance, Robert. 1986. *The Rise of the Trading State: Commerce and Conquest in the Modern World.* New York: Basic Books.

Rubenfeld, Jed. 2003. "The Two World Orders." *Wilson Quarterly* (Autumn). Available at: http://www.thelatinlibrary.com/imperialism/readings/rubenfeld.html.

Ruggie, John. 2004. "American Exceptionalism, Exemptionalism and Global Governance." In Michael Ignatieff (ed.). *American Exceptionalism and Human Rights.* Princeton: Princeton University Press.

Sands, Philippe. 2005. *Lawless World. America and the Making and Breaking of Global Rules.* London: Penguin.

Sapir, André. 2005. "Globalisation and the Reform of European Social Models." *Background Document for the Presentation at ECOFIN Informal Meeting in Manchester* (September 9). Available at: http://www.bruegel.org/Repositories/Documents/publications/working_papers/SapirPaper080905.pdf.

Sbragia, A.-M., and D. Damro. 1999. "The Changing Role of the European Union in International Environmental Politics; Institution Building and the Politics of Climate Change." *Government and Policy* 17 (1): 53–68.

Schaffer, Gregory. 2000. "The WTO under Challenge: Democracy and the Law and Politics of the WTO's Treatment of Trade and Environment Matters." *The Harvard Environmental Review* 24 (2).

Schimmelfennig, Franck. 2005a. "Democracy in the Post-Communist World: Unfinished Business. What Has Been Learned and How Can It be Applied." Club of Madrid: IV General Assembly at Prague (November). Available at: http://www.clubmadrid.org/cmadrid/fileadmin/Nov05_WG3_Frank_Schimmelfennig.pdf.

———. 2005b. "European Regional Organizations, Political Conditionality, and Democratic Transformation in Eastern Europe." Club of Madrid: IV General

Assembly at Prague (November). Available at: http://www.clubmadrid.org/cmadrid/fileadmin/Nov05_WG3_Frank_Schimmelfennig.pdf.

———. 2005c. "The International Promotion of Political Norms in Eastern Europe: A Qualitative Comparative Analysis." Center for European Studies. Harvard: Central & Eastern Europe Working Papers Series. Working Paper 61. www.ces.fas.harvard.edu/publications/docs/pdfs/Schimmelfennig.pdf.

Schimmelfennig, Franck, Stefan Engert, and Heiko Knobel. 2003. "Costs, Commitment and Compliance: The Impact of EU Democratic Conditionality on Latvia, Slovakia and Turkey." *Journal of Common Market Studies* 41 (June).

Schimmelfennig, Franck, and Sandra Lavenex. 2006. "Relations with the Wider Europe." *Journal of Common Market Studies* 44 (1): 137–154.

Schimmelfennig, Franck, and Ulrich Sedelmeier. 2004. "Governance by Conditionality: EU Rule Transfer to the Candidate Countries of Central and Eastern Europe." *Journal of European Public Policy* 11 (4): 669–687.

Schmitt, Carl. 1992. *La notion de politique. Théorie du partisan*. Paris: Flammarion.

———. 1998. *Le* nomos *de la Terre*. Paris: PUF.

Schneider, Catherine. 2004. "L'Union Européenne et la conditionnalité politique." Forum of Nijni Novgorod (July).

Sloss, David. 2003. "International Agreements and the Political Safeguards of Federalism." *Stanford Law Review* 55 (May).

Smith, Karen. 2006. "Speaking With One Voice? European Union Coordination on Human Rights Issues at the United Nations." *Journal of Common Market Studies* 44 (1): 97–121.

———. 2003. *European Foreign Policy in a Changing World*. Cambridge: Cambridge University Press.

———. 2005. *Still "Civilian Power EU"?* European Foreign Policy Unit. Working Paper 1. Available at: http://www.arena.uio.no/cidel/WorkshopOsloSecurity/Smith.pdf

Solana, Javier. 2003. *A Secure Europe in a Better World*. European Security Strategy. Brussels (December 12). Available at: http://ue.eu.int/pressData/en/reports/76255.pdf

Soule, Edward. 2000. "Assessing the Precautionary Principle." *Public Affairs Quarterly* 14 (4).

Stephan, Paul. 2000. "International Governance and American democracy." *Chicago Journal of International Law* (Autumn).

Stiglitz, Joseph, and Andrew Charlton. "A Development Round of Trade Negotiations?" Available at: http://www2.gsb.columbia.edu/faculty/jstiglitz/download/2004_Charlton_Stiglitz.pdf

Szymanski, Marcela, and Michael Smith. 2005. "Coherence and Conditionality in European Foreign Policy. Negotiating the UE-Mexico Global Agreement." *Journal of Common Market Studies* 43 (1): 171–192.

Tapiola, Kari. 2002. "Core Labor Standards and Globalization" (July). Available at: www.adb.org/SocialProtection/tapiola.pdf

Therborn, Göran. 1997. "Europe in the Twenty-First Century." In Peter Gowan and Perry Anderson (eds.). *The Question of Europe*. London: Verso.

Toffel, Michael W., and James E. Heyman. 2002. "An Atlantic Divide? European and American Attitudes on Genetically Engineering Foods." Haas School of Business, University of California, Working Paper (February).

Tomuschat, Christian. 1997. "International Law as the Constitution of Mankind." *International Law on the Eve of the Twenty-First Century* 47. New York: United Nations.

Triscritti, Fiorella. 2007. "Free Trade and New Economic Powers: The Worldview of Peter Mandelson." EUI Working Paper.

Vachudova, Milada Ana. *The Leverage of International Institutions on Democratizing States: Eastern Europe and the European Union.* EUI Working Papers.

Van den Hoven, Adrian. 2004. "Assuming Leadership in Multilateral Economic Institutions: The EU's 'Development Round' Discourse and Strategy." *West European Politics* 27 (2): 256–283.

———. 2004. "Assuming Leadership in Multilateral Economics Institutions: The EU's Development Round: Discourse and Strategy." *West European Politics* 27 (2): 256–283.

Védrine, Hubert. 2003. *Face à l'Hyper-puissance.* Paris: Fayard.

Verdier, Daniel, and Richard Breen. 2001. "Europeanization and Globalization: Politics against Markets in the European Union." *Comparative Political Studies* 34 (3): 227–262. Available at: http://www.nuff.ox.ac.uk/Sociology/Group/Breen%20papers/comp_pol_studs_01.pdf

Verhofstadt, Guy. "Open Letter: The Paradox of Anti-globalisation." Available at: http://www.tni.org/george-docs/verhofstadt.htm

Vig, Norman J., and Michael G. Faure (eds.). 2004. *Green Giants? Environmental Policies of the United States and the European Union.* Cambridge, MA: MIT Press.

Virmani, Arvind. 2005. *A Tripolar Century: USA,China and India.* New Delhi: India Council for Research on International Economic Relations (March). Available at: www.icriev.org

Vogel, David. 2003. "The Politics of Risk Regulation in Europe and the United States." *Yearbook of European Environmental Law* 3.

Vogel, David, and Diana Lynch. 2001. "The Regulation of GMOs in Europe and the United States: A Case Study of Contemporary European Regulation Politics." NewYork: Council on Foreign Relations. Available at: http://www.cfr.org/publication/8688/regulation_of_gmos_in_europe_and_the_united_states.html

Vogler, J. 1999. "The European Union as an Actor in International Environmental Politics." *Environmental Politics* 8 (3): 24–48.

Von Bogdandy, Armin. 2004. "Globalization and Europe: Law to Square Democracy, Globalization and International Law." *EJIL* 15 (5): 885–906. Available at: http://www.ejil.org/journal/Vol15/No5/2.pdf

Wallace, Helen. 2000. "Europeanisation and Globalisation: Complementary or Contradictory Trends." *New Political Economy* 5 (3): 369–382.

Wallace, William. 2003. "Looking for after the Neighbourhood: Responsibilities for the EU-25." *Policy Papers* 4. Groupement d'études et de recherches "Notre

Europe" (July). Available at: www.notre-europe.eu/uploads/tx_publication/Policypaper4_01.pdf

———. 2005. "Is There a European Approach to War?" European Foreign Policy Unit, Working Paper 2 (March).

Waters, Sarah. 2004. "Mobilizing against Globalization: ATTAC and the French Intellectuals." *West European Politics* 25 (5): 854–874.

Weiler, Joseph. 1995. "Une révolution tranquille. La CJCE et ses interlocuteurs." *Politix* 32: 119–138.

The White House. 2002. *The National Security Strategy of the United States of America*. Available at: http://www.whitehouse.gov/nsc/nss.html

Whitman, Richard.1998. *From Civilian Power to Superpower?: The International Identity of the European Union*. New York: St. Martin's Press.

Wolfers, Arnold. 1962. Discord and Collaboration. Essays on International Politics. Baltimore: Johns Hopkins Press. Available at: www.mtholyoke.edu/acad/intrel/pol116/wolfers.htm

Woolcock, Stephen. 2007. "European Union Policy towards Free Trade Agreements." EUPE. Working Brussels Papers 3.

Woolfson, Charles. 2006. "Working Environment and 'Soft Law' in the Post-Communist New Member States." *Journal of Common Market Studies* 44 (1): 195–215. Available at: http://papers.ssrn.com/sol3/papers.cfm?abstract_id=885428

World Public Opinion. *Views of European Union's Influence*.

Young, Alasdair. 2004. "The Incidental Fortress: The Single Europe Market and World Trade." *Journal of Common Market Studies* 42 (2): 393–414.

Youngs, Richard. 2004a. "Normative Dynamics and Strategic Interests in the EU's External Identity." *Journal of Common Market Studies* 42 (2): 415–435.

———. 2004b. "Europe's Uncertain Pursuit of Middle East Reform." Working Paper 45. Carnegie Endowment for International Peace. Carnegie (June). Available at: http://www.carnegieendowment.org/publications/index.cfm?fa=view&id=1532

Zizek, Slavoy. 2005. *Que veut l'Europe? Réflexions sur une nécessaire réappropriation*. Paris: Climats.

INDEX

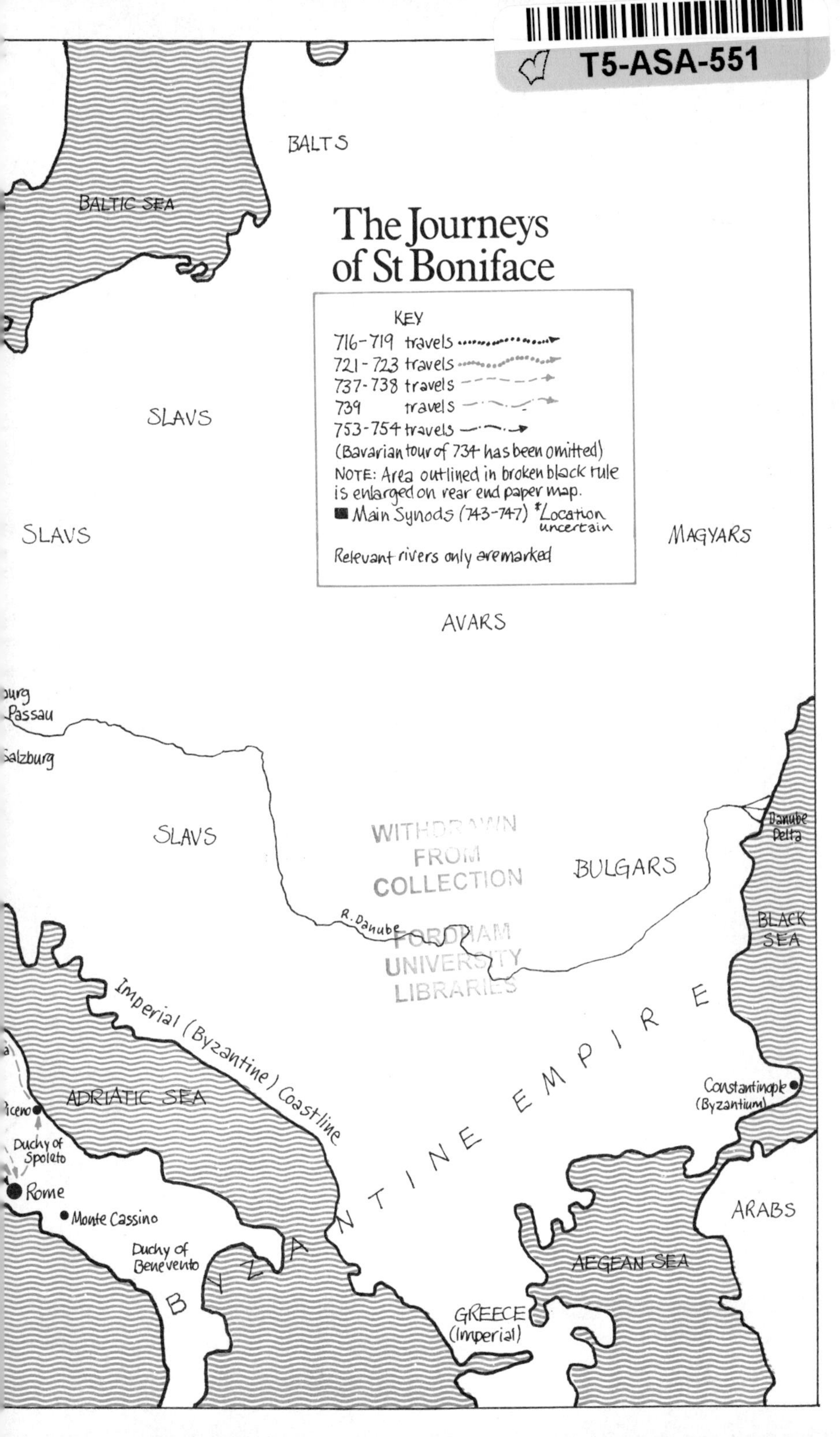
The Journeys of St Boniface
KEY
716–719 travels
721–723 travels
737–738 travels
739 travels
753–754 travels
(Bavarian tour of 734 has been omitted)
NOTE: Area outlined in broken black rule is enlarged on rear end paper map.
Main Synods (743–747) *Location uncertain
Relevant rivers only are marked
BALTS
BALTIC SEA
SLAVS
SLAVS
MAGYARS
AVARS
Passau
Salzburg
SLAVS
Danube Delta
BULGARS
R. Danube
BLACK SEA
Imperial (Byzantine) Coastline
BYZANTINE EMPIRE
ADRIATIC SEA
Constantinople (Byzantium)
Duchy of Spoleto
Rome
Monte Cassino
Duchy of Benevento
ARABS
AEGEAN SEA
GREECE (Imperial)

The Greatest Englishman
Essays on St Boniface and the Church at Crediton

THE GREATEST ENGLISHMAN: ESSAYS ON ST BONIFACE AND THE CHURCH AT CREDITON

edited by

TIMOTHY REUTER

Lecturer in History at the University of Exeter

EXETER

THE PATERNOSTER PRESS

ISBN: 0 85364 277 X

AUSTRALIA
Emu Book Agencies Pty., Ltd.,
63 Berry Street, Granville, N.S.W., 2142

SOUTH AFRICA
Oxford University Press
P.O. Box 1141,
Cape Town

British Library Cataloguing in Publication Data
The greatest Englishman
1. Boniface, *Saint, Abp of Mainz* – Addresses, essays, lectures
I. Reuter, Timothy
270.2'092'4 BX4700.B7
ISBN 0–85364–277–X

Typeset by Input Typesetting Ltd., London and printed and bound in Great Britain by Redwood Burn Limited, Trowbridge and Esher for The Paternoster Press Ltd., Paternoster House, 3 Mount Radford Crescent, Exeter, Devon.

Contents

Preface

The date of the birth of St. Boniface is uncertain. (So, indeed, is its location). Modern scholarship would suggest that 680 AD may be some years too late. But tradition and legend are often more compelling and persitent than the history from which they spring and surely even the most austere scholar would feel that a celebration of Boniface's 1300th anniversary comes better late than never. When it was suggested that the Department of History at the University of Exeter might wish to join in Crediton's diverse programme of commemoration with a series of academic lectures on themes associated with Boniface's life, work and legacy my response was immediately positive. The Department has its own strong record of interest in the history at all periods of the south-west of England and, even more emphatically, of contributions to early medieval studies. Heads of Department have included R. R. Darlington and, happily still active in research and writing, Professors Emeriti David Douglas and Frank Barlow. It was clear at once that by calling on present and past members now living in the Exeter area we could without any difficulty put on a comprehensive and appealing course of lectures.

Discussions with colleagues and the directors of the Paternoster Press who enthusiastically offered to publish the lectures enabled the rapid drafting of the programme of topics and contributions. This book is the outcome. Professor Frank Barlow ('The English Background') was my predecessor as Head of the Department from 1953 to 1976. His many books include *The English Church 1000–1066* and *Edward the Confessor.* He is presently writing on the reign of William Rufus. Professor Christopher Holdsworth ('Saint Boniface the Monk') was formerly Reader in Ecclesiastical History at University College, London; he joined the Department here as Professor of Medieval History in 1977. As a specialist in monastic history he has edited *The Rufford Charters* and is now engaged on a study of St. Bernard. Mr. George Greenaway ('Saint Boniface as a Man of Letters') taught in the Department from 1930 to 1968. His works include *St. Boniface: Three Biographical Studies*, and the second volume (1042–1189) of *English Historical Documents* (with David Douglas). Dr. Nicholas Orme ('The Church in Crediton from Saint Boniface to the Reformation') joined the Department in 1965. Now a Senior Lecturer in History, he is the author of *English Schools in the Middle Ages*, and he is currently investigating aspects of the history of Exeter Cathedral in the later Middle Ages. The Editor of this volume, Dr. Timothy Reuter, who also contributes a lecture on 'Saint Boniface and Europe', has been a lecturer in the Department since 1971. He has recently translated and edited a collection of articles on *The Medieval Nobility*, and is now writing a history of medieval Germany.

The lectures on St. Boniface were delivered under the auspices of the University during the Lent Term 1980. Publication has been arranged to coincide with the completion of the series. I must express the thanks of the Department of History to the University for including St. Boniface in its heavy programme of public lectures, to the Paternoster Press for producing the volume in such an attractive format and to Dr. Timothy Reuter for taking on its editorship. Above all I am grateful to colleagues, past and present, for being ready, willing and able to contribute to what I am sure will be a lasting as well as a more or less timely reminder of the achievement and aspirations of one of the South-West's greatest sons.

Ivan Roots

Department of History
The University of Exeter

List of Abbreviations

EHD	*English Historical Documents, 500–1042*, ed. D. Whitelock (London, 1955)
Ep., epp.	*S. Bonifatii et Lulli epistolae*, ed. M. Tangl (*MGH Epistolae selectae*, I, Berlin, 1916), cited by number
Levison	W. Levison, *England and the Continent in the Eighth Century* (Oxford, 1946)
MGH	*Monumenta Germaniae Historica*
AA	*Auctores antiquissimi*
Cap.	*Capitularia regum Francorum*
Epp.	*Epistolae*
SRG	*Scriptores rerum Germanicarum*
SRM	*Scriptores rerum Merovingicarum*
Talbot	C. H. Talbot, *The Anglo-Saxon Missionaries in Germany* (London, 1954)
Vita	*Vita Bonifatii auctore Willibaldo*, in *Vitae Sancti Bonifatii*, ed. W. Levison (*MGH SRG*, Hannover, 1905), 1–58.

THE ENGLISH BACKGROUND

Frank Barlow

CHAPTER 1

The English Background

St Boniface, 'the apostle of Germany', was born in Wessex about 675,[1] and died, with fifty-two others, a martyr to the Christian faith at Dokkum, in what is now Holland, in 754 or 755. When the heathen burst into his tent he shielded his head with the book of the Gospels he was reading, the book he had taken as his lifelong guide.

Boniface was one of the heroes of an heroic age. It was an age of heroes not only because heroism was the ideal of the noble classes, but also because the depicters of the scene shared that belief and painted it in those colours. At the base of society were the *laboratores*, the workers, the farmers and their labourers, whose lives were far from heroic according to the ideas of the time; and the mass of the clergy, whether living in communities in secular minsters or in monasteries, had little opportunity for heroism. But it was acknowledged by all thinking men that there were in this visible world two kinds of armies: the armies of the temporal princes and the army of Christ; and the ideal put before all soldiers was the heroic. It was also, therefore, an age of saints.

The times in which Boniface lived are among the best known of the Anglo-Saxon period because he was almost an exact contemporary of the Venerable Bede, who was born in Northumbria about 673 and died in his monastery at Jarrow in 735. Bede's *Ecclesiastical History of the English People*, which he completed in 731, is a relatively long work in five books, and illuminates the English scene in an unprecedented, and for many centuries unique way. The Northumbrian monk was not, of course, primarily concerned with Wessex; and although he obtained some information about its history from Daniel bishop of Winchester (705–44), and Boniface and others of his circle kept in touch with friends in Wessex and Mercia after he had gone abroad in 718, it is not altogether surprising that Bede did not mention Boniface in his *History*.[2] That is one reason why this west-country missionary finds no place in the *Anglo-Saxon Chronicle* which King Alfred founded towards the end of the ninth century, and in which earlier material for the history of Wessex was incorporated. Indeed, Boniface was unknown to English historians until the mid-twelfth century, when William, monk of Malmesbury, who had a keen nose for Englishmen abroad, brought him briefly into his story.[3]

Boniface lived the early part of his life on the frontier between an English and a British kingdom; and we also know something of British society at this time. The famous book *On the Ruin of Britain* was written by the Welsh cleric, Gildas, over a century before Boniface's birth. But a contemporary of Boniface, St Adamnan, abbot of Iona, a reconciler whom Bede admired, wrote a Life of the Irish missionary, St Columba, the founder of the community at Iona who died in 597, the year in which St Augustine arrived in England from Rome and began to convert the heathen in Kent.

There is much social history in Bede and Adamnan, and even more illuminating, because fiction, is the poem *Beowulf.* This poem, the longest (3,182 lines) and in many ways the most important Old English poem to have survived, was composed probably in the eighth century. It is concerned with the heroic exploits of princely warriors. And, as it must have been written down, and possibly composed, in a monastery, and transmitted through monastic libraries, it shows how Germanic pagan ideals had been largely accepted and assimilated by the church. Beowulf, nephew of Hygelac, king of the Geats, a tribe which lived in southern Sweden, went in search of adventure and fortune to the court of Hrothgar, king of the Danes. There he slew the monster Grendel, and later, while killing another dragon, met his own death. In the words of the poem, 'To any warrior death is better than a life of dishonour . . . The hero's last day had come. The king of the Geats had perished nobly . . . Music of the harp will not awake the heroes. But the black raven flapping over the dead shall speak much and tell the eagle of its luck at dinner, when along with the wolf it plundered the slain.'[4] In a similar way, the religious heroes, the missionaries, men like Columba, Augustine, and Boniface, went out to slay dragons, although of a different kind: they went to overturn the heathen idols in the temples and destroy the pagan gods. They too went with followers, a hearth-troop, who did not always match the heroism of their leader. Indeed, heroic literature tells us much of the cowardice, if only momentary, of lesser mortals. It is not only a touch of realism, but also a heightening contrast.

Britain in the seventh and eighth centuries was a land fit for heroes to live in. In the fifth century Roman Britain, no longer with an effective central government and breaking up again into native principalities, was overrun in the east and south by German marauders and settlers drawn from rebel mercenaries and garrisons and tribesmen from the whole Continental seaboard from Frisia to Jutland.[5] By the end of the seventh century the newcomers controlled most of Britain south of the Firth of Forth except for a few internal pockets and the western extremities. The conquerors had been as disorganized as the conquered: there had been no one great Germanic leader, as had often happened on the Continent; and the result was a congeries of petty kingdoms created by nobles or military adventurers partly out of conquests from the natives, partly by imposing their rule over scattered Germanic settlements. By the end of the sixth century the most powerful king of the time often was the overlord of the others; but a unified England was not to come before the tenth and eleventh centuries. The mass of the settlers in the fifth century are believed to have been largely of Saxon origin and to have come from the area between the River Ems and the Baltic (what is now the North German plain). But most of the new kings and perhaps much of the nobility seem to have been of Anglian origin, with roots in Angeln (known to us as Schleswig–Holstein), to the north of the Saxon homelands. All but one of the new royal dynasties traced back to Woden, the god of war, who may have been an Anglian hero. As a result the Germans in Britain, although called 'Saxons' by most outsiders (including the Scots and archaeologists), preferred on the whole to call themselves and their language 'English'. Bede, we notice, although he knew of Angles, Saxons, and Jutes among the settlers, nevertheless wrote the ecclesiastical history of the *English* nation.

Among the kingdoms created in the sixth century was Wessex. The founder of the royal dynasty, a man with the British name Cerdic (which is equivalent to the Welsh Ceredig), but who claimed to be descended from Woden, is said to have landed on the Hampshire coast, possibly in 514.[6] He and his descendants pushed inland through Jutish settlements and established their rule over Angles and Saxons who had reached the Upper Thames and the Chilterns by various routes from the East coast. Cerdic's great-grandson, Ceawlin (another with a British name), who ruled from 560 to 592, both completed the amalgamation of the settlements in Hampshire, Wiltshire, Berkshire, and Oxfordshire, and also expanded westwards against the Britons. But between the death of Ceawlin and the emergence of Caedwalla (again a British name) in 685, shortly after Boniface's birth, Wessex was without a famous leader and a memorable history. Nevertheless, it remained one of the great pioneering kingdoms, for it had inviting British territory to the west. (It may help us to understand the position if we have in mind the 'moving frontier' in North America and the penetration and settlement of Indian lands, provided we remember that the Romano-British were at least as 'advanced' as the English.)

The names of the several English kingdoms were, of course, made in Britain, and were probably invented by those who found it necessary to distinguish them. Bede may have played a part with his *History*. Originally some of the new nations called themselves after an eponymous ancestor of the royal family. For example, the East Anglian royal dynasty was known as the *Wuffingas*, after the sixth-century founder-hero, Wuffa. In the case of Wessex, Bede says that its original name was the kingdom of the *Gewissae*. And in the royal genealogy which was recorded (and perhaps partly fabricated) in the ninth century Gewis appears as sixth in descent from Woden and the great-grandfather of Cerdic. But few historians believe that Gewis ever existed, and prefer to think that *Gewissae* is a folk-name, not a patronymic.[7] It is possible that this nation did not choose to call themselves after their founder, Cerdic, because of his partly British origins, which show up clearly in the personal names of him and his descendants. However that may be, Bede also referred to this people as the West Saxons, which in process of time displaced the other title. It was named in relation to the East Saxons with their kingdom of Essex and the South Saxons in Sussex. If the kingdom centred on the upper Trent was ever the land of the West Angles or North Saxons, those names are not recorded: instead, it was the frontier kingdom, the kingdom of the marches, Mercia.

Royal genealogies have been preserved for most of the English kingdoms, and it is known that these falsify the descent of the kingdoms by giving a false impression of linear transmission.[8] Under Germanic law all members of a family had a claim on the family estates. It seems that in Wessex, until at least the time of Alfred at the end of the ninth century, the principality was divided into provinces ruled by different branches of the royal family, and that civil war and attempts by the ambitious to dominate, or even destroy, the rest, were not uncommon. Similar conditions existed in other English kingdoms and also in the British areas. With such internal disunity, the external boundaries of the kingdoms were most unstable. Wessex lost its northern territory to Mercia and became confined to south of the Thames and the Somerset

Avon. In the seventh century the most powerful kings in England were the Northumbrian; the eighth century was the age of Mercia. Three great midland kings, Wulfhere (657–74), Æthelbald (716–57), and Offa (757–96), overshadowed their neighbours, absorbed some of the lesser kingdoms, and were sometimes the overlords of Wessex.

In 672, about the time of Bonface's birth, King Cenwealh of Wessex died. According to the *Anglo-Saxon Chronicle* he was succeeded for a year by his widow, Queen Seaxburgh, then by three short-lived kings in turn, one of whom, Centwine, we shall meet again. But this is official history. According to Bede, after Cenwealh's death sub-kings divided up the kingdom between them and ruled for about ten years until Caedwalla got rid of them and ruled for two years.[9] This glimpse of a widowed queen trying to hang on to her dead husband's power, possibly in the interest of her own sons against the claims of elder step-children, and of the partition and then civil war between competing members of the royal family carries us into the even more familiar world of the sixth and seventh-century Merovingian kings in Gaul, as described by Gregory of Tours and Fredegar.[10] Out of this struggle for existence between princely seedlings and saplings emerged occasionally a great tree which destroyed all its competitors. Caedwalla in the space of two or three years rooted out all his rivals in Wessex and also conquered the Isle of Wight (which was still heathen), Sussex, Surrey, and Kent, all independent kingdoms. But in 688 he resigned, went to Rome, was baptized by Pope Sergius, and given the name of Peter. Seven days later he died, still clad in his baptismal robes, and was buried in St Peter's basilica. Crispus, archbishop of Milan, composed the long epitaph for his tomb.[11] Caedwalla's was a brief, meteoric, and doubly heroic reign. He was succeeded by Ine (688–726), from a collateral line, the son of an under-king, probably of Dorset. Ine re-established Caedwalla's empire for a time and reorganized the settlements in the West in which Boniface was born. He also issued a collection of West-Saxon laws, a revision necessitated by the changes in the nature as well as in the extent of the kingdom.

The conquests of Caedwalla and Ine in the south-east of England were not without considerable influence on the later history of Wessex; but for the seventh and eighth centuries the colonization in the west was of greater importance. The shift in the kingdom's centre of gravity is shown by the creation of new ecclesiastical dioceses. Its first bishop, Birinus, established his see in 634 at Dorchester on Thames, near Oxford. This came under Mercian influence, and by 670 the see-town of the *Gewissae* was Winchester.[12] In 705 the diocese of Sherborne was created by Ine for the new lands in the west; and in 909 King Edward the Elder established the dioceses of Wells and Crediton.

In the west the kingdom of the *Gewissae* pushed against the British kingdom of Dumnonia. Aldhelm, polymath and one of the most influential authors of this age, who died as bishop of Sherborne in 709, was in correspondence with King Geraint, whom he addressed as 'the most glorious lord, wielder of the sceptre of the western kingdom';[13] and the two kingdoms can be regarded as roughly equal in size and similar in social system and political organization. Both were branches of the great Indo-European family, both Christian, and the British had fallen, and the English had risen, to a similar economic and cultural level. Bede's contempt of most of the British because of the Easter controversy can be misleading. But there can be no doubt that the English were the rising, and the Britons the falling power. Even though the *Anglo-Saxon Chronicle* lists only English victories and never defeats, the last great defeat of the English in the west recorded in the British Annals was at *Mons Badonicus*, possibly Badbury Rings on the Stour in Dorset, about 500; and the frontier moved, if not steadily, at least inexorably west.

Its movement, however, cannot be charted with any precision. The *Anglo-Saxon Chronicle* records battles, presumably English victories, in 614, 658, 661, and 682. The location of all these is controversial.[14] The temptation is to make them mark the progressive stages of the English expansion to the west. But as such battles were probably fought as a result of an invasion by either side, and hence far to either the west or the east of the frontier, a linear progression westwards may be completely wrong. When Cenwealh gave battle at *Peonnan* in 658 and drove the Britons in flight as far as the River Parret, it is possible, as Professor W. G. Hoskins has argued, that the battle was fought at Pinhoe, just outside Exeter; but, if so, the result was to drive the enemy some forty miles north-eastwards across English settlements, and in completely the wrong direction. In 682, shortly after Boniface's birth, King Centwine 'put the Britons to flight as far as the sea', a description so vague that only those who are convinced that the battle site is to the west of those they have already located, would venture to explain it.

More persuasive for the stages of the westward expansion is the ecclesiastical evidence, which Hoskins also used. In 672

Cenwealh gave lands near Taunton to an English abbot of Glastonbury. By that time west Somerset must have been under English rule; and King Ine built towns at Somerton, Petherton, Taunton, and Wellington, all in south Somerset, to consolidate and protect the English settlements. The early charters of Exeter abbey have been lost; but on the evidence of Boniface's early life there was a Benedictine abbey [14a] at Exeter by the period 677–685, just about the time when Centwine drove the Britons in flight to the sea. Hoskins would put the boundary between the two kingdoms at this juncture on the upper reaches of the River Taw which rises on Dartmoor.

The English advance westwards into what the West Saxon laws call the lands of the Welsh (so we will now abandon the name 'British') took two forms: the relatively peaceful colonization by farmers and herdsmen, and the military conquests by kings and their lieutenants. Each produced its typical social unit. The independent colonists, usually simple freemen, set up enclosed homesteads and farmed their separate fields with the help of a few labourers and slaves, thus forming areas of hamlets. But where the king took a large demesne for himself he usually shared it with the church and his noble followers (*gesiths*), and hence created a number of large estates, each organized to support a military or ecclesiastical aristocrat and his household and followers.

We can get some idea of the social scene from the laws which King Ine of Wessex issued when Boniface was a boy. Both English and Welsh society was divided into similar social classes, basically noble, free, and slave. These divisions were definite and of the utmost importance. They affected many aspects of a man's life – primarily the amount of money which had to be paid to his kinsmen if he were slain (his *wergild*), but also his status under the law. The highest nobility had a *wergild* of 1200 shillings, the lesser nobility 600, and ordinary freemen 200. The nobles were called *gesiths*, which means 'companions', and they owed their nobility to their proximity to the king. The ordinary freeman was a *ceorl*, a churl.

The ranks were hereditary, but not immutable. Changes of status could occur because of capture in war or through legal penalties. Bede tells the story of Imma, one of King Ælfwine's *gesiths*, who, badly wounded and unconscious, survived the death of his lord in a battle on the Trent against the Mercians in 679. At first, either through shame at his survival or to save his life, he pretended that he was a peasant who had only brought provisions to the army; but, while he recovered from his wounds, his nobility was suspected, and in the end, when promised his life, he confessed that he was indeed a royal servant. Whereupon his noble captor sold him as a slave to a Frisian trader in London. Finally he was ransomed by the king of Kent and returned to Northumbria.[15] There were also the hazards of the law. According to a law of Ine, 'If a slave works on Sunday at his master's command he is to be free . . . If a freeman works on that day without his lord's command, he is to forfeit his freedom.'[16] Accordingly, in a dangerous, pioneering age, and with a legal system which freely altered status as a punishment or reward, there was probably a good deal of social mobility.

The Welsh were given their appropriate place. It is clear that in western Wessex a good number of natives remained on the land, and the creation of large estates probably disturbed the existing inhabitants even less than the colonization by smaller men. They were not recognized as complete social and legal equals of the conquerors; but their position was defined and brought into the system. For instance, a Welshman with an estate of 5 hides was allowed a *wergild* of 600 shillings, that of an English second-class nobleman; and a Welsh rent-payer, presumably an independent farmer, a *wergild* of 120 shillings, which made him a sort of second-class freeman.[17] But royal service could improve the position even of the Welsh. According to another law, 'The king's Welsh horseman who can carry his messages shall have a *wergild* of 200 shillings.' – that is to say he was brought up to the status of an ordinary English farmer.[18]

The laws also regulate some aspects of the land tenure of the nobles, the *gesiths*, into whose ranks it is possible that Boniface was born. Estates rated at 20, 10, and 3 hides are mentioned.[19] As a hide was regarded as the amount of land needed to maintain one free household, these estates were not of the greatest size or value. And they were burdened with what look like quite heavy rents paid to the king. The food rent (*feorm*) for an estate of 10 hides was 10 vats of honey, 300 loaves, 12 ambers of Welsh ale, 30 of clear ale, 2 full-grown cows or 10 wethers (castrated rams), 10 geese, 20 hens, 10 cheeses, an amber of butter, 5 salmon, 20 units of fodder, and 100 eels.[20] The *gesith* who abandoned his estate had to leave it fully cultivated, and could take with him only his reeve (farm manager), smith (chief craftsman), and his children's nurse.[21] Presumably his stock and seed as well as his land had been provided by the king.

The main subject of Anglo-Saxon laws was, however, violence and theft, and how they were to be atoned for, with regard to the status of the parties. Boniface was born not only into a violent age but also in a particularly lawless area, the frontier. According to the laws of Ine, "We call up to seven men 'thieves', from 7 to 35 'a band'; above that it is 'an army'." [22] Another clause reads, 'If a man from a distance or a foreigner [i.e. a Welshman] goes through the wood off the track, and does not shout or blow a horn, he is assumed to be a thief, and can be either killed or ransomed.' [23] Again, 'The horn of an ox is valued at 10d., that of a cow 2d., the tail of an ox 1s., that of a cow 5d., the eye of an ox 5d., that of a cow 1s.' [24] – strange arithmetic, but reminding us that we are in rustler country, and that 'Taffy is a Welshman, Taffy is a thief'.

We cannot place Boniface exactly in this scene. According to his first biographer, the Englishman Willibald, his parents owned estates and his father was the lord of a village who entertained visiting preachers.[25] If this means that there was no permanent church on the estate, it would seem that the settlement was either recent or of modest size. All the same, the later tradition, found in the Fulda martyrology of *c.* 900 and the 'third Life', that Boniface was of noble birth,[26] is probably correct. Boniface was baptized Wynfrith, a typical two-syllable Old English name, *wyn* meaning pleasure or joy, *frith* peace. One element was probably taken from his father's name, the other from his mother's. There was a Wynfrith bishop of Mercia about 672, and the name is similar in formation to Wilfrid, carried by a bishop of York of undoubted aristocratic origins. Hence, although it is unlikely that Boniface sprang from the highest nobility, he certainly came from a landed and prosperous family; and on balance it would seem that he was born into the 600 shillings rather than the 200 shillings class.

Although the Anglo-Saxons are sometimes regarded as a pessimistic, even gloomy, race. moralists thought that the joys of this world were far too highly prized. Pessimism, indeed, is as likely to encourage hedonism as gloom. The perils of illness, captivity, death, and the many other misfortunes which could afflict even the noble, were seen only as shadows on the good life, the rumours of the tempests which raged outside the warmth and security of the lord's hall in which brave men sheltered for a little while.[28] The hero who went boldly through the hazards which beset him acquired much happiness and glory on the way; and he might find everlasting fame. The acceptance of Christianity in the seventh century at first produced more an alternative way of life than a consistent change of heart. Most of the Christian virtues were so contrary to the aristocratic *mores* that they could be accepted only through dramatic and total conversions. To give up wearing a sword and riding a fine horse, to abandon pride in the various treasures and pomps of the world, to become humble and accept injuries and insults without retaliation, meant a change of life in the manner of St Paul. It was not unknown for even baptism to be postponed until the time came for total conversion as we have seen in the case of King Caedwalla. We know from the way in which English kings of this period abdicated and went on pilgrimage to Rome that the nobility could become obsessed by the terrors of hell and convinced of the need to take the final cure of total abasement as a penance for their sins. There was high drama in religion as well as in the world of secular heroes.

A good number of men and women who observed the literal rules of religion under monastic discipline were, however, sacrifices offered by their parents, and primarily for the salvation of their parents' souls. Boniface is said by his biographer to have had during infancy a strong personal inclination towards the monastic life and from the age of four or five to have discussed religion with the itinerant preachers who visited their house.[29] Be that as it may, the effective cause of Wynfrith's oblation to the Benedictine abbey at Exeter was his father's serious illness, an affliction from which he subsequently, perhaps consequently, recovered. The sacrifice had been effective, and, according to the biographer, it had been a real and painful sacrifice. Wynfrith was the favourite son, and his father had wished to make him his heir to his estates and possessions. But before the age of seven he was arbitrarily transferred to an alternative father, Abbot Wulfhard,[30] and set to follow another road, *via regia*, the royal road, according to monastic writers.

The church was becoming an alternative career for the children of the aristocracy and the free classes. The landed nobility were building churches on their estates to provide for worship by themselves and their dependants; and sometimes in this period, as Bede informs us, they even turned their homestead into a monastery, with the head of the family becoming the abbot, in order to avoid royal taxes.[31] Monasteries were, in both the English and the Welsh lands, private and hereditary property; and it was a matter for family decision which of its members should enter these institutions and who should rule them. Boniface's parents, however, do not seem to have owned a church, let alone a monastery; and they presumably chose the nearest convent for their son. Several factors were involved in the giving of children to be brought up as monks. Noble families were usually quite large. Boniface had several brothers (and although sisters are not mentioned they could have existed.) Multiple marriages and polygamy and the use of wet-nurses resulted in many births. Despite the opportunities in an expanding, pioneering world, too many children could be an embarrassment. All had some claim on the patrimony, and provision for the marriages of both sons and daughters could dissipate a family's wealth. These debits had to be put against the credits of a possibly valuable marriage and the construction of a network of useful relationships – the creation of a macro-family. Moreover, in that dangerous world some sons had to be kept in reserve against the inevitable losses. All the same, some artificial method of population control had to be practised, and one of these was enforced celibacy, especially by making some of the children monks, nuns, or priests.

Children with a physical defect, boys unfit for a military career and girls unlikely to marry, were obvious candidates for the religious life. But there were also the real sacrifices, the oblation of a favourite son, like Wynfrith. These were almost predestined to leadership in the church. It is a stereotype of saints' lives that the hero was not only of noble birth, but also handsome and of fine physique. And, indeed, to endure the rigours of the ascetic life were required an iron constitution and a serene purpose.

During the missionary period in England monasteries were founded to serve as centres for the propagation of the faith and as schools for training a clergy. They were the powerhouses of the new religion. And because missionaries came to England from almost every great centre of Christian learning, the converts were offered a diet of extraordinary richness and variety. From Ireland came the saints who had preserved the archaic Roman-British-Gaulish traditions. Some of their evangelical fervour became a characteristic thread in the Anglo-Saxon church. Frankish influence was inevitable, and, in the case of the double monastery – associated male and female communities ruled by an abbess – important.[32] From Rome itself came St Augustine and his followers to introduce the authentic ritual and the great body of patristic and classical learning. Christian music was taken up by the English with enthusiasm: Bede often mentions it, and he records that in 679 Benedict Biscop brought back from Rome no less a person than John, precentor of St Peter's, to instruct the cantors of Jarrow and Wearmouth in the practices of chanting observed in that basilica.[33] Even more unlikely was Pope Vitalian's dispatch to England in 668 of Theodore of Tarsus to be archbishop of Canterbury. Theodore, a Greek monk in exile at Rome because of Arab conquests, was accompanied by an African abbot named Hadrian and their helpers. Theodore, who created a united English church, not only introduced a powerful Greek stream into English Christian culture but also, because of his partial detachment from the Roman-British controversies, was tolerant of some insular customs, both English and Celtic, and sympathetic to their social problems. The famous and influential Penitential ascribed to him often records Greek as well as Roman practices, and tempers the wind to the shorn lambs.[34] The archbishop was, for example, remarkably sympathetic to the plight of those deprived of their spouse through no fault of their own (e.g. through captivity) and allowed divorce and remarriage in a way which was quite unacceptable to the medieval church.

For a time a few scholars in England could learn to read and write Greek and Latin, and were thereby given the keys to two great civilizations. These were, of course, too vast and too advanced to be exploited to the full. Bede's lifelong work of making Christian scholarship available to his brother monks, although a great achievement, was only a start – and, as it turned out, was not to be built upon. The immediate results of these cultural stimuli were, however, quite dazzling. In Wessex the new learning can be exemplified by Aldhelm, a relation of King Ine, who became abbot of Malmesbury about 675 and first bishop of Sherborne in 705. He received his earliest education at Malmesbury, which was an Irish foundation, and later visited Canterbury to imbibe from Theodore and Hadrian Roman and Greek learning. A copious writer in both prose and verse, he has earned the dubious reputation of being the founder of a Latin style of prodigious obscurity in both vocabulary and syntax and the popularizer of riddles and cyphers. With Bede the new culture had a rather plain and utilitarian stamp. Aldhelm made it a mystery cult, hermetic, bizarre, confined to the elite, *obscurum per obscurius*, a don's delight.[35]

Boniface, when he reached manhood, found the educational resources of Exeter inadequate for his purpose and migrated to the Benedictine abbey at Nursling, near Southampton, in the West-Saxon heartlands. There he acquired further education of the new type as influenced by Aldhelm; and it is interesting to note that in addition to the sound learning he imparted to the Germans, he also taught such sidelines as the art of secret writing or cryptography.[36]

Within the same Christian framework, but at the other end of the cultural scale, Caedmon, the illiterate Yorkshire cowherd with a British name, received in old age the gift of making songs in English to be recited to the harp. He was taken up by the Abbess Hild of Whitby and instructed in sacred history so that he could turn it into verse. Bede considered him an incomparable poet and wrote lovingly of him.[37]

Religion can be the opium of the people; but in some circumstances it can be an energizer, a tonic. The Roman and Greek missionaries to England taught their converts many basic intellectual skills, such as reading and writing, arithmetic, astronomy, and how to compose legal documents. They also reintroduced building in stone and all the arts of furnishing. English missionaries passed some of these on – and all the other skills of their newly-acquired superiority. That typical Yorkshireman, Bishop Wilfrid, after converting the South Saxons taught them how to cast nets to catch fish in the sea.[38] Such men, even if their heads were in heaven, had their feet firmly on the ground.

The richness of culture in seventh and eighth-century England was caused initially by movements directed from without. But there started almost immediately a reciprocal movement of Englishmen themselves going abroad in search of education. Benedict Biscop travelled five times to Gaul and Rome. Bede tells of many who went to Ireland as a preparation for missionary work in their ancient homelands on the Continent: Egbert who was frustrated, Wihbert and Willibrord who went to Frisia, the two priests named Hewald who were martyred in Old Saxony, and Swithbert who became bishop of the tribe of the *Bructeri*.[39] Boniface, we may note, joined Willibrord, by then archbishop of Utrecht, in 719. Bede also described the missionary work of his compatriot Wilfrid. The monk of Jarrow was making a point. The Britons had never preached the gospel to the English who came to live among them. The English, on the other hand, as soon as they received the good tidings, were anxious to share the gift with others. The point, however, cannot be pressed too hard: English missionary work was mainly confined to heathens of their own race.

It is no belittlement of Boniface to say that he was very much a man of his own time. They were, after all, glorious times. Bede thought that the age of Theodore and Hadrian, in which Boniface spent his youth, was a golden age. 'Never', he wrote, 'had there been such happy times since the English first came to Britain: with brave Christian kings, they were a terror to all the barbarian nations; the hopes of all men were set on the joys of the heavenly kingdom of which they had only recently heard; and all who wished to be instructed in the Holy Writ had teachers ready to hand.'[40] Bede died before the full importance of the contribution of English missionaries to the spread of Christianity in northern Europe and to the renaissance of Christian culture in Gaul was apparent. In 735, although Boniface had become archbishop of all Germany east of the Rhine, he had still to organize a church in that province; and in the last twenty years of his life he was to accomplish much. It was in the very year of Bede's death that Alcuin, who in many ways built on the work of Boniface and other English pioneers in the Frankish empire, was born at York.

Bede in his last years was conscious of deterioration in England.[41] He was probably right. And it may be that the country was harmed by the export of some of its best talent. But England's loss was Europe's gain. The debt has been repaid by the fruitful interest always shown by German scholars in English language and history. And if Boniface is today still better known on the Continent than in his native land, he has not been neglected in Wessex since the commemorative activities of 1954–5. In 1960 the new nuclear power station at Nursling was called Winfrith, a name which, although at first sight surprising, is not completely inapt.

Appendix: The Date of Boniface's Birth

The date of Boniface's death is known; and as he was certainly an old man in 754, it is likely that he was born before 685. Various attempts have been made at greater precision. One of the more elaborate investigations is Franz Flaskamp, 'Das Geburtsjahr des Wynfrith-Bonifatius', in *Zeitschrift für Kirchengeschichte* 45 (1926), 339–344. He argued that Boniface was born in 672–3 because after he became a priest at the age of 30 he probably attended a council held at Brentford in October 705, and that he reached the age of 50 in 722, when he first refused and then accepted episcopal orders.

The weakness in the latter argument is that although Boniface's biographer Willibald (*Vita*, cc. 5–6, pp. 24, 28–30), states that he refused to become a bishop (c. 722) because he was not yet 50, there is little evidence that 50 was generally regarded in the west as the minimum age for becoming a bishop, and no reason why the pope should not have overcome any scruples Boniface may have had.

The first argument seems completely fanciful. According to the *Vita*, c. 4, pp. 13–15, after Boniface had become a priest at the age of 30 (c. 3, p. 12), a synodal council was held by the church of Wessex on the advice of King Ine because of a novel dissension (*nova seditio*) which had arisen. After the meeting, which from the description was a national assembly, it was decided to send legates to Archbishop Beorhtweald of Canterbury lest the prelates be blamed for their presumption in taking action in this matter without his counsel. On the proposal of three abbots, including Boniface's own superior, he was selected for the task, went to Canterbury and returned with a favourable answer. After that the monk's reputation was so high that he was usually present at synods. We may think that these were those of his own West Saxon church; and to make on this evidence alone Boniface attend a peace conference which it was proposed to hold at Brentford in Middlesex in October (?705) to settle various, apparently secular, disputes between the king of Wessex and the rulers of Essex, seems hazardous in the extreme. There is not even any evidence that the meeting actually took place: we know of the proposal only from a letter from the Bishop of London to the archbishop asking his advice on whether he should attend.[42] It will be seen that the only scrap of fairly reliable information in all this supposition is that Boniface when at least thirty years old conveyed the decision of a West Saxon synod to Canterbury. But we have no knowledge of the nature of the business transacted and no way of dating the council usefully. If it was concerned with the proposal to create the see of Sherborne, which came to fruition in 705, we should, of course, have something to go on. But this suggestion is as rash as the other.

In 1946 Wilhelm Levison, who knew more about Boniface and his times than anyone before or since, preferred the date 'about 675' for the saint's birth.[43] I have followed him.

NOTES

1. For the date see Appendix, below, p. 26.
2. His martyrdom is entered under 754 in the continuation in the Moore MS: Bede, *Historia Ecclesiastica*, edd. B. Colgrave and R. A. B. Mynors (Oxford, 1969), 574–5.
3. *Gesta Regum*, ed. W. Stubbs (Rolls Series, London, 1887), i, 79–83; *Gesta Pontificum*, ed. N. E. S. A. Hamilton (Rolls Series, London, 1870), 11–12.
4. Lines 2890–1, 3023–7.
5. The latest survey of the evidence is in P. H. Sawyer, *From Roman Britain to Norman England* (London, 1978), Chapter I: 'The seventh century and before'.
6. K. Harrison, 'Early Wessex annals in the Anglo-Saxon Chronicle', *English Historical Review* 86 (1971), 527.
7. H. E. Walker, 'Bede and the Gewissae: The political evolution of the Heptarchy and its nomenclature', *Cambridge Historical Journal* 12 (1956), 185.

8. Cf. D. N. Dumville, 'Kingship, genealogies, and regnal lists', in *Early Medieval Kingship*, edd. P. H. Saywer and I. N. Wood (Leeds, 1977), 72–104.
9. *Anglo-Saxon Chronicle*, edd. D. Whitelock and others (London, 1961), 22–3; Bede (as note 2) iv. 12, pp. 368–9.
10. Cf. Joan Nicholson, '*Feminae gloriosae*: women in the age of Bede' and Janet L. Nelson, 'Queens as Jezebels: the careers of Brunhild and Balthild in Merovingian history', in *Medieval Women* (Rosalind Hill *Festschrift*) ed, D. Baker (Oxford, 1978).
11. Bede 'as note 2) v.7, pp. 468–473.
12. Bede iv. 15, pp. 380–1.
13. Aldhelm, *Opera*, ed. R. Ehwald (*MGH AA*, 15), 480 no. 4.
14. Cf. W. G. Hoskins, *The Westward Expansion of Wessex* (Department of English Local History, Occasional Papers, no. 13, University of Leicester, 1960).
14a. It is unlikely that the monastery followed the Rule of St Benedict exclusively; but it was probably closer to that pattern than to the Celtic. It had an abbot with an English name, and if it had been recently set up by the 'ascendancy' it may well have been aggressively English in tone. See, further, Christopher Holdsworth, below, p. 54
15. Bede (as note 2) iv. 22, pp. 400ff.
16. c. 3: *EHD*, 364.
17. cc. 24,2; 23,3; 32: *EHD*, 367.
18. c. 33: *EHD*, 368.
19. cc. 64–6: *EHD*, 371.
20. c. 70,1: *EHD*, 371.
21. cc. 63–3: *EHD*, 371.
22. c. 13,1: *EHD*, 366.
23. c. 20: *EHD*, 366.
24. cc. 58–9: *EHD*, 370.
25. *Vita*, c. 1, pp. 5–6. For travelling preachers see Bede (as note 2) iv. 27, pp. 432–3, on St Cuthbert.
26. For *gesiths* building churches see Bede v. 4–5, pp. 462ff. But this argument cannot be pressed hard. Bede also, in his letter to Archbishop Egbert written in 734, makes it quite clear that in Northumbria at that time there were few resident village priests. Itinerant preachers were the rule, at least in remote areas: *EHD*, 737.
27. *Vitae S. Bonifatii*, ed. W. Levison (*MGH SRG*, Hannover 1905), 59, 79.
28. Cf. Bede (as note 2) ii.13, pp. 183–5.
29. *Vita*, c. 1, pp. 4–5.
30. *Vita*, c. 1, pp. 6–7. Bede was given at the age of seven: v. 24, pp. 566–7. According to Isidore, *Etymologiae*, XI.ii.2, it was the age at which infancy ended.
31. Bede's letter to Egbert (734): *EHD*, 740–2.
32. Levison, 22–3.
33. Bede (as note 2) iv. 18, pp. 388–9; cf. iv.2, pp. 334–5.
34. Printed in A. W. Haddan and W. Stubbs, *Councils and ecclesiastical documents relating to Great Britain and Ireland* (London, 1871), iii, 173ff.
35. Michael Lapidge, 'The hermeneutic style in tenth-century Anglo-Latin literature', *Anglo-Saxon England* 4 (1975), 67. The misuse of 'hermeneutic' is unfortunate and should not be followed: 'hermetic' would be more correct.
36. Levison, 290ff.
37. Bede (as note 2) iv. 24, pp. 414ff.
38. Bede iv.13, pp. 374–5.
39. Bede v. 9–11, pp. 474ff.

40. Bede iv.2, pp. 334–5.
41. Letter to Egbert (734): *EHD*, 735.
42. Printed and dated in Haddan and Stubbs (as note 34), 274–5.
43. Levison, 70.

SAINT BONIFACE AS A MAN OF LETTERS

George Greenaway

CHAPTER 2

Saint Boniface as a Man of Letters

This aspect of the life and activities of St. Boniface is, I believe, an integral part of his constructive work for the establishment of a distinctive Christian culture in the lands beyond the Rhine and the Scheldt, which he evangelized. It seems to me that modern historians, especially those of his native land, have paid insufficient attention to this. For the most part it has been left to German scholars, preeminently Michael Tangl and Wilhelm Levison, to do justice to St. Boniface's achievements in this sphere.

Actually Levison's Ford Lectures at Oxford in 1943 were delivered in English and published three years later under the title of *England and the Continent in the Eighth Century*, but the form and content of this magisterial work, with its textual compression, extensive footnotes and elaborate appendices, render it more profitable to students and scholars than to the ordinary educated Englishman, interested in the period and desirous of learning more about St. Boniface and his fellow-workers in the German mission field. With the notable exception of Sir Frank Stenton's illuminating pages in his *Anglo-Saxon England*, among historians writing in English within the last half-century only Christopher Dawson in his remarkable synthesis, *The Making of Europe*, and the American, Eleanor S. Duckett, in the charming biographical study contained in her *Anglo-Saxon Saints and Scholars*, have made appreciable and positive contributions to the subject.

It is indeed surprising that modern English writers should have so neglected this particular legacy of St. Boniface, since already in his own day and for centuries afterwards it received due recognition among English churchmen. Within a few months of the saint's death Cuthbert, archbishop of Canterbury, wrote to the Englishman Lull, Boniface's successor in the see of Mainz, an official letter of condolence, in which he characterized the martyred apostle in these terms: '*this gifted student of heavenly learning, this noble soldier of Christ,* sent forth by the English nation, together with so many disciples, well taught and trained'.[1] You will observe that the archbishop makes no distinction between Boniface's role of Christian missionary and that of an exponent of the traditional Anglo-Saxon religious culture of his age. Nor would Boniface himself have drawn one. To him, as to his contemporaries, both were vital elements in his vocation as a preacher of the Gospel. We must keep this in mind if we are to do justice to his achievements in learning, while appreciating the limitations imposed by the unfavourable conditions of his work in Germany and the Frankish kingdom: the scarcity of books and manuscripts, the almost total lack of the tools of scholarship. Once he had left the shelter of his Wessex cloister to embark on his heroic career as an evangelist, his life was that of a busy and adventurous 'man of action'. He had scant leisure for reading and study, and used the pen only when it was necessary for him to do so; when he had some urgent problem of faith or morals or Christian order to deal with and needed help and advice from friends or his ecclesiastical superiors. This point is particularly relevant to his correspondence, as will be seen later.

It should not be difficult to determine the place of St. Boniface in the history of medieval learning. Unquestionably he was the chief agent in the transmission of Anglo-Saxon religious culture to the continent in the eighth century, mainly through the schools and libraries attached to his numerous monastic foundations in Germany. His literary works, his sermons and homilies – assuming that at least a proportion of those ascribed to him are genuine – and notably his letters, also played their part in reinforcing and developing that tradition. Though never a distinguished Latin stylist, he none the less excelled all his Anglo-Saxon contemporaries except Bede, and may be acclaimed the forerunner of that other great English teacher and man of letters who also spent the greater part of his life on the continent, Alcuin of York, the friend and counsellor of Charlemagne. The spread of Anglo-Saxon religious culture on the continent, which Boniface initiated and championed, Alcuin and the other scholars at Charles' court and in the Frankish abbeys fostered and brought to fruition. This is certainly not the least valuable part of Boniface's services to western Christendom. His personal contribution to this intellectual revival was considerable, though largely indirect and unconscious. No other 'man of action' in the 'dark ages', not excepting Charlemagne and King Alfred, left a richer cultural legacy.

A few words on the early life and training of the young Wynfrith – to give him the Anglo-Saxon name of his baptism

– will make clear both the nature of his literary talents and the influences that shaped its development. According to his biographer, the Anglo-Saxon priest, Willibald,[2] Wynfrith, in his tender years, was nourished on the lives and legends of the saints, by which was possibly meant Celtic lore infiltrating Devon from across the Tamar. Certainly in later life Boniface was more indebted to the Celtic saints and scholars than he ever acknowledged. Willibald categorically states that Wynfrith's desire to apply his talents to 'Divine Learning' was one of the motives impelling him to embrace the monastic life, though of course it is difficult to decide how much weight to attach to this remark in a Life which, in the fashion of the age, is not far removed from hagiography. Nor do we know anything about the education the young novice received in his first monastery at Exeter. The house was small and of recent foundation, probably sadly lacking in library facilities. The standard of learning could not have been high in this frontier outpost of Wessex Christianity. With Wynfrith's departure in early manhood to the Benedictine abbey of Nursling (situated between Winchester and Southampton) we are on firmer ground. He went there in search of more advanced knowledge and more competent teachers. There, under the benign and scholarly guidance of Abbot Winbert, he devoted himself to the study of letters, both sacred (the Vulgate Bible and the Latin Fathers) and secular (the Latin Classics). He soon became a proficient Latin scholar and, from evidence in his correspondence, he also acquired a smattering of Greek. His fame as a teacher soon spread far beyond the confines of his own monastery, especially after he had become head of the abbey school. In exposition and commentary of the Bible he was unsurpassed in his immediate circle, and he attracted many pupils from other religious houses, both of monks and nuns. His acquaintance and friendship with some of the learned nuns who eventually either joined him in Germany or remained behind in England to become cherished correspondents probably originated in these early years. His work as a teacher necessarily in that age involved attempts at original composition. There were very few books or manuals, and the progressive teacher had perforce to write his own. Wynfrith compiled a Latin grammar and a treatise on metrics, both intended for use in the class-room. He also composed Latin elegiac verses, a few specimens of which are extant. He tried his hand at Latin riddles and acrostics, and did much to popularise on the continent both these artifices and that peculiar cryptographic form of writing characteristic of Anglo-Saxon – or should it be Anglo-Irish? – literary dilletanti in that age. Examples of his acrostics and cryptograms are to be found, says Levison,[3] in the Vienna manuscript of the correspondence of Boniface and Lull. Rhabanus Maurus in the ninth century, the ablest pupil of Alcuin of York, who himself wrote a treatise on the cryptographic art, asserts that it was first practised on the continent by Boniface, who taught it to his disciples. Now Rhabanus was successively abbot of Fulda and archbishop of Mainz, and was therefore in the best position to know. It is pleasant to imagine Boniface whiling away his all too infrequent leisure hours in the medieval equivalent of crossword puzzles.

Born and bred in Wessex, it was only gradually, and mostly in his later years, that Wynfrith felt the impact of the distinctive Northumbrian religious culture that flowered, as if by a miracle, in the life and writings of Bede. Wynfrith had no personal contacts with Northumbrian Christianity, and his knowledge and appreciation of the manifold and diverse writings of the 'Father of English Church History' were derived, as will be shown later, from manuscripts acquired by him in Germany from friends and correspondents in England. A closer and more potent stimulus during his cloister life at Nursling was provided by Aldhelm, abbot of Malmesbury and later bishop of Sherborne, the presiding genius of West-Saxon learning, and indeed the most learned man of his age, next after Bede. Wynfrith's youthful literary exercises are but servile imitations of the ornate and pompous style of the master. He was slow to emancipate himself from Aldhelm's literary conceits, for we read in Willibald's Life that on the occasion of his second visit to Rome in 722, when Pope Gregory II consecrated him bishop, Boniface presented the written profession of orthodoxy required of him in polished and eloquent Latin.[4] (One may draw one's own conclusions as to the implications of the phrase.) Nevertheless, one can detect, as one works through the saint's correspondence, a growing power of self-expression, an increasing mastery of diction, until in the letters of his later years he had become capable of writing clear, fluent and forceful Latin. But perhaps the chief point to note in Willibald's account of Wynfrith's progress as student and teacher at Nursling is that it affords, in S. J. Crawford's words, 'a valuable glimpse of the extensive range of studies pursued at a comparatively small Anglo-Saxon monastery in the early eighth century'.[5]

It was this traditional culture of Wessex and Northumbria, of Aldhelm and Bede, that Boniface proceeded to inculcate into the infant churches of central and southern Germany. Everywhere in the course of his far-flung missionary labours in Hesse and Thuringia, Franconia and Bavaria, he set up schools and seminaries for the training of priests, lay teachers and women workers from among the ranks of his native Christian converts. Each of his monastic foundations, large or small, ranging from the earlier communities of Amöneburg, Fritzlar and Ohrdruf to the larger and more prosperous houses of Heidenheim and Fulda, had a school or seminary attached to it. By this means Hesse and Thuringia were sprinkled with centres of religious education, where the native converts could be taught the rudiments of letters as well as religious faith. This ambitious programme of 'cultural evangelization', as it may be called, necessitated a constant process of reinforcement in proportion to the expansion of Christian territory in Germany. Boniface needed not only more priests and preachers, but also more lay teachers and experts in education. He sent out an appeal for help to the bishops and clergy of his native land and the response was magnificent. A trickle of helpers had begun to flow from Wessex soon after his early successes in Hesse. By 732 the trickle had become a flowing stream, by 746 it had assumed the proportions of a flood. Willibald tells us that the first band of ardent disciples contained 'readers and writers and learned men trained in the liberal arts'.[6] Many of them were already professed monks, and those who were not were exhorted by Boniface to take the vows of the religious life. They were put to work in scattered groups in Hesse and Thuringia, preaching and teaching in towns and villages as the Gospel spread in ever-widening circles. Some of these early pioneers and disciples are well-known to us, and many of them figure prominently among the saint's correspondents. In the first group were Wigbert, a monk from Glastonbury, who became the first abbot of Fritzlar; Burchard, later made bishop of Würzburg; and Lull, Boniface's successor as head of the German mission and in the see of Mainz, and probably also a former pupil of his at Nursling. Both Lull and Burchard had formerly been monks at Malmesbury, and here we have an interesting and perhaps significant link between Boniface and the school of Aldhelm. Later there arrived on the scene Willibald (not the biographer) and his brother, Wynnebald, distant cousins of Boniface, who by devious routes and diverse experiences had both been drawn into the apostolic charmed circle. All these men were proficient scholars, who whether as bishops or abbots became the leaders and organisers of the German churches in the next generation.

Nor should we forget the galaxy of Anglo-Saxon nuns and noblewomen, though most of them only arrived in Germany at a later date, probably not earlier than 746. Among these were Lull's aunt, Cunihild, and her daughter Bergit, who worked as teachers among the women of Thuringia. Others were Cunitrude, put to a similar task later in Bavaria, and Walpurgis (St. Walburg), who became abbess of a double monastery at Heidenheim and after her death suffered a strange metamorphosis into the legendary figure of German folklore celebrated on Walpurgis night. Finally there were the saint's own two female relatives, Thecla, who presided successively over the monasteries of Kitzingen and Ochsenfurt, and the unique and admirable Lioba (or Leofgyth), the brightest star in this fair constellation, and the best beloved in Christ among Boniface's women helpers. Lioba became abbess of another double monastery at Tauberbischofsheim, some thirty miles from Würzburg, and was closely associated with Boniface during the later years of his life. She survived her master by many years, and was often consulted by the Frankish bishops on matters of faith and order. Her judgement on these questions invariably commanded respect. Her biographer, Rudolf,[7] a monk of Fulda, lays special stress on her mastery of the Scriptures and mentions also her knowledge of canon law and her interest in problems of chronology.

To such men and women of dedicated life and heroic self-sacrifice the rapid spiritual and cultural progress made by the native Christians of Germany is chiefly due. But there were hundreds more, whose names are unknown to us, but whose teaching labours helped to disseminate Christian learning far and wide in central Europe. It is a highly important aspect of the impact of Anglo-Saxon religious culture on the continent in the eighth century. It is the considered opinion of Hauck that the German provincial church established by Boniface 'surpassed all the provincial churches of the Frankish realm, both in religious and intellectual life'.[8] It is an arresting judgement, but one not devoid of truth.

But perhaps the strongest guarantee for the safe harvesting of this promising crop of learning was the existence of the great religious houses which Boniface founded, especially the abbey of Fulda. He sent both Sturm, the first abbot, and Lull to Monte Cassino for short periods to study the Benedictine life at first hand, while Wynnebald, his cousin, had spent long years there as a monk prior to coming to Germany. Indeed, in respect of learning and the arts, Fulda soon outdistanced St. Benedict's original foundation, for in the eighth and ninth centuries it became the chief centre of Carolingian culture on the continent, while at the same time preserving all that was best and most original in Anglo-Saxon traditions. Its personnel made it almost an Anglo-Saxon 'religious colony'. Alcuin's pupil, Rhabanus Maurus, was abbot of Fulda for twenty years (822–842), while Rhabanus' pupil, Walafrid Strabo, poet, grammarian and author of biblical commentaries, who became abbot of Reichenau, received part of his early education at Fulda. The numerous poets and scholars of the abbey of Reichenau owed almost everything to Fulda and the diligent labours of its copyists in its famed scriptorium. The astonishing multiplication of manuscripts of the Latin Fathers and of biblical *codices*, which is a notable feature of the ninth century, thus also derives ultimately from Boniface's pioneer efforts to spread and organise 'Divine Learning' on the continent in harmony with Anglo-Saxon tradition. The revived culture of the Carolingian age centred in the Carolingian abbey, and Fulda was outstanding among the abbeys in the German domains of Charlemagne's Empire. This is not the least impressive part of the cultural legacy of St. Boniface.

★ ★ ★

'A Man of Letters'. The appellation may be taken quite literally, as well as in a wider connotation. For Boniface, considering his busy and adventurous life, was a prolific letter-writer. Over one hundred and fifty letters are printed in Tangl's Latin edition of the combined correspondence of Boniface and Lull,[9] and many others, as we can tell, have perished in the course of the centuries. The letters have been described by Sir Frank Stenton as 'the most remarkable body of correspondence which has survived from the Dark Ages',[10] They provide first-hand evidence for Boniface's manifold interests and activities, and they are also indispensable to any attempt to recreate his personality. The collection contains letters from his correspondents as well as his own. A good proportion of them consists of letters written to and by the popes, and the importance of these for the history of the German mission and Frankish politics can scarcely be exaggerated. The remainder were addressed to, or received from, an astonishing variety of correspondents, drawn from all ranks and classes of society, and Boniface's fellow-countrymen of both sexes figure prominently among them. For Boniface maintained a large circle of friends and acquaintances in his homeland and continued to take a lively interest in its affairs. Indeed, his English correspondence shows the surprising extent to which he relied on his countrymen at home for material aid, no less than for spiritual succour; for books, food and clothing, as well as for prayer and intercession.

It is with these material and intellectual needs that we are here primarily concerned. For the letters provide additional evidence of Boniface's love of learning and his efforts to transplant Anglo-Saxon religious culture in the soil of continental Europe.

The demand for books frequently crops up in his letters to England. In 735 he wrote to Nothelm, archbishop of Canterbury, asking him to obtain for him a copy of the famous questionnaire sent by St. Augustine of Canterbury to Pope Gregory the Great and of the pope's answers:

> I pray you in the same way to obtain for me a copy of the letter containing, it is said, the questions of Augustine, first archbishop and apostle of the English, and the replies made to them by Pope Gregory I. In this letter it is stated among other things that marriages between Christians related in the third degree are lawful. Will you have a careful search made to discover whether or not this document has been proved to be an authentic work of St. Gregory? For the registrars say that it is not to be found in the archives of the Church at Rome among the other papers of the said pope.[11]

Boniface subsequently pursued the subject further, for we have a letter addressed to him by Cardinal-deacon Gemmulus from Rome[12] apologising for the delay in sending a copy of Pope Gregory's *Register* and promising to do so forthwith. The letter to Nothelm is evidence of Boniface's interest in Anglo-Saxon precedent for the solution of the knotty matrimonial problems with which he was continually confronted in the German mission field.

The next letter[13] is to a certain Abbot Dudd, of whom nothing is otherwise known, reminding him of their old association as master and pupil – presumably at Nursling – and begging the loan of a commentary of St. Paul's Epistles:

> Though I was but poorly equipped as a teacher, yet I tried to be the most devoted of them all, as you yourself know. Be mindful of my devotion and take pity on an old man worn out by troubles in this German land. Support me by your prayers to God, and help me by supplying me with the Sacred Writings and the inspired works of the Fathers. It is well known that books are most helpful to those who read the Holy Scriptures, so I beg you to procure for me as an aid to sacred learning part of the commentary on the Apostle Paul which I need. I have commentaries on two Epistles – that to the Romans and the First to the Corinthians. If you have anything in your monastic library which you think would be useful to me and of which I may not be aware, or of which I have no copy, pray let me know about it; help me as a loving son might an ignorant father, and send me also any notes of your own.

This touching request may be paralleled by two letters written in that same year (735) to Eadburg, abbess of St. Mary's Minster in the Isle of Thanet and the daughter of a former king of Wessex. The first[14] is a brief note thanking Eadburg for her gift of books to himself, 'an exile in Germany', and asking for her prayers. The second[15] contains a more specific request of considerable interest:

> I pray Almighty God, the rewarder of all good works, that when you reach the heavenly mansions and the everlasting tents He will repay you for all the generosity you have shown to me. For many times by your useful gifts of books and vestments you have consoled and relieved me in my distress. And so I beg you to continue the good work you have begun by copying out for me in letters of gold the epistles of my lord, St. Peter, that a reverence and love of the Holy Scriptures may be impressed on the minds of the heathen to whom I preach, and that I may ever have before my gaze the words of him who guided me along this path.

In, or soon after, 742, in one of his many letters to his friend and former diocesan, Daniel, bishop of Winchester, describing the difficulties he was encountering in his work in Germany, Boniface begs the bishop to send him *The Book of the Prophets* which had belonged to his late master, Abbot Winbert of Nursling:[16]

> There is one other comfort for my missionary labours that I should like to ask from you. May I be so bold as to beg you to send me the *Book of the Prophets* which Winbert, of revered memory, my former abbot and teacher, left behind when he departed this life? It contains the text of the six prophets bound together in one volume, all written out in full with clear letters. Should God inspire you to do this for me, no greater comfort could be given me in my old age, nor could any greater reward be earned by yourself. Such a book cannot be procured in this country, and with my failing eyesight it is impossible for me to read small abbreviated script. I am asking for this particular book because all the letters in it are written out clearly and separately.

Quite often the saint's letters contain similar passages of human interest.

In 746, and the years immediately following, a new star had begun to rise above Boniface's literary horizon. The fame of Bede was now, nearly fifteen years after his death, widespread throughout Anglo-Saxon England, and echoes of it had evidently penetrated the continent. Boniface, who seems to have had as yet little or no knowledge of his great compatriot's works, was now eager to acquire them. A number of letters to correspondents in England illustrate this newly found interest. He writes to Hwaetbert, Bede's own abbot at Jarrow, begging him for a copy of Bede's commentaries on Holy Scripture:[17]

> I beg you to be so kind as to copy and send me the treatises of the monk Bede, that profound student of the Scriptures, who, as we have heard, lately shone in your midst like a light of the Church.

A similar request is made in two letters to Egbert, archbishop of York, probably written within a year of each other:

> Have copied and sent to me, I pray you, some of the treatises of Bede, whom, we are told, God endowed with spiritual understanding and allowed to shine in your midst. We also would like to enjoy the light that God has bestowed upon you.[18]
>
> We beg you from the bottom of our hearts to comfort us in our sorrow, as you have done before, by sending us a spark from that light of the Church which the Holy Spirit has kindled in your land; in other words, be so kind as to send us some of the works which Bede, the inspired priest and student of Sacred Scripture, has composed – in particular, if it can be done, his book of homilies for the year (because it would be a very handy and useful manual for us in our preaching), and the Proverbs of Solomon. We hear that he has written commentaries on this book.[19]

Incidentally the first of these two letters proves that Boniface had by this time succeeded in obtaining a copy of Pope Gregory's *Register* from Rome. He is now forwarding it for the archbishop's inspection, accompanied by suitable presents for him and his monks. The second letter also closes with the mention of a present, which manifests the saint's humanity and tolerance:

> We are sending you by the bearer of this letter two small casks of wine in token of mutual affection, beseeching you to use them for a merry day with the brothers.[20]

Boniface's correspondence with the Anglo-Saxon nuns who were his kinswomen or old acquaintances in England, is among the most charming and intimate in the whole collection. These letters display the saint in gentler mood and illustrate the striking appeal which his personality made to women. Foremost among his correspondents in this group are the two abbesses, Eadburg and Bucge. It hardly seems safe to identify these two women, as some recent editors and translators of the correspondence have done, including C. H. Talbot. There is no variation or interchange of name in Boniface's own letters: the two are kept distinct throughout. Eadburg was the recipient of a further letter[21] from Boniface, besides the two about books and presents already quoted.[22] In this he pours out his heart to her concerning the many crosses he has to bear:

> On every side is grief and labour, fightings without and fears within. Worst of all, the treachery of false brethren exceeds the malice of pagan unbelievers.

He concludes, as so often before, by asking for her earnest and unceasing prayers.

The name of the other abbess, Bucge – apparently a diminutive or pet-name common among Anglo-Saxon girls – first appears in an early letter[23] written in 719 or 720, and is coupled with that of her mother Eangyth, abbess of a double monastery of unknown location, probably in Kent. Boniface is asked for his opinion on the advisability of mother and daughter undertaking a pilgrimage to Rome. Boniface had strong views on the subject, and we might make a good guess at the kind of answer he returned, although his reply is not extant. A year or so later Bucge wrote again, this time in her own name, congratulating Boniface on the success of his mission preaching in Frisia. It is a confident letter[24] for a young girl and filled with the spirit of joy and loving friendship:

> The power of my love grows warm within me, now that I recognise that it is through your prayers that I have reached this haven of peace and quiet. I have been unable to procure the Martyrology for which you asked me, but I will send it as soon as I can come by it. And you, beloved, comfort my lowliness by sending me some select passages from Holy Scripture, as you promised in your sweet letter . . . I am sending you fifty shillings and an altar frontal, which are the best gifts I can manage. Small as they are, they are sent with great affection.

Other letters evidently passed between them, and it may be that a regular correspondence ensued. In one of these missing letters Bucge returned to the project of a pilgrimage to Rome – apparently *without* her mother! In his reply,[25] to be dated in, or a little before, 738, Boniface refused to commit himself. He left the decision to the lady. He recognised the purity of her motives and evidently had a good opinion of her commonsense. He wrote:

> Be it known to you, dear sister, that in regard to the matter on which you have sought my advice, I cannot presume on my own responsibility either to forbid your pilgrimage or to encourage it.

The letter concludes:

> In regard to copying out the passages of Scripture for which you asked me, please excuse my neglect. I have been so much occupied in preaching and travelling that I could not find the time to complete it. But when I have finished it, I will send it on to you. Thank you for the presents and the vestments which you have sent; I pray that God may reward you with eternal life . . . I beseech you to pray for me, because for my sins I am wearied with many trials and vexed both in mind and body. Rest assured that the long-standing friendship between us shall never fail; farewell in Christ.

The letter is a model of tact and prudence, but in his heart he knew she would go to Rome – and go she certainly did! From evidence in a letter of King Æthelbert II of Kent,[26] a friend to both parties, it is certain that she and Boniface met in Rome, probably on his third visit in 738–9. Many years later, when they had both grown old and their ways had long since parted, Boniface wrote again to the abbess, an exquisite letter,[27] breathing the pure spirit of Christian charity:

> In compassion for your tribulations and mindful of your kindnesses and of our old friendship I am sending you a brotherly letter of consolation and encouragement . . . Rejoice and be glad always, beloved sister, and you will not be confounded. Scorn earthly trials with your whole soul, for all soldiers of Christ, of both sexes, have despised the storms and troubles and infirmities of this world, and counted them as naught . . . Rejoicing in the hope of a heavenly fatherland, hold fast, beloved, the shield of faith and patience against all adversities of mind and body. With the help of Christ, your bridegroom, perfect in your beautiful old age to the glory of God the building of that tower of the Gospel, which you began in early youth, so that when Christ shall appear, you may be found worthy to meet Him in the company of the wise virgins, bearing your lamp with the oil burning.

This is the saint's last letter to her. The date of her death is uncertain, but she may have survived him for many years.

It is unfortunate that only one of Boniface's letters to his cousin, Lioba, has survived. This is a brief and colourless note written to her in her capacity as abbess of Tauberbischofsheim shortly before his last expedition to Frisia in 754. The single letter[28] we possess from Lioba herself is a gem and well worth quoting in full. It was written while she was a young nun at Wimborne Abbey in, or soon after, 732:

> To her most revered master, Boniface, endowed with the insignia of the highest rank, most dear in Christ and related to her by blood, Lioba, the lowliest servant among those bearing the easy yoke of Christ, sends wishes for eternal salvation.
>
> I beg you of your kindness to remember the friendship which bound you long ago in the West Country to my father, Dynne. It is now eight years since he was taken out of this world, so cease not, I beg you, to pray for his soul. Remember also my mother, Aebbe, who is your kinswoman, as you well know. She is still alive, but has long been suffering from a grievous infirmity. I am my parents' only daughter, and though unworthy, I would I might consider you as my brother, for there is no other man in my family whom I feel I can trust as much as you. I venture to send you this little gift; not that it deserves your attention, but that it may remind you of my humble existence and bind us more closely to each other for all time in true affection, despite the great distance which

> now separates us. I entreat you, dear brother, to protect me with the shield of your prayers against the envenomed darts of the hidden enemy. Would you also be so kind as to correct the rustic style of this letter and send me a few gracious words of your own as a pattern? I do so long to hear from you. I composed the little verses appended here according to the rules of prosody, not in presumptuous vein, but in the endeavour to exercise any slender talent I may possess and conscious of the need for your help. I learned the art from my mistress, Eadburg, who continues unremitting in her study of the Scriptures.

The letter closes with an invocation of the Blessed Trinity in four lines of laboured Latin hexameters reminiscent of Aldhelm at his worst.

There are many other letters of abiding human interest in this precious collection, but even this abbreviated and selective treatment should indicate that the letters made a notable contribution to Boniface's literary reputation. For one thing they gained a wider publicity than he himself had either intended or foreseen, so many and various were his correspondents. Assuredly Bucge and Eadburg were not the only ones to take their master's treasured writings as models for their own compositions. His friends and disciples everywhere, and their pupils after them, turned them to similar profitable, if utilitarian, account. In this way the letters made a distinctive, if limited contribution to the literary side of the Carolingian revival. This is surely a component part of Boniface's cultural legacy to medieval Christendom, and one not to be depreciated. It reinforces the claim often and rightly made on other grounds for his inclusion among the select company of 'Makers of the Middle Ages'.

NOTES

1. *Ep*. 111, pp. 239–40. Tangl's edition of St Boniface's correspondence established the definitive text and the correct chronology.
2. *Vita*; English translation in Talbot, 25–62.
3. Levison, 291ff.
4. *Vita*, c. 6, p. 28 (Talbot, 44).
5. S.J. Crawford, *Anglo-Saxon Influence on Western Christendom, 600–800* (Oxford, 1933), 50.
6. *Vita*, c. 6, p. 34 (Talbot, 47)
7. Rudolf's *Life of St Lioba* is given in an English translation in Talbot, 205–226.
8. A. Hauck, *Kirchengeschichte Deutschlands*, I (Fourth edn., Leipzig, 1904), 461.
9. *Epp*.; selections from the letters in English translation are given in the

following: E. Emerton, *The Letters of St Boniface* (New York, 1940); Talbot; E. Kylie, *The English Correspondence of St Boniface* (London, 1924)

10. F.M. Stenton, *Anglo-Saxon England* (Second edn., Oxford, 1947), 171.
11. *Ep*. 33 (Talbot, 89)
12. *Ep*. 54.
13. *Ep*. 34(Talbot, 90–1).
14. *Ep*. 30 (Talbot, 88).
15. *Ep*. 35 (Talbot, 91).
16. *Ep*. 63 (Talbot, 118).
17. *Ep*. 76 (Talbot, 128).
18. *Ep*. 75 (Talbot, 127).
19. *Ep*. 91 (Talbot, 138).
20. *Ep*. 91 (Talbot, 139).
21. *Ep*. 65.
22. See above, p. 41.
23. *Ep*. 14.
24. *Ep*. 15 (Talbot, 69–70).
25. *Ep*. 27 (Talbot, 83–4).
26. *Ep*. 105 (Talbot, 143).
27. *Ep*. 94.
28. *Ep*. 29 (Talbot, 87–8).

SAINT BONIFACE THE MONK

Christopher Holdsworth

CHAPTER 3

Boniface the Monk

The justification for devoting one lecture to Boniface as a monk scarcely needs labouring since for nearly the whole of his life he was one. We can, indeed, scarcely visualise him without other monks, and nuns, near him, or close to his thoughts, and yet a great deal about the kind of monastic life he led is extremely obscure. This may seem a very strange assertion; do we not have a considerable body of letters associated with him and a Life written within at most fifteen years of his death? Indeed, we do, and a number of other sources of equal antiquity, astonishing in their range when one considers how long they have survived, but they often fail us and account for the hesitations and qualifications which one must make at many a crucial point in the story.[1] Let me illustrate my generalisation by a brief look at the longest consecutive narrative source, the *Vita* by Willibald.

After a preface addressed to two of Boniface's friends, Lull, who succeeded him as bishop of Mainz, and Megingoz, who had been a monk at Fritzlar, a house founded by Boniface, and became bishop of Würzburg, Willibald begins his Life with a chapter headed 'How in childhood he began to serve God'.[2] The searcher after specific detail, for the boy's parentage, his place of birth, or the very date of that event, are nowhere gratified. Instead we are given an almost incredible account of how by the age of four or five he had come to wish to serve God and even to consider the advantages of becoming a monk. We would, I think, be wrong in deducing that Willibald did not know, or could not discover, the facts we would like to know, for he does tell, admittedly in a very uncircumstantial way, how the boy's father lost his struggle to keep his favourite son by him so that he finally fell in with his desire to become a monk. The details that we would like to know were irrelevant to Willibald's purpose; he was composing not a biography to instruct, or even amuse, but the life of a saint, to serve as a model leading his readers towards a better life.[3] Certainly, by his time, the *genre* of saint's life was well-developed and had many branches.[4] It seems possible that Willibald was particularly influenced by the branch represented by classic early lives of saintly bishops, those of Cyprian by Pontius and of Augustine by Possidius, and by the life of an early western enthusiast for monasticism, Honoratus of Lérins.[5] In all three cases personal details are sparse in the extreme, and there is almost a complete absence of miracle, both characteristics of Willibald's work. Whether it does belong to this tradition or not, it is true that above all Willibald planned his work in such a way as to show his hero as a latter-day St Paul, a modern apostle to the Gentiles.[6] The clearest evidence of this is the series of quotations from Paul's writings chosen to end each chapter of the *Life,* apart from the first and last of the *Life* proper. I say the *Life* proper because it would appear that the ninth chapter was an afterthought to the original plan, added to tell a story about a posthumous miracle, told to the author by Lull.[7] The preceding eighth chapter looks much more like an end, closing as it does with a dating of Boniface's death in three ways, by the number of years he had spent in Francia, by the year of the Incarnation, and by the number of years he had been a bishop. Then comes a final encomium, and a doxology closed by a single 'Amen'.[8] It is not irrelevant to point out that the date Willibald produced for the saint's death, 755, has not commended itself to most modern historians, who prefer 754, the date recorded, not long after he wrote, at Fulda, Boniface's late, but very significant, monastic foundation.[9] One, at least, of the people to whom he dedicated the book, Lull, must be responsible for a telling silence in the book: its lack of any mention about the struggle which occurred over the saint's body. In those days possession of such a relic was a weighty matter, since where it was the saint lived on, able, it was held, to bless or blast those who cherished or attacked the community where he lay. It is from another source, the Life of Sturm, that we learn of Lull's attempt to keep the body by him at Mainz;[10] Willibald glosses over the story, but makes it clear that what those who received the body were to have in Boniface was an advocate forever, *in posterum perpetualiter patronum.*[11] Here again, incidentally, Willibald chose his words carefully – there is at one and the same time a Biblical reminiscence, (St John's 'If any man sin, we have an Advocate with the Father') and an allusion to that most powerful of forces in the secular society of his day, lordship.[12] So we must read Willibald bearing in mind the combined effects of purpose, *genre* and contemporary strains which helped to shape his work.

We can only read the evidence aright, too, if we bear in mind the world in which Boniface worked, and here the post-war years have brought very considerable changes. In the area of our concern one may say that a major reassessment has occurred.[13] The period between the time of Benedict of Nursia (c. 480 to c. 550) and the late eleventh century, when new religious orders began to arise, used to be called the Benedictine centuries; now the situation looks much more complicated. We see that Benedict's Rule had many forerunners, many rivals, like those of Caesarius of Arles or Cassian, or later on that of the Irish wanderer, Columbanus, and that these were not outpaced by Benedict overnight. A key figure in that process was a monk-statesman of the Carolingian Empire, a second Benedict, of Aniane, who managed to persuade the emperor, Louis the Pious, to try to impose the Rule of the first Benedict on all the monks and nuns of the Empire. Boniface's work has emerged as in some sense a prelude to this achievement, but where his commitment to the Rule came from, and what exactly it meant is not so easy to answer, for the past years have changed our understanding of early monasticism in these islands too. Whereas until recently it was confidently stated that Benedictine monasticism arrived in these islands with the first missionaries sent from Rome by Pope Gregory, and that therefore most monks (and nuns) here from then on were in a real sense followers of Benedict's Rule, now this can no longer be asserted. It is generally held that the monasticism established by Augustine, or under his influence, imitated the way of life practised in the urban monasteries of Rome, themselves not Benedictine, and that Wilfrid's monastery at Ripon, founded about 660, over sixty years *after* Augustine's arrival, was the first place where the Rule was followed.[14] The 'new look' on early monasticism here gives more emphasis too to the abiding influence of the monks who brought Christianity to the north from Scotland, to Aidan and his followers who went on to work in so many parts of this island. The northern missionaries came from a tradition, very different from that of Rome or Monte Cassino, which by the seventh century flourished not only in the so-called Celtic lands, Scotland, Wales, and Ireland, but also, thanks in the main to men from Ireland, in parts of Francia and Italy. And we see that the century of Boniface's life was a period of fusion, when the rules of one great monastic teacher were often combined with those of another, so that it is now called by monastic historians the period of the mixed rule, *regula mixta*.

The past thirty years have however not merely altered our knowledge of the internal tempo of monasteries, but enriched our understanding of how monasteries fitted into the world around them.[15] The emphasis of recent historians on the economic bases of society, 'the getting and spending', has shown us much more about how monks managed their affairs and has also directed attention to the abiding interest of founders and patrons in the communities they favoured. Monks and nuns might in theory, – here I quote Willibald on Boniface – renounce 'all worldly and transitory possessions for the sake of acquiring the eternal inheritance', but their relatives often retained a very real hold over the communities in which they lived.[16] Monks, too, might have withdrawn from the world, but bishops, and others, often wished to draw them out of it, or at the least, retained a considerable interest in their doings. Monastic wealth and monastic manpower, so to speak, were too important not to have attracted the interests of those who lived outside monasteries in positions of influence.

Now, having set the scene, I hope at not too excessive length, let me get nearer to Boniface the monk. I wish first to look at his native background and early monastic life, and then to move on to his work as a missionary monk and bishop, where I shall particularly draw attention to his work as a founder of monasteries and protagonist of the Rule of St Benedict.

★ ★ ★

Let us turn, then, first to look for a moment at Boniface in his home setting, though here we should rather call him Wynfrith, since he was given the name of an early Roman martyr only in 719, when he was at least in his fortieth year, adopting the chronology implied by these commemorations, or, using the more widely accepted dating, forty-four years old.[17] What can we know of Wynfrith's life on this side of the Channel where he spent, whatever date one accepts for his birth, about half his life?

The answer, in many senses, is precious little; we do not know, as I have already pointed out, the names of his parents, nor beyond any shadow of a doubt, the place of his birth, although the tradition that he was born in Crediton has much to commend it.[18] Wynfrith himself once said he was a sprig from a non-noble stem (*ignobili stirpe procreatum*), but I think this may be a literary turn of phrase, rather than a clear description, since there are plentiful indications that he had noble relations.[19] The nun Leoba, with whom he had the warmest friendship (did he not hope that she would be buried in his tomb?), is called noble by the man who wrote her life, and she was related to Wynfrith on his mother's side.[20] Other noble relatives were the brothers Willibald (not to be confused with his biographer) and Wynnebald, who, like Leoba, followed him to Germany.[21] Wynfrith seems to have been well-connected. It is, therefore, not stretching the sparse information we have to believe that he was brought up in a fairly substantial house where it would have been easy for him to talk with visiting preachers who had turned there for hospitality.[22] He came from a family which would have given him a solid position in the world, so that it would not have been unnatural for him to speak with the great, on terms if not of equality, of easy familiarity. But as is obvious from the fact we remember him as a monk and bishop, he turned aside into the monastic life.

Before trying to answer the question what sort of a life that may have been I want to emphasise one other aspect of Wynfrith's world, its precarious newness in more than one sense. He was born in newly conquered land and belonged to a people who were but newly Christian, yet these people had gained control of a land which was old, whose inhabitants had long been Christian.[23] Much of Devon was conquered by the West Saxon kings only during Wynfrith's childhood; he lived, that is to say, on a slowly advancing frontier, which may have shifted not a little one way or another as either side had the advantage. One must not, of course, think of this frontier as a continuous line, power rested upon the control of families and rural communities of one kind or other, yet the position of Wynfrith's family can hardly have been secure. They were part of a confederation of peoples, the West Saxons, only recently won to Christianity; the first of their kings to become a Christian was baptised in 635, forty years before Wynfrith's birth. It is surely indicative of the situation that it was not thought necessary, or perhaps possible, to create a bishopric to oversee the new western territories until well into Wynfrith's adulthood, in 705 to be precise. But these lands west of old Wessex, so to say, were not deserted, nor pagan. They had been part of the kingdom of Dumnonia, whose roots lay back in the period when Roman imperial authority had broken down in the late fourth and early fifth centuries, a kingdom whose people may well have been Christian from rather earlier. But these Christians, like their contemporaries to the north in what we call Wales, or still further north in the area which now divides England and Scotland, seem to have held themselves aloof from those who were laying hold to areas where they had ruled themselves before the Saxons came. Who can blame them? Long after Wynfrith had become Boniface, when a West

Saxon king wished to give land at *Cridie,* that is to say Crediton, to the church at Sherborne, he drew the boundary of his gift in such a way as to exclude a sector of land which appears to have been held then, as late as 739, by British people over whom he had not the same control as over the rest of the area.[24] Relations between Saxons and British must have been tricky at the levels of loyalty, and of co-operation in winning a living from the soil, and there is clear evidence that as Christians the groups did not get on well either. In 705, that is to say when Wynfrith was already a grown man, the learned and forceful abbot of Malmesbury, Aldhelm, soon to become first bishop of Sherborne, wrote to Geruntius, whom he calls ruler of the western kingdom, castigating him and his people because they kept outside the catholic church, criticized the shape of tonsure worn by the Saxon monks, celebrated Easter at the wrong time, and refused to sit down to eat with Saxon priests.[25] The aim of the letter, which won Bede's praise, was to invite Geruntius and his people to accept the authority of priests and bishops who had received their marching orders from Rome, to re-enter the catholic fold, but his tone was scarcely conciliatory.[26] Wynfrith and his church were upstarts and newcomers to those who could look back on perhaps two centuries and more of Christian life, and I do not think we have to look far in his later life to see one kind of reaction to this side of the environment in which he grew up.

Undoubtedly, however, the most potent institution which formed him was the monastery, but what sort of a monastery did he join at Exeter as a young boy? He would, I think, be a brave man who would try to answer this question in simple terms. We know the abbot had a Saxon name, Wulfhard, and bearing in mind the tense relationships between Saxon and British Christians I think it is doubtful whether the monastery can have been of old, British, foundation.[27] It seems much more likely that it was a new house, recently founded as the Saxons entered into the conquered land. We know too, as George Greenaway has already told us, that it provided a setting which encouraged Wynfrith to develop his intellectual capacities, and in particular to study the Bible.[28] More than this can I think scarcely be said, though the great Levison, who has been followed by many others, stated that here, and later at Nursling (of which more anon), 'he was trained in the spirit of St Benedict'.[29]

The difficulty that faces us here, as in so many cases, is in not taking what did happen as inevitable and in ignoring the other possibilities which might have come to pass and so reading one meaning into a source which it may not rightly bear. When trying to discover what kind of monastic life may have shaped Wynfrith as an adolescent and young, mature adult it is tempting to assume that because he was a promoter of the Rule of St Benedict in his later life, he was shaped by this way, and only this way from the start. It is, I would suggest, for such reasons that words in Willibald's *Life* have been, perhaps, stretched too tightly in one direction. Let us look at what is said of Exeter and then of the probably larger, and certainly more learned, community which Wynfrith moved to at Nursling, between Southampton and Winchester.[30]

Recounting the matter in which the young boy's request to be admitted at Exeter was received Willibald says that first Wynfrith presented a petition to be admitted, and then

> The father (i.e. the abbot) of the monastery took advice from the brethren and accepted it, as the right order of monastic life lays down, and then approved his proposal with blessing.[31]

Levison, the editor of the *Vita,* against the phrase *sicut regularis vitae ordo poposcit,* directed the reader to the third chapter of St Benedict's Rule 'Of calling the Brethren to Council'.[22] Is this what Willibald had in mind?

That particular chapter begins: 'As often as any important business has to be done in the monastery, let the abbot call together the whole community'; it then goes on to explain how advice is to be obtained and that ultimately the abbot has to make up his mind 'in the fear of God and observance of the Rule'. Nothing is said in the chapter to define what matters should be considered 'important', and although we may well consider that the admission of a novice or oblate (a youth offered by his parents, to which category Wynfrith would seem to have belonged) is important, in fact the chapters of the Rule which concern such matters, Chapters 58 and 59, say not a word about consultation with the brethren.[33] Where, if anywhere, is the question of admission linked with the taking of counsel?

So far I have not been able to find such a provision in any monastic rule before, contemporary with, or soon after Boniface's time, but I have found it, and this may not be particularly significant, in the mid-eleventh century customs followed at Cluny.[34] There it is specifically stated that the abbot shall consult the brethren before admitting anyone. What this small example can usefully remind us, I would suggest, is that no set of regulations laid down at some particular point in time can serve to cover every eventuality, and it was to fill these gaps that abbeys developed their own customs, or turned to other rules and adopted parts of them to their own use. I would more tentatively suggest that when the abbot at Exeter consulted his monks about Wynfrith's admission he may have been moved by the Rule of Columbanus, for the Irishman had laid down: 'Do nothing without taking advice' (*Sine consilio nihil facias*).[35]

Whatever combination of custom and rule may lie behind the manner of Wynfrith's acceptance, a similar blend appears behind the way he moved from the house of his youth to Nursling. We are told that it was the lack of teachers which induced him to ask permission from his abbot and community to transfer, a situation certainly not envisaged by St Benedict, who provided only for two cases for mitigation of the vow of stability, that is to say the promise to remain until death in the house of profession, the desire to go on pilgrimage, or the desire to become a hermit.[36] But what, apart from teachers and books, did he find in his new home?

Here the evidence appears, at first sight, to be straightforward for Willibald writes that Wynfrith strove to work every day with his hands and to perform the offices in an orderly manner *secundum praefinitam beati patris Benedicti rectae constitutionis formam,* 'according to the prescribed shape of the regulated law of the blessed father Benedict'.[37] Here, for the first time, we have a clear statement that a house where Wynfrith lived followed the great Italian rule. Its interpretation seems simple, since it is well known that Benedict stressed the significance of manual work (chapter 48), and that much of his work concerns the right ordering of the *Opus Dei,* services in church. But there are two other indications in the *Life* that Nursling, like Exeter, lived according to a mixed rule, did not follow exclusively the directions of Benedict.

In the first place we are told that after Wynfrith became a priest at the canonical age of thirty 'he received various gifts' so that 'in so far as the limitations of a regular monastic life allowed' he gave himself up 'to alms-giving and works of mercy'.[38] This statement accords oddly with Benedict's strict prohibition of the reception of presents,[39] whilst Wynfrith's rejection of the use of alcohol ('he drank neither wine nor beer') went far further than Benedict had expected his monks to go.[40] In this respect, indeed, we seem to be pointed back to the austerities practised by some of the Irish, to some communities in Gaul and Italy before Benedict's time, and even further back to Anthony in the desert, in our search for examples which may have affected Wynfrith.[41]

Does the picture which is emerging of Exeter and Nursling

as places where Benedict was sometimes tempered and sometimes strengthened with other ways, fit into the picture of monasticism in the England of that day? I would claim that it does. Our clearest evidence comes from Monkwearmouth and Jarrow where Benedict Bishop built up a way of life made up from the best of the customs of the seventeen houses which he had visited; a mixed rule indeed.[42] Even Wilfrid, the first as we have seen to use Benedict's Rule, understood parts of it in an eccentric way. In particular, as Hugh Farmer has put it, 'he did not think (as he was dying) that the time had come for his monasteries to elect their abbots in accordance with the procedure of St Benedict's Rule'.[43] Much closer to Wynfrith, the great Aldhelm, whose elaborate, not to say self-conscious, style has made it so hard for us to read him, appears to have had a great respect for the Rule,[44] but since the Malmesbury where he became a monk was presided over by an Irishman, Mailduibh, it is likely that he was used to Benedict with some additions.[45] No one knows whether Mailduibh came direct to Wessex from Ireland or not: I incline to believe he did not, but came like two of the first bishops of the west Saxons from Francia. Agilbert and his nephew Hlothere, or Leutherius, who occupied their sees between 650 and 660, and 670 and 676 respectively, were connected with monasteries in Francia which followed a rule which combined Benedict with Columbanus, the very mixture we can see signs of in the two houses where Wynfrith passed so much of his life.[46]

As we all know, the Anglo-Saxon monk left England to spend the second and better-documented half of his life in Francia, as missionary bishop and organiser of the church in frontier provinces, not entirely unlike his native heath. How did this drastic uprooting come about? We do not know what precise channels developed in him a longing to get away from the company of his relatives and friends and to seek foreign places rather than the lands of his upbringing, but we can make some fairly plausible suggestions.[47]

By 716, the year Wynfrith first left England, other Englishmen, notably the Northumbrian Willibrord, had been working in Frisia for a quarter of a century; a tradition, that is to say, of missionaries going to work in some of the areas from which originally their forebears had come, was established.[48] By then, too, a way of describing this sojourn in terms of a pilgrimage, or *peregrinatio,* had won favour, with its echoes of the wanderings of Abraham who had set out on his journey, as the writer of the Epistle to the Hebrews put it, not knowing where he was going.[49] The monks of Ireland, with whom Willibrord had spent twelve years, had particularly developed the spiritual value of *peregrinatio* as a means of growing in discipleship. Something, at least, must have been known to Wynfrith of Columba, of Columbanus, and of those Scots missionaries nurtured in Columba's tradition at his monastery of Iona who came to England, so his decision to take up a not dissimilar way of life was scarcely surprising. He may have been moved to leave in 716 by news of the difficulties which Willibrord was experiencing when the Frisians rebelled against the overlordship of the Franks. In fact Wynfrith found on this first journey overseas that conditions were unpropitious, so that he returned to Nursling within a year. He may well have learnt from this apparent failure that the propagation of the Gospel was unlikely to succeed without the support of a strong secular power. Be that as it may, he returned to Europe in the spring of 718, but decided this time to seek papal approval for his plans, and from then on his course was to run in Francia.

There is not time to describe at length the course of his life there; I am not, for example, going to say anything about his rôle as an organiser of bishoprics, or the secular church, since aspects of these things are the major concern of other lectures in this series, but before closing this lecture by speaking specifically of his monastic work, I want to say a word on one characteristic of Boniface's life in Europe. He remained to the end conscious that he was a stranger and that those from England who answered his call for help, were strangers, in a difficult situation. Their 'pilgrimage' was no easy journey, and so, we see him, for example, writing towards the end of his life to Fulrad, abbot of St Denis, and chaplain to Pippin, asking him to find out what the king proposed for his followers when Boniface was no longer there to be their shepherd. 'They are almost all foreigners' (*Sunt enim pene omnes peregrini*), and for them he begs of Pippin that he would be advisor and patron (*ut habeant mercedis vestrae consilium et patrocinium celsitudinis vestrae*).[50] The same strength is implied here, we may note, as that which Boniface's biographer believed that his body provided after death to those who kept it at Fulda. Without a lord the prospects of safety and the means of existence were small indeed.

As we have seen, Boniface himself came from a background which was not at all settled: he had been born almost a stranger to Devon, and so it is, I think, not surprising that he reacted to his situation in Francia in a particular way. On the one hand he did his best to obtain the secular protection, patronage, lordship, of the rulers, and on the other he turned to Rome for support and direction. He was not the first Anglo-Saxon to do either of these things, and there are hints here and there that Willibrord succeeded better with lay powers than Boniface did; certainly, however, both of them sought the authority of Rome for their actions.[51] In this respect they were both, perhaps, typical of their church which had, after all, been beholden to a pope, Gregory the Great, not so long before their day, for their faith. But, as Dom Hallinger has recently shown, we should not imagine that devotion to Rome and a high estimation of the customs of Rome in liturgy or law, were foreign to the lands where Willibrord and Boniface worked.[52] The Anglo-Saxons, however, undoubtedly had this characteristic deeply imbedded, and of them Boniface, perhaps just because he was a frontiersman, had it above anyone else. So we find him consulting successive popes over difficult issues where he felt the path forward was uncertain, and we also find him writing home to his friends for help in his exile.[53] In this way he obtained direction and counsel; solace and refreshment no doubt, came mainly from monks and nuns, particularly from the communities he himself helped to establish.

At least four communities of monks and three of nuns looked upon Boniface as their founder, all of them within what can be called north-central Germany, in Hesse, Thuringia or Franconia. In this they reflect the activity of Boniface between 721 and 735, before he moved southwards to be concerned with the organisation of the church in Bavaria; with one exception they seem to be founded within the latter part of this period.[54] When they were established the surrounding countryside was not still entirely pagan, but there was much work to be done teaching the new faith. Fritzlar, and to a lesser degree, Fulda, seem to have been placed with the aim of opening up the almost entirely untouched Saxony; an area which was not in fact to be converted until after Boniface's death. Boniface seems to have considered the monasteries as preaching centres, not entirely unlike the use Cuthbert made of Melrose, and as schools where potential priests could be taught. All this has been well discussed by others; what I want to return to is the evidence these foundations provide for Boniface's relationship to the Rule of St Benedict.

The earliest point in time in a description of the way of life in these monasteries comes in Willibald's *Life,* where he states that under Wigbert, an Anglo-Saxon monk, who guided both Fritzlar and Ohrdruf, the latter, that is to say Ohrdruf, was a house where the monks worked with their hands. He comments that they did this 'in apostolic manner', which seems a reference back to St Paul's claim in the First Epistle to the Corinthians that he had come to them as one who had toiled with his hands. Bearing in mind the 'Pauline tone' which Wilibald was so concerned to give his work, it is difficult to know how much weight to give to the fact that he does not refer to the way that the practice at Ohrdruf fulfilled the Rule.[55] We learn much more, however, from what Boniface wrote to the community at Fritzlar about 747 telling them how they should govern themselves now that Wigbert was dead.[56] The significant paragraph is short and worth quoting in full:

> With fatherly love I entreat you, my friends, now that father Wigbert is dead, to try to keep the tenor of your monastic life even more strongly. Wigbert the priest and Megingoz the deacon shall instil into you your rule and keep the offices *(spirituales horas)* and calender of the Church and admonish the others, be teachers of the children and preach the Word of God. Hiedde shall be prior (*prepositus*) and admonish the servants; Hunfrid shall help him whenever there is need. Sturm shall work in the kitchen. Bernard shall be master of works (*operarius*) and build whatever cells are needed. As in everything, whenever there is need, let abbot Tatwin be asked, and whatever he indicates, do.

Two things immediately strike one, an 'officer' is mentioned in the monastic family for whom there is no precedent in the Rule of St Benedict, the master of works, and the prior, a considerable figure in that Rule, has the job of keeping the servants under control, whereas Benedict put such affairs in the hands of the cellarer.[57] Fritzlar, whatever it may have become later, can scarcely at this stage be described as a Benedictine house, if by that we mean a house following exclusively the Rule of St Benedict. We are instead looking at a place where a mixed rule is followed, probably very like the 'mixture' at Nursling and Exeter, and since we know that both Fritzlar and Ohrdruf shared an abbot at first it is reasonable to deduce that a similar situation existed there.

Evidence for the internal life of all the rest of Boniface's foundations is lacking, with one exception, Fulda, which was not founded until 744.[58] By that time Boniface had played a leading role in the calling of two synods to consider the affairs of the church in Austrasia, in 742 and 743, both of which in slightly different terms emphasised the Benedictine Rule as the appropriate one for monks and nuns.[59] The earlier synod laid down that they should try to order their monasteries and conduct their lives *iuxta regulam sancti Benedicti,* 'according to the Rule of St Benedict', whilst the later meeting said that abbots and monks had received the Rule of the holy father Benedict 'to restore the tenor of regular life' (*ad restaurandam normam regularis vite*).[60] It would be wrong to read into these phrases the intention that religious should follow a particular rule exclusively; the words suggest instead the use of one rule as a standard by which the life of religious communities shall be reformed. And this interpretation fits in with the impression we are gaining of the place that Rule had in the life of Boniface, the vital spirit in the two synods.

It must, at any rate, have been during these years, 742 and 743, that the fairly protracted events took place which led to the establishment of a new monastery at Fulda. The first impulse towards it was of a different kind, since the monk and priest Sturm conceived the idea of leaving Fritzlar for the loneliness of the desert, *eremi squalore,* to become, in fact a hermit.[61] Such an intention fitted in with Benedict's concept of hermits whom he described as those who had spent time learning in community how to fight the devil, and then went out *ad singularem pugnam heremi,* 'to the solitary combat of the desert'.[62] Boniface, according to Eigil, author of the *Life of Sturm,* approved the idea, chose two companions for him and told him to go off and find somewhere where 'the servants of God might live'.[63] First they settled at a lonely spot (where later the monastery of Hersfeld was established), but after they had lived there 'for a long time', Boniface urged them to go further into the woods.[64] This new search was protracted and during it, if not before, it emerged that Boniface was not so much interested in establishing a hermitage but a new centre of community life in the wilderness, *'monachicam in solitudine instituere conversationem'.*[65] It is, I believe, absolutely right to connect the emergence of this plan with Boniface's work in the synods of 742 and 743, and to see in Fulda his attempt to create a house where the Rule should be used as the guide for what monastic life should be. But it is also quite clear that faithful to his upbringing, he still added to it practices derived from other sources. The most obvious example of these at Fulda was the decision to abstain from all strong drink, and to take only weak beer – a relaxation, it is true, of Boniface's own practice at Nursling, but a more severe practice than that allowed by Benedict.[66] Four years after the community began it had reached a point where it decided to send a group to visit older houses to learn to improve their following of the Rule. As a result Sturm and two monks spent over a year in Italy between 748 and 749, where according to Sturm's *Life* we are told they spent time in Rome and Tuscany.[67] Another source tells us that they visited Monte Cassino, which seems extremely likely on a number of counts; it would have attracted them as the oldest house founded by Benedict, and within a very few years Boniface was in correspondence with the abbot.[68] In any case on the travellers' return Sturm instructed the community about what he had seen, and generated great enthusiasm to carry out in all things (*ad omnia*) the Rule of St Benedict which they had vowed to follow. It is, therefore, not surprising to find that when Boniface wrote to the pope commending Fulda to his protection in 751 he described the monks there as living 'under the rule of the holy father Benedict', adding that they abstained from wine and meat, had no servants and worked with their hands.[69] With this reference to manual work we return to a side of Boniface which was first singled out when Willibald described his life at Nursling, nearly forty years earlier; in this sense, at least, his life was all of a piece.

Wynfrith/Boniface, younger man and old man, emerges from our examination as devoted to the Rule of Benedict, but at neither age did this attention divert him from other customs. It may be fair, however, to believe that attachment to one rule increased as his life progressed, for in the complex, luxuriant variety of monastic customs which he found in Francia, Boniface could well have turned increasingly to one standard as a guide to be held up before all monks whether they came from the Irish, or older Gallic, traditions. One Rule may have appeared to him as more and more significant through its connection with Rome, though this angle too may have changed. At first it was perhaps Gregory, the apostle of the English and preacher of Benedict, who attracted his attention, whereas later it was his own experiences of the monastic world which he found in Italy on his journeys to Rome; here it is surely relevant to remember that the last pope whom he visited, Zachary (741–52), was later remembered as the man who returned an autograph copy of the Rule to Monte Cassino.[70] In this light Boniface's devotion to the Rule belongs to the same part of his feelings as his adherence to Rome as the fountain of law by which the church should govern its affairs.

If one tries to sketch a comparison of his approach with that of other monastic patrons and founders of his day a series of contrasts and similarities emerge, whose proper delineation would take us beyond the scope of one lecture. The most interesting, and well-explained, comparison is that with Pirmin, who himself founded three monasteries, of which the best-known is Reichenau, and whose pupils founded at least five others.[71] Geographically the foundations of the two men did not overlap: with one exception the 'Pirminian' houses were in Alsace or Schwabia, but the kind of inner tempo of their houses was not dissimilar. Both of them followed a mixed rule, but the strong 'Irish' tradition to which Pirmin belonged produced one very significant difference in the relationships they cultivated with bishops. On the one hand Pirmin tried to establish his monasteries as islands independent of the local bishop, where, for example, monks wishing to be ordained were free to seek ordination from whatever bishop they liked, even including a monk bishop member of their own community, but Boniface planned otherwise. True he tried to protect the property of Fulda from any future bishop's interference by obtaining a privilege from the pope, but he in no way weakened episcopal control over monasteries in general.[72] Indeed the relevant decrees of synods held under his influence were designed to strengthen the hold diocesan bishops should have over all priests, monk priests included. So the two emerge as protagonists of what one may, for shorthand, call the monk's church, on the one side, and the bishop's church on the other. Yet in other respects, their relationship with lay patrons or protectors, their treatment of their own foundations, they are not far apart.

These last words are an inadequate hint at a complex situation, for it has been my main concern to try to explain in what sense we can now call Boniface a Benedictine, and how his work makes the achievement of the Carolingian age more intelligible. Boniface may not have been a Benedictine in the sense that Benedict of Aniane was to be, but he clung, perhaps increasingly tenaciously as he aged, to the old Italian rule as a standard and guide. And here as we leave him, we may dare to imitate his biographer Willibald and see Boniface in his seizure of the Rule to have been following Paul, who had saved himself from drowning at Malta by clutching some plank on which he floated to shore.[73] That such a simile might please Boniface himself is suggested by one of his earliest letters to a young monk in which Wynfrith, taking up a well known figure, likened life to a dangerous tempest through which one could gain the most blessed shore of Paradise only by holding fast to the book of the law.[74] At that time he may indeed have had in mind the life-giving support given by a study of the Bible, but it is not far-fetched to see here a parallel to his relationship to a monastic rule. Life appeared very hard, guides and standards were needed to avoid disaster, and in an age when men looked for something more universal than a charismatic word from a holy man, an old, prestigious rule had its appeal.[75] Boniface was not by any means the only monk who turned to Benedict but he was almost certainly the most significant man who did so between Benedict's time and the ninth century.[76]

NOTES

1. [*S. Bonifatii et Lullii*] *Epistolae,* ed. M. Tangl (*Monumenta Germaniae Historica, Epistolae Selectae,* I, Berlin, 1916); *Vita [Bonifatii auctore Willibaldo]* in *Vitae Sancti Bonifatii* ed. W. Levison (*MGH SRG,* Hannover and Leipzig, 1905), 1–58. The volume also contains five later *Lives* which, in the main, depend on Willibald. Translations of some of the letters and of Willibald are in Talbot. My versions of Willibald generally follow this.
2. *Vita,* 1–4, 4–7 (Talbot, 25–26, 27–28).
3. *Vita,* 4: *legentibus praebens exemplum . . . et ad meliora profectus perfectione perducitur* (Talbot, 26).
4. The classic work on the early history of hagiography is Hippolyte Delehaye, *The Legends of the Saints* (originally published in French, 1905). I am indebted in what follows to the essay by Patrick Wormald, 'Bede and Benedict Biscop' in *Famulus Christi,* ed. Gerald Bonner (London, 1976), 141–169. There is as yet no adequate study of the literary background to Willibald's *Vita,* but there are some excellent paragraphs by Pius Engelbert in his *Die Vita Sturmi des Eigil von Fulda* (Veröffentlichungen der Hist. Kommission für Hessen und Waldeck, 39, Marburg, 1968), 23–24, 37–39.
5. To be found respectively in *Corpus Scriptorum Ecclesiasticorum Latinorum,* iii (3) (Vienna, 1868), xc–cx; Migne, *P[atrologia] L [atina,]* xxxii, cols. 33–66; Migne, *PL,* l, 1249–72. It was to this tradition that Wormald suggested Bede's *Historia Abbatum* belonged. There is as yet no evidence that this work was known by Willibald, or by anyone else in the middle ages outside England. The MSS tradition is entirely insular; C. Plummer, *Bedae Opera Historica,* (Oxford, 1896), i, cxxxii–cxxxviii.
6. Cf. Engelbert, *Vita Sturmi,* 37.
7. *Vita,* c.9, pp. 56–57 (Talbot, 61–62).
8. *Vita,* c.8, pp. 55–56 (Talbot, 60). Engelbert (as note 4), 26 notes the significance of this early use of dating by the year of the Incarnation, which Bede popularised.
9. Cf. the discussion by Theodor Schieffer, *Winfrid-Bonifatius und die Christliche Grundlegung Europas* (Freiburg, 1954), 272, or in Levison, 90 note 2.
10. *Vita Sturmi,* c. 16, p. 149 (Talbot, 194).
11. *Vita,* c.8, p. 54 (Talbot, 60).
12. 1 John, 2.1. This passage should be compared with Willibald's description of how Boniface himself accepted the *dominium* and *patrocinium* of Charles Martel: *Vita,* c. 6, p. 30 (Talbot, 45), and Charles' own letter about this: Ep. 22, pp. 36–8 (Talbot, 75).
13. A brief impression is to be found in David Knowles, *Christian Monasticism* (London, 1969), 25–61. There is also good material in Wormald (as note 4). A useful summary of the complex situation in Francia is S. G. Luff, 'A survey of Primitive Monasticism in Central Gaul', *Downside Review* 220 (1952), 180–203. P. Riché, *Education and Culture in the Barbarian West* (Columbia, S. Carolina, 1976, being a translation by J. J. Contreni of the work first published in French in 1962), 335–6.
14. On Wilfrid see D. H. Farmer in *Saint Wilfrid at Hexham,* ed. D. P. Kirby (Newcastle upon Tyne, 1974), 35–9. Mr. Farmer's suggestion that the

oldest surviving MS of the Rule (Oxford, Bodleian Library, Hatton MS 48) may have been commissioned by Wilfrid has not won universal acceptance; see his *The Rule of St Benedict (Early English Manuscripts in Facsimile,* 15, Copenhagen 1968), 23–4 and P. Engelbert, 'Paläographische Bemerkungen zur Faksimileausgabe der ältesten Handscrift der Regula Benedicti . . . ', *Revue Bénédictine,* 79 (1969), 399–413.

15. Cf. J. M. Wallace-Hadrill, 'A background to St. Boniface's mission', *Early Medieval History* (Oxford, 1975), 138–154.

16. *Vita,* c.1, p. 7 (Talbot, 28).

17. *Epistolae,* no. 12, 17–18 (Talbot, 68). For the date of his birth see Levison, 70, and Schieffer (as note 9), 103.

18. The foundation of a minster and later a bishopric at the place may itself be witness to the weight his fame gave: Susan Pearce, *The Kingdom of Dumnonia* (Padstow, 1978), 102.

19. Levison, 70. The phrase comes in the prefatory letter to a grammatical work by Wynfrith.

20. Rudolf of Fulda, *Vita Leobae, (MGH Scriptores,* xv. i) 129, 124, 126 (Talbot, 224, 210, 214).

21. Huneberc of Heidenheim, *Vita Willibaldi, (MGH Scriptores,* xv. i), 88 (Talbot, 154). The tradition that the brothers were Wynfrith's relatives does not seem strong, appearing clearly only in the *Vita Tertia Willebaldi* (*Acta Sanctorum,* Julii, II, 516) whence it was taken into the *Vita Quinta Bonifatii* (in *Vita,* 108). Huneberc does not mention the relationship in her Life of Willebald, but in that of Wynnebald she may be alluding to it when she says the saint asked Wynnebald to help him in Germany, 'ut adminiculum tanti laboris et solacium episcopatus in divine verbis ammistratione illo foret, qui carnale propinquitatis et sanguini copulatione illo fuerat sociatus'. (*MGH Scriptores,* xv. i, 109).

22. *Vita,* c.1, p. 5 (Talbot, 27).

23. Cf. H. P. R. Finberg, 'Sherborne, Glastonbury, and the Expansion of Wessex', in *Lucerna* (London, 1964), especially 99–104 and W. G. Hoskins, 'The Westward Expansion of Wessex' (Leicester University Department of English Local History, Occasional Papers, 13, Leicester 1960), which gives a slightly different picture from the same author's *Devon* (Newton Abbot, 1954), 41–45.

24. H. P. R. Finberg, 'The Early Charters of Devon and Cornwall' (Leicester Occasional Papers, 2, 1953), 20–25.

25. Aldhelm, *Opera,* ed. R. Ehwald (*MGH AA,* xv), 480–86.

26. Bede, *Historia Ecclesiastica,* v. 18, ed. Plummer (as note 5), 320–1.

27. *Vita,* c.1, p. 6 (Talbot, 28). Hoskins, *Devon* (as note 23) 41 note suggested it can't be ruled out that it was a Celtic foundation, but later asserted a foundation, c. 670 ('Westward Expansion' [as note 23], 17).

28. *Vita,* c.2, p. 8 (Talbot, 29).

29. Levison, 71; Schieffer (as note 9), 105 (cf. 142).

30. *Vita,* c.2, p. 9 (Talbot, 30).

31. *Vita,* c. 1, p. 7 (Talbot, 28). I have translated a slightly amended version of the Latin here which seems to fit better, but does not affect the point at issue. *Cui protinus pater monasterii, inito fratrum consilio et eorum accepto* (edition: accepta), *sicut regularis vitae ordo poposcit, benedictione, consensum praebuit et effectum?*

32. *Regula S. Benedicti,* c. 3 (ed. Justin McCann, London, 1952, 24).

33. McCann, ed., 128–134.

34. Bernard of Cluny, *Consuetudines* I, xv, in M. Hergott, *Vetus Disciplina Monastica* (Paris, 1726), 164–7.

35. Migne, *PL,* lxxx, col. 215 (translated in Ludwig Bieler, *Ireland, Harbinger of the Middle Ages,* London, 1963, 34).
36. *Vita,* c. 2, p. 9 (Talbot, 30); *Reg. S. Benedicti,* cc. 1, 58, 61 (ed. McCann [as note 32], 14, 130, 138.
37. *Vita,* c. 2, p. 10 (Talbot, 30–31).
38. *Vita,* c. 3, p. 12 (Talbot, 32–3).
39. *Reg. S. Benedicti,* c. 54 (ed. McCann [as note 32], 122).
40. *Vita,* c. 3, p. 13 (Talbot, 33); *Reg. S. Benedicti,* c. 40 (ed. McCann [as note 32] 96).
41. Adalbert de Vogüé and Jean Neufville, *La Règle de Saint Benôit* (Sources Chrétiennes, 186, Paris, 1972), vi, 1159–69, and Engelbert, *Vita Sturmi* (as note 4), 92. Cf. Columbanus (as note 35), cap. III 'cibus sit vilis . . . et potus ebrietatem'.
42. Bede, *Historia Abbatum,* para. 11, ed. Plummer (as note 5), 374.
43. *Wilfrid at Hexham* (as note 14), 57.
44. Aldhlem, *De Virginitate,* c. xxx, ed. Ewald, *MGH AA*, xv, 268 and 390. I do not think one can be certain that the words mean that 'St. Aldhelm claimed to live by the Rule' (Wormald [as note 4), 146). Ewald in his note to 390 said 'Regulam Benedicti iam tunc receptam esse in Britannia neque ex hoc loco neque ex eis, quae in prosa affert (i.e., 268), concludi potest'.
45. Henry Mayr-Harting, *The Coming of Christianity to Anglo-Saxon England* (London, 1972), 192.
46. Wormald (as note 4), 145–6. He calls the two men cousins, which seems a slip, for Bede uses *nepos* for Hlothere; *Hist. eccles.* iii. 7 (ed. Plummer, [as note 5], 141).
47. *Vita,* c. 4, 15 (Talbot, 34).
48. Levison 45–69 still provides the best account in English.
49. Hebrews, xi, 8, cf. Genesis xii, 1–4. A. Angenendt, *Monachi peregrini. Studien zu Pirmin und den monastischen Vorstellungen des frühen Mittelalters* (Münstersche Mittelalter – Schriften 6, Munich, 1972), and his later 'Pirmin und Bonifatius' in *Mönchtum Episkopat und Adel zur Gründungszeit der Abtei Reichenau,* ed. A. Borst (Vorträge und Forschungen . . . 20, 1974), 251–304, especially 267–270.
50. *Ep.* 93, pp. 212–14 (Talbot, 139–40), and see p. 50 above.
51. Angenendt (as note 49), 232.
52. Kassius Hallinger, 'Römische Voraussetzungen der Bonifatianischen Wirksamkeit im Frankenreich', in *Sankt Bonifatius. Gedenkgabe zum 1200 Todestag* (Fulda, 1954), 320–361. The essay by Stephanus Hilpisch, 'Bonifatius als Mönch und Missionar', in the same volume seems to me to over-emphasise the degree to which Boniface's inspiration was 'Benedictine', and to undervalue the influence of ideas which are fundamentally Biblical rather than specifically Benedictine. For relations between England and Rome see also J. M. Wallace-Hadrill, 'Rome and the early English Church' (as note 15), 115–137.
53. *Epp.* 24, 26, 45, 50, 51 to and from Popes and 23, 32, 33, 78, with English correspondents.
54. Cf. Levison, 76–77. Schieffer (as note 9), 184 suggests Boniface was also responsible for the establishment of Benedictine monks in the cathedral chapters of Salzburg, Regensburg, Freising and Passau, but can only give tradition and analogy as authority.
55. *Vita,* c. 6, p. 34 (Talbot, 47). The reminiscence is to I Cor. iv. 12. See p. 50 above for the Pauline tone of the Vita. *Reg. S. Benedicti,* 48 deals with work.
56. *Ep.* 40, p. 65 (Talbot, 92–3). The dating of this letter is now put a decade later than in the edition; cf. Engelbert, *Vita Sturmi,* 74–75.

57. *Regula S. Benedicti,* cc. 65 and 31 (ed. McCann [as note 32], 148–150, 80–82). Admittedly Benedict has two minds about the desirability of having a prior at all. In these paragraphs I follow Engelbert, *Vita Sturmi,* 94–95.
58. Schieffer (as note 9), 222–25, and Engelbert, *Vita Sturmi,* 81–90.
59. There has been some dispute about the dating of the synods:– see Engelbert, 81 note 41 and Timothy Reuter, below p. 92 note 73.
60. A letter of Carloman gives a text of the synodal decisions: *Ep*. 56, pp. 98–102. The passages quoted are on 101.
61. *Vita Sturmi,* c. 4, p. 133 (Talbot, 182).
62. *Reg. S. Benedicti,* c. 1 (ed. McCann [as note 32], 14).
63. *Vita Sturmi,* c. 4, p. 134 (Talbot, 183).
64. *Ibid,* loc. cit. 'manseruntque illic tempus non modicum' . . .
65. *Ibid.*, c. 6, p. 138 (Talbot, 185), and Engelbert's introduction, 81.
66. *Vita Sturmi,* c. 13, p. 145 (Talbot, 190); *Reg. S. Benedicti,* c. 40 and p. 56 above.
67. *Vita Sturmi,* c. 14, pp. 145–7 (Talbot, 191–92).
68. *Vita Leobae* (as note 20), 125 (Talbot, 213–14); *Ep*. 106, pp. 231–2.
69. *Ep*. 86, p. 193 (Talbot, 136).
70. P. Meyvaert, 'The Problems Concerning the "Autograph" MS of Benedict's Rule', in *Benedict, Gregory, Bede and Others* (London, 1977), chapter III.
71. See Angenendt, *Monachi peregrini,* 216–24 and his 'Pirmin und Bonifatins' (both as note 49), whom I follow in this paragraph.
72. *Ep*. 89, pp. 203–205 Talbot, 136–37).
73. Acts xxvii. 44.
74. *Ep*. 9, p. 6.
75. Cf. Philip Rousseau, *Ascetics, Authority, and the Church in the Age of Jerome and Cassian* (Oxford, 1978), 2, where he calls Cassian 'a link between the charismatic but transitory influence of the desert father and the greater rigidity of later monastic rules'.
76. Cf. Wormald (as note 4), 146 for whom Boniface 'was the most important single figure in the history of the Rule between St. Benedict himself and his Carolingian namesake.'

SAINT BONIFACE AND EUROPE

Timothy Reuter

CHAPTER 4

Saint Boniface and Europe

'Boniface and Europe' is perhaps too all-embracing a title. It is true that the most recent large-scale biography of Boniface carries the title 'Boniface and the Christian Foundations of Europe',[1] and we shall see later how far the claim implicit in such a title can in fact be justified, but we should remember that the immediate range of his activities was much narrower. As a missionary, he was active in Frisia (which extended considerably further south than the modern Dutch province of Friesland)[2] and in the lands to the north of the Main. He was active here also as a church reformer and organizer, as well as in Bavaria and in the Frankish kingdom proper between Rhine and Loire. His work was thus confined to the Frankish Empire and its dependencies – though he also gave advice and encouragement to Anglo-Saxon church reformers – and even here large parts of it were hardly touched by his work: Alemannia, Aquitaine, Burgundy.[3] There were also great local variations in his influence. To understand why this was so – and it was a source of much anger, frustration and heart-searching in Boniface's career – we must begin by taking a look at the Frankish Empire and its church.

The Franks began as a small tribal confederation around the lower Rhine. In the fourth and fifth centuries they moved gradually southwards and westwards into the Low Countries, but real expansion began under Clovis at the end of the fifth century. In the thirty years of his rule the Franks conquered the rump of 'Roman' Gaul, Syagrius' kingdom in the Paris basin; most of Visigothic Gaul south of the Loire; and some territory from the Alemanni, who at that time seem to have held lands along both banks of the Rhine from Worms southwards.[4] His sons followed these conquests by absorbing the kingdom of the Burgundians and taking Provence from the Ostrogoths. The large Thuringian empire was destroyed in a Frankish campaign of 531; some of Thuringia was incorporated into the Frankish empire, some given to the Saxons, who became tributaries of the Franks.[5] Bavaria and the Alemanni also became attached to the Frankish empire in a loose but definite dependency.[6] Frankish armies also intervened in Italian politics, sometimes as mercenary allies of the Byzantines, sometimes independently. The Lombard rulers who had established themselves in northern and central Italy after 568 paid intermittent tribute to the Franks during the two centuries of the Lombard kingdom's independent existence.[7] So also did the Bretons. Frankish relations with the rich and powerful kingdom of Visigothic Spain were complex and fluctuating: the Franks were usually able to have their way in the series of feuds engendered by the marriages which took place between members of the Frankish and Visigothic royal families, but Spain was never a Frankish tributary. The Franks also had diplomatic and commercial relations with the kingdoms of Anglo-Saxon England, and played some role in their conversion to Christianity.[8]

By the end of the sixth century the Franks had achieved a position of virtual hegemony in Western Europe. Along the way there had been two important developments. First, Clovis had eliminated his rivals for Frankish kingship and established the Merovingian dynasty. Many of these rivals seem to have been related to him, so that it is not entirely clear whether the Merovingians were the victors among several Frankish royal families, or the victorious branch of a large Frankish royal clan.[9] In any event, they were victorious, and Merovingian blood enjoyed such prestige that Merovingian kingship continued long after Merovingian power had passed to others. Only in Boniface's own time was the dynasty finally supplanted. This did not, however, mean rule by a single Merovingian. Merovingians were prolific, and no distinction in throne-right was necessarily made between sons born to lawful queens and those born from more casual liaisons.[10] Clovis' kingdom was divided amongst his four sons, and after being briefly reunited under the one who lived longest was again divided into four. Gradually these divisions took on a permanency of their own; by the end of the sixth century, Francia was divided into three regions: Neustria in the west, Burgundy in the south, and Austrasia in the east. Aquitaine was initially divided so that each subkingdom had a portion attached to it. After the early seventh century, when it briefly became a subkingdom for Dagobert's brother Charibert II, it went its own way, politically. But the ties of land and family between it and the three parts of Francia proper remained important.[11]

The other important development of the sixth century was the Franks' acceptance of Christianity. Like the Anglo-Saxons, and unlike the other German tribes who invaded the former Roman Empire, they accepted the Catholic form, without going through an intermediate stage of Arianism. This had important political consequences. The Frankish conquest of Gaul had left the former Roman elite relatively undisturbed in their possessions and in their political control especially of the cities.[12] The Franks' acceptance of Christianity made it possible for Frankish and Roman elites not only to cooperate but to merge. The barbarian kingdoms of southern Europe were based, initially at least, on a fairly strict segregation of invaders and natives, often going as far as separate and parallel systems of government, separate laws, and prohibition of intermarriage. None of this happened in Francia. As late as the early seventh century it was still possible to say that a man was a Roman, or a Frank, or a Burgundian; but this was not a fact of very great signficance.[13] Frankish magnates and old Roman senatorial aristocrats intermarried, shared political power, and collectively formed a supra-regional governing elite, characterized, as the old senatorial aristocracy had been in the days of the Empire, by widely-scattered land-holding.

Frankish acceptance of Christianity did not mean any very substantial change in their way of life. It was an adherence to a new god, accompanied by the gradual dropping of the old ones. This indeed had been the general pattern of conversion to Christianity from the fourth century onwards; it was inevitable once Christianity had ceased to be the religion of a select and persecuted minority and become the religion at first favoured and later enforced by those who held political power. The conversion of the Franks was not essentially different from the mass conversion of the Roman Empire. Clovis was converted – not without misgivings as to whether his Frankish warriors would follow him – as Constantine had been.[14] The conversion of the Frankish elite followed as that of the Roman elite had done, though with less resistance; there was no Frankish Symmachus. The conversion of the 'ordinary Frank' was a much slower process. A century after the conversion of Clovis Pope Gregory the Great could write to the Merovingian Queen Brunchildis urging her to suppress pagan sacrifices, tree-cults, and 'sacrileges with the heads of animals' (probably ritual processions); Frankish rulers from the sixth to the eighth centuries ordered the destruction of idols.[15] Paganism as a religion, a system of belief, ended quite quickly (we do not in fact know how strong it was among the Franks by the time of Clovis' conversion). Pagan practices survived far more tenaciously.[16] Nor were these confined to unreconstructed Franks. The mass conversion of the Roman Empire had been possible because of the importance of cities in Roman civilization. Not much progress had been made with the conversion of the countryside: indeed, a pagan was precisely the inhabitant of the *pagus*, the countryside.[17]

It would be wrong to suppose that the Frankish church neglected its task, simply because we can show that pagan practices survived. Nor was missionary activity in the Frankish empire confined to the Anglo-Saxons of the late seventh and eighth centuries, and before them the Irish. Not all bishops were like the one who Boniface claimed had 'so far neglected to disseminate the word of teaching among the people, out of laziness'.[18] The seventh century saw a good deal of missionary activity by Frankish bishops and abbots.[19] For some of it we have direct evidence; more can be deduced from later conditions. The Low Countries were evangelized by Eligius, who became bishop of Noyon in 641, Amandus and Remaclus, who founded monasteries at Saint-Amand (Elne) and Stavelot-Malmédy respectively, and by Audomarus and Bertinus, whose names survive in Saint-Omer and Saint-Bertin. These men were Franco-Romans, not Irishmen, though they had contacts with the so-called 'Irofrankish' monasticism which spread from Columban's foundation of Luxeuil.[20] From Luxeuil Columban and his disciple Gallus set out in the early seventh century to preach in the Zürich and Bregenz regions. A later abbot of Luxeuil, Eustasius, went to Bavaria as a missionary. Nor were the bishops of the old Roman cities in the Rhineland inactive. Kunibert of Cologne began missionary activities among the Frisians from Utrecht (a fact which was to cause some trouble for the later Anglo-Saxon mission based there)[21] and among the tribes in Westfalia from Soest, or at least intended to do so.[22] The bishops of Mainz spread Christianity up the Main valley as far as the Nidda, probably also to the Wetterau and southern Thuringia, and south-eastwards to the Spessart. The bishops of Speyer and Worms were active in the Neckar valley;[23] it was from Worms that Kilian set out for Thuringia and Rupert for Bavaria at the end of the seventh century.[24] Along with the bishop of Strasbourg, they also conducted missionary activity in Alsace. Alemannia proper – the Black Forest and the plateau to the east of it – was the responsibility of the old(?) bishopric of Augsburg and the new one of Constance. It is by no means certain that the bishopric of Augsburg had a continuous existence between Roman times and the eighth century,[25] and certainly no missionary activity can be attributed to it. The bishopric of Constance is equally problematic: it was founded at the beginning of the seventh century, the only certainly new bishopric in the Frankish empire before the coming of the Anglo-Saxons, but little is known about the first century and a half of its existence, and the reasons for its foundation are still a matter of dispute.[26] Probably neither Constance nor Augsburg were able to do much in the Alemannic lands east of the Rhine, and the Alemanni were at least as pagan at the beginning of the eighth century as the Hessians and Thuringians.[27] Certainly they were more pagan than the Bavarians. Here there may have been some survival of Roman Christian communities, for example at Passau.[28] The ducal family of the Agilolfings, possibly Frankish by origin and probably owing its position initially to the Merovingian rulers of Francia, was also Christian.[29] There are traces of missionary activity from across the Alps, from Aquileia, in the sixth century;[30] in the seventh century we have Lives of three missionaries – Haimhramn (Emmeram) from Poitiers, Corbinian from near Melun, and Rupert from Worms.[31] By the early eighth century the land was sufficiently Christian for the then duke, Theodo, to ask the pope for permission to erect bishoprics.[32] A legate with power to do this was duly sent out, but for reasons now unknown the plan was not carried through, and it was left to Boniface twenty years later to give Bavaria a diocesan organization (though there were bishops there from the late seventh century).

It can, of course, be misleading to talk of Frankish bishops: not everything that was done by way of spreading the faith under, say, a bishop of Worms was done by him personally or even at his direction. But it cannot be doubted that in almost all the areas with which Boniface had to deal there had already been some missionary work before his time. The evidence from Boniface's own letters and Willibald's Life is confirmed by the evidence from inscriptions, church dedications, and excavations. By the time of Boniface's consecration as bishop in November 722 only northern Frisia, Saxony, and perhaps northern Thuringia and parts of the Black Forest remained untouched by Christianity. What kind of Christianity is another matter. There were two kinds of difficulties. First, there was a shortage of trained priests and of the means for their support. If we examine the conversion of Saxony later in the eighth century, we see that it was possible because Charlemagne could draw on and direct the resources of a united Frankish church which had been undergoing reform for two generations, and which he controlled, and indeed owned, in a way that his predecessors, Carolingian and Merovingian, had not.[33] Nevertheless, it was an immense effort, which demanded great material support from the king (and from the Saxons themselves),[34] and which seems to have exhausted the Frankish church – further missionary work among Avars, Slavs and Danes was by comparison limited and timid. The conditions of the seventh and early eighth centuries were much less favourable, and indeed it is surprising that individual bishops managed to do so much. Even the material existence of priests was difficult to provide for before the Carolingians made the payment of tithe general and compulsory.[35] Much depended on monasteries in the period before 800. Boniface himself used monasteries as the basis for his missionary activity, as did his older contemporaries Willibrord and Pirmin.[36] Even these required endowments, and hence some degree of support from the great men of the region to be converted.

The other difficulty lay in the nature of the Christianity which was transmitted. The initial stages of conversion consisted essentially in baptism – with some preparation, but without anything like the long catechumenate of the early church. – and the abjuration of pagan beliefs and practices. The text of a Carolingian formula to accompany baptism[37] shows what was entailed:

Do you reject the devil? I reject him.

Do you reject sacrifies to the devil? I reject them.

Do you reject the works of the devil? I reject them (and his words, and Donar and Wodan and Saxnot and all their evil companions).

Do you believe in God the almighty father? I believe in God the almighty father.

Do you believe in Christ, God's son? I believe in Christ, God's son.

Do you believe in the Holy Ghost? I believe in the Holy Ghost.

The inner conversion which entailed acquiring some understanding of Christian belief and ethics was a very long-term process; but until it was present, there was a constant danger that a superficial Christianity would simply co-exist with other beliefs and practices, especially as these often had important social functions.[38] The danger was still greater where no regular church organization existed. Boniface's world was one of lapsed and backsliding converts.

It was also a world of lapsed and backsliding ecclesiastics. I have already pointed to some of the difficulties which Frankish bishops and abbots faced in their missionary work; but it is in a way surprising that any of them found any time to do it. Bishops had for a long time dominated their cities, in effect both as the agents of the king and the representatives of the local noble families.[39] After the rapid decline in Merovingian power following the death of Dagobert in 638, this dominance developed into virtual independence. The cities became 'aristocratic republics with episcopal heads'.[40] These aristocratic families also fought on a large scale for control of the court, and especially of the important office of mayor of the palace. The patterns of alliance and enmity shifted rapidly, but they were to some extent determined by the new regionalisms which had developed, as we have seen, at the end of the sixth century. Neustria, Burgundy, and Austrasia ceased simply to be terms for parts of the Frankish kingdom governed by particular Merovingians, and became focuses of loyalty in themselves. The family which was ultimately to rise to the top, the Arnulfing (later Carolingian) family, established a dominant position after the victory of Pippin II and the Austrasians at the battle of Tetry in 687, but it was not until Charles Martel had emerged from the succession crisis which followed Pippin II's death in 714, having defeated rivals both from within the Armulfing family and from the Neustro-Burgundian nobility, that the position of the Arnulfings could be said to have been finally established.[41] Even then, there was much to be done by way of weakening or eliminating rival power-bases. Pippin II and Charles Martel are remembered as the Frankish leaders who reestablished Frankish control over the Germanic tribes east of the Rhine, and this was indeed important, as well as being an essential precondition for the work of Boniface and other missionaries.[42] But they were also the men who broke episcopal power within Francia. They had no pattern or policy in this. Some 'episcopal republics' – Trier, for example – were in the hands of families who supported them, and these they allowed to continue.[43] Others were handed over more or less intact to their supporters.[44] Elsewhere again they stripped bishoprics of much of their land and power, and these they gave to followers. The men they put in also had followings to satisfy, and these were rewarded with church lands and the lands of defeated rivals; and besides all this there was a general process of asset-stripping without any direction from above. Without all this the Arnulfing mayors of the palace would not have been able either to protect Boniface and other missionaries, or to begin the ecclesiastical reforms which Boniface thought so necessary. But the initial effects were, first, to impoverish a number of bishoprics and monasteries (though not in general those nearest to Boniface's field of mission),[45] and second, to fill bishoprics and monasteries with men whose concerns were often very secular. They were not necessarily or normally irreligious: they often endowed monasteries, and if they did not take up episcopal orders they arranged for a *chorepiscopus* to perform the spiritual functions of a bishop.[46] But demands for missionary work and for the observance of canonical order and discipline were at best an irrelevance to them and at worst a serious threat to their position.

It was in this world then, a world incompletely and imperfectly Christian, and one undergoing rapid political change whose effects were felt heavily by the Church, that Boniface began his work. About Boniface's years in England earlier lecturers have already spoken. For us, his history really begins with his first journey to Rome in 718–9, after an earlier and unsuccessful attempt to work in Frisia in 716. Here he was given the task of preaching to the heathen. He returned by way of Thuringia and the Rhine to Frisia, where he worked for a while with Willibrord, who had been established there – with the blessing and support of the pope and of the Arnulfings – since the 690s.[47] In 722 he made a second journey to Rome and was ordained bishop. On his return he moved to Thuringia and Hesse, regions in which Willibrord had also been interested. Here he worked for some twelve years, beginning with the dramatic felling of the sacred oak at Geismar, and proceeding with the conversion and reconversion of the peoples north of the Main. Monasteries were founded at Fritzlar, Amöneburg and Tauberbischofsheim. In 732 Boniface received the pallium from Pope Gregory III, and we hear for the first time of plans to consecrate further bishops. In 735 or thereabouts Boniface went to Bavaria, and for the next four years, which included his third and last visit to Rome, he was largely concerned with the reorganization of the Bavarian church, which he completed in 739 with the setting up of four bishoprics at Salzburg, Freising, Regensburg and Passau.[48] Meanwhile, a campaign by Charles Martel in 738 had made the position of Frankish central Germany much more secure from Saxon attack. Boniface seems to have hoped for a time that it might be possible to evangelize the Saxons, but Frankish power was not yet great enough for this.[49] What did become possible was the establishment of bishoprics in central Germany, and in 741 or 742 (the date is not simply of antiquarian interest)[50] bishops were consecrated for the new sees of Würzburg, Büraburg, and Erfurt. In 741 Charles Martel, who had protected Boniface, died, and the Frankish kingdom was divided between his two sons Carloman and Pippin. Both of these took up the idea of ecclesiastical reform, Carloman with enthusiasm, Pippin more cautiously. A series of synods met from 742 (or 743) and began the long process of restoring canonical order to the Frankish church. The inspiration and leadership for these synods came very much from Boniface. But he faced difficulties. He was unable to become archbishop of Cologne and head of an Austrasian church province, and had to content himself with Mainz. The Franks vacillated about their decision to begin the restoration of a provincial organization in the Frankish church. Only one of the three newly-founded bishoprics, Würzburg, survived, the others being incorporated by Boniface himself into his own bishopric of Mainz.[51] And in 747, Carloman, who was much closer to Boniface than Pippin, and perhaps a more enthusiastic supporter of reform, followed the example of several Anglo-Saxon rulers of the seventh and eighth centuries in abdicating, going to Rome as a pilgrim, and becoming a monk.[52] Carloman should have been succeeded by his son Drogo, but Pippin was able to take over almost noiselessly, and was thus now sole ruler of Francia. In 749–50 the pope sanctioned a constitutional change recognizing this, namely the deposition of the last Merovingian, Childeric III, and his replacement as king by Pippin. Boniface may have taken part in Pippin's ordination as king by performing the ceremony of anointing in the autumn of 751 – a novelty in Frankish history, though there were Visigothic and possibly Irish and Anglo-Saxon precedents.[53] But he seems to have largely retired from active involvement in Frankish politics, ecclesiastical or otherwise. In 753 he handed over Mainz to his disciple Lull, and returned to Frisia; after a summer of missionary activity and a winter spent in the Frankish outpost of Utrecht, he again proceeded into pagan Frisia in the summer of 754. On June 5 he and his companions were attacked and killed, apparently by brigands rather than by fanatical pagans.[54]

We are accustomed to think of Boniface as a great missionary, who for a time towards the end of his life was also active as a church reformer. 'After so many years of missionary activity a new epoch of Boniface's life began; it was shorter than the previous period, but its importance was even greater', wrote Levison, in a chapter with the subtitle 'German mission and reform of the Frankish Church'.[55] Schieffer also makes a distinction between Boniface the missionary and Boniface the reformer. This is useful for us, but for contemporaries, and probably for Boniface himself, it was not so clear. Boniface felt himself to be just as much an exile and a pilgrim in a hostile world among the Frankish bishops as he did when preaching among the pagan or semi-pagan.[56] Willibald, in his life does indeed mention the organizational and reforming activities of Boniface – though he devotes far less space to them than modern biographers – but Willibald saw them as part of Boniface's preaching activities. The same kind of language is used to describe the effects of Boniface's missionary work among the Hessians and Thuringians, his reorganization of the Bavarian church, and his restoration of synodal activity in the Frankish church in the 740s.[57] All is summed up in the phrase: *cumque quoddam canonicae rectitudinis speculum omnibus ad exemplum gradibus bene vivendi opponeret*[58] – 'since he held up a mirror, as it were, of canonical rightness as an example of righteous living to men of all classes'. Boniface's work was done in lands either controlled by or under the influence of Christian rulers. The existence of pagans in these lands was one of many offences against the right order of things, a serious one it is true, but not qualitatively different from other breaches of order. What Boniface was concerned to do was not simply to bring Christianity to those who had never heard of it, but by example, by legislation, and by enlisting the support of those who held power, to see that the Christianity practised by all was brought nearer to *canonica rectitudo*, canonical rightness.[59] Getting Bishop Gewilib of Mainz deposed for pursuing a blood-feud was not a different kind of activity from converting pagans; it was all part of Boniface's duty as a bishop and after 738 as a legate of the people, his duty of *praedicatio*, which is probably better translated as teaching than as preaching.[60]

Other scholars have attempted to put a different kind of pattern on Boniface's career. It has been argued that he really wished to devote himself to the Frisian mission; that he left Frisia because of differences with Willibrord, and planned to return from 738 onwards, leaving his work in Germany to other hands, but was prevented by Gregory III and Zachary.[61] I find this difficult to believe. It is true that Willibald's life says that Boniface returned at the end of his life to Frisia, 'the land which he had once indeed left in body, but never in his heart',[62] but this is the kind of commonplace one would expect at this point. There is no evidence that Boniface had any contact with the Frisian mission between 722 and Willibrord's death, and there was little contact after that until the 750s.[63] It seems to me that his final return to Frisia is characteristic of his whole career in a different sense. He was a man conscious of his calling and his gifts, who was quick both to seize opportunities and to meet difficulties as they arose. The Frisian mission seemed threatened in 752–3, and he stepped in to protect it,[64] just as in 735 he had accepted the invitation of Duke Hucbert to reform the Bavarian church, and in 742 had moved quickly to exploit the possibilities opened up by the attitude of Carloman to church reform. It is this almost opportunistic sense for what was possible which marks Boniface, and in view of it I find it also very difficult to accept that his real goal was the conversion of the Saxons. There can be no doubt that this was something which Boniface very much wished for; he discussed it with Pope Gregory II and Pope Gregory III, and wrote to friends back in England asking for their prayers. But there is no firm evidence that he even began missionary work among the Saxons.[65] He knew how essential it was to have secular support: 'I am not able to prevent heathen customs or the sacrilege of idolatry in Germany without the orders of and the fear inspired by the prince of the Franks'.[66] Charles Martel, Carloman, and Pippin all conducted campaigns against the Saxons, but these were of a punitive and retaliatory kind, and were not sufficient to be the basis for missionary work.[67] Boniface asked not for help or advice in the conversion of the Saxons, but for prayers that this might come about; it was something to hope for, not to begin work on.

If Boniface's aim was the restoration of *canonica rectitudo*, who were his opponents? It is clear that he felt himself to be a man with many enemies, but can we say anything more about who opposed him and why?[68] The answer, I think, is that more has been said than can be said with confidence, and some at least of what has been said is supported by conjecture and anachronistic or circular arguments. This is true even at the highest level. We have already seen something of Boniface's relations with Pippin and Carloman.[69] His relations with their father Charles Martel are much more obscure. We know that Charles took Boniface under his protection at the beginning of Boniface's career, an important and indeed essential support for his missionary work.[70] We know also that at some point in his reign Charles prohibited idolatry. This may have been at the request of Boniface or other missionaries, or it may simply have been a continuation of an earlier Merovingian practice.[71] Beyond this all is guesswork. We know that in 732 Boniface was given the pallium and the right to consecrate bishops;[72] yet it was not for nine or ten years after this that the first bishops of central Germany were consecrated. Was the delay due to opposition by Charles Martel, or to opposition by Frankish bishops which Charles was unwilling or unable to overcome? We do not know, though that has not prevented some scholars from writing as if we did.[73] It is clear that Charles' consent was essential for the erection of new bishoprics,[74] but so was a sufficient degree of Christianization and of security from pagan incursions, and it may equally be that these were the cause of the delay.[75] Certainly there does not seem to have been much opposition to the new dioceses once they were set up. The fact that only one, Würzburg, survived, was due to Boniface's own actions, as we have seen.[76]

As for opposition by the Frankish episcopate and nobility, this was more substantial, though it was certainly less deep-rooted and uncomprising than might appear from a reading of Boniface's correspondence with the popes and with his English friends. For instance, Boniface wished to restore in Francia the provincial system of church organization, whereby dioceses were grouped together into provinces under a metropolitan bishop, and to add to this the Anglo-Saxon refinement whereby the metropolitan could exercise his rights only after receiving the pallium, a liturgical garment, from the pope.[77] The Frankish episcopate agreed to this for the bishops of Rouen, Sens and Rheims, but later it was decided just to ask for the pallium for the bishop of Rouen, and in the end the whole idea seems to have been dropped.[78] It was also agreed that Boniface should have the bishopric of Cologne, that this should become an archbishopric, with the bishops of Liège, Utrecht, Worms and Speyer as suffragans. But again 'the Franks did not fulfil what they had promised', and Boniface had to be content with Mainz as his see instead of Cologne, and without a provincial organization (though he himself was an archbishop).[79] Boniface was angry at these difficulties; but the main function of provincial organization was legislation, and this had now been taken over by 'national' synods. Otherwise it was difficult even for Pope Zachary to explain to Pippin what metropolitans were meant to do.[80] Theoretically they were supposed to supervise the election of their suffragans, but, as Boniface knew very well, control over the choice of bishops was firmly in the hands of the Carolingians.

Again, Boniface thought that his initial successes in the question of restoration of church lands had quickly been reversed, and he was considerably troubled by this. An annual rent for church lands held by laymen was put forward as a compromise, after the first reform council under Carloman had simply decreed that alienated church lands were to be restored. Yet though Boniface had scruples about accepting the rent and the compromise, even to have got this much was a considerable feat, in view of the huge amounts of land involved and the very large demands already being made on them. Certainly Pope Zachary thought that Boniface had done well and need not press further. We may also say that without a fairly general degree of goodwill towards Boniface and towards ecclesiastical reform even such a compromise would have aroused more opposition than it apparently did.[81]

Boniface's real difficulty lay in those ecclesiastics who in their very existence and way of life constituted opposition to his work. 'Milo and his like' (referring to Milo, bishop of Trier, and, until 748, also of Rheims) was the phrase used by Boniface in his last letter to Pope Zachary.[82] Such men had been a source of concern to Boniface at the outset of his career. It may have been he himself who inserted in his episcopal oath of 722 the promise not to communicate with bishops who did not observe the rules laid down by the fathers but either to prevent their activities or to report to the pope on their behaviour.[83] Complaints about such men – rarely named – run right through Boniface's correspondence from his early years in Thuringia to the end of his career.[84] Yet though Boniface himself may not have thought that much had been done about such men, we can see that they were ceasing to be a common type even during his own lifetime. The bishops who replaced them were generally of a different stamp. Some, like Burchard, the first bishop of Würzburg, and Lull, Boniface's successor in Mainz, were Boniface's own pupils. More significant for the future was the way in which new appointments were made from members of those families which had once produced Boniface's *bêtes noires*, yet were now turning out a different type of bishop. Boniface was beaten to Cologne by Agilolf, and it might well seem that this was a good example of the established Frankish aristocracy's refusing to accept the new ways promulgated by Boniface, and insisting on an important bishopric's going to one of its own members. We know little about Agilolf except his name, but that, coupled with the area in which he became bishop, suggests that he was related to a group of families which had dominated the mid-Rhine area since at least the early seventh century, and from which Gerold and Gewilib of Mainz also came. But we also know that Agilolf was not an opponent of reform; he attended the last council known to have been held in association with Boniface, in 747.[85] Boniface's successor as archbishop in Francia, Chrodegang of Metz, was also perhaps related to this group of families.[86] The Frankish aristocracy, from which the great majority of bishops were drawn, was not, so to speak, hostile to the new technology. It insisted only that the old ways should be eliminated through natural wastage rather than redundancies. Even here it was not entirely successful. Milo had to give up Rheims; Boniface managed to get Gewilib of Mainz and at least one other bishop deposed.[87] These were the first bishops to be removed from office for canonical rather than political reasons in Francia for a very long time.[88] It is not even clear that Boniface was shut out by a reaction against his work in the last years of his life. The synod of 747 is the last one known to have been held in his lifetime, but both it and the one of 745 are only known from references to them in his correspondence with Pope Zachary. As Boniface's correspondence becomes much more fragmentary in the years after 748, it is at least possible that there were later synods.[89] It would be surprising if Pippin's elevation to kingship were not accompanied by a Frankish synod, even though this is nowhere indicated in the sources. Boniface was on good terms with one of the Franks who were to lead ecclesiastical reform after his death, Fulrad of Saint-Denis, though he had no known contacts with Chrodegang of Metz.[90] He secured the succession of Lull in his own bishopric of Mainz. He was perhaps associated with the change of dynasty in 749–51, and certainly with the canonization of Kilian in 752.[91] He managed to defeat Cologne's claims to Utrecht. None of this suggests defeat or exclusion, and it is dangerous to infer it from the tone of his few surviving letters from this period and from the gaps in the sources.

What, then, was Boniface's achievement? Clearly, his work east of the Rhine and in the Frankish church was of immense importance for the development of Germany and consequently of Latin Christendom. The eighth century saw the full incorporation of Germany into the Frankish empire. Without a conversion of the German tribes to Christianity and the setting up of a proper church organization this would not have been possible. The later history of Frankish relations with the Slavs and Avars show this: without Christianization, all that could be done to enforce the status of tributary on such tribes. The conversion of the Germans was not, as we have seen, solely the work of Boniface and his followers. Something had been done before his time, and much remained to be done afterwards. Yet his work was vital. He saw clearly that missionary results could not be consolidated and preserved without a church organization in the converted areas, and his organizational work in Hesse, Thuringia and Bavaria was an important for the future of Christianity in those regions as his missionary work. It is also very doubtful whether the conversion of the Saxons would have been possible without the reform of the

Frankish church initiated by Boniface. As it was, it took many years and much work; it could not have been done at all with pre-Bonifatian methods. And of course the reform of the Frankish church itself, however incomplete and imperfect, was a great achievement. Boniface himself was conscious mainly of how much he had failed to do, and was at times overwhelmed by this sense of failure. With hindsight we can realize how much he did do, and how remarkable this was.

Other achievements are more controversial. Johannes Haller, the great Protestant historian of the medieval papacy, wrote of the early medieval papacy:

'The papacy in the Roman Empire . . . was a papacy for the bishops, not for the individual Christian. In those things which concerned the ordinary man – certainty of redemption, penitence, forgiveness of sins, eternal life – the Roman pope had no more to offer than any other bishop or priest. . . . How different, when we enter the world of the converted Germans! For them the power of the bishop of Rome is a matter of faith. The heir and representative of St. Peter is for them not just the chief among the judge over his fellow-bishops, but the guarantor and mediator of temporal and eternal salvation for all. . . . No other bishop could compete with this fullness of power. Above all, the pope of Rome was, with his unlimited power over all souls from the beggar to the king, the lord of Christendom.'[92]

This change he ascribed to the work of Boniface in particular and the Anglo-Saxons in general, whom he saw as taking their special relationship with St. Peter with them to the continent. This view has been subject to much revision in recent years. Eugen Ewig and Kassius Hallinger have shown that the links which the pre-Bonifatian Frankish church had with Rome were more significant and more substantial than Haller had supposed. The Anglo-Saxon missionaries did not bring a cult of St. Peter to Francia and Germany; they found it there already.[93] Indeed, as Michael Wallace-Hadrill has reminded us, the leader of the Roman party at the Northumbrian synod of Whitby in 664, at which King Oswiu of Northumbria decided in favour of the Roman method of reckoning Easter, was a Frank; yet Haller had taken this episode as typical of the Anglo-Saxon veneration of St. Peter as the doorkeeper of heaven![94] I think, though, that the reaction against Haller's thesis has gone too far. It is not quite to the point to show that the Merovingian church acknowledged the pope's authority in matters of church organization and discipline, though it is a useful corrective to the older view that Boniface threatened the independence of the Frankish church from Rome.[95] This was not something that Haller denied; he argued that from Boniface's time the popes meant something more. And indeed they did: within Boniface's own lifetime popes were sanctioning changes of dynasty in Francia and summoning Frankish armies to fight for them in Italy. It is difficult not to feel that Boniface, with his authority as papal legate, and his constant referring to papal authority on all kinds of matters – not just on questions of church organization, but on those of marriage, diet and behaviour – must have done a lot to bring about this change. Of course he was not the only person or force working towards it. Of course he did not create a new attitude from nothing. The preconditions were there; but he developed them. This was not his primary intention, nor was it the result of papal initiative,[96] but it happened. We can see it in the Carolingians' rise to power. When Grimoald wanted his son to become king he had him adopted by the Merovingian ruler Sigibert III, though without lasting success. Charles Martel seems to have had a similar idea in mind when he left the throne vacant on the death of the Merovingian Theuderic IV in 737 and had his son Pippin adopted by the Lombard king Liutprand.[97] Pippin himself, as we have seen, took the quite different and revolutionary step of approaching Pope Zachary to legitimize the change of dynasty. With this, the papacy had begun to be something more than a bishop among bishops, had begun to be the spiritual leader of all Christians in western Europe. And with the unification of a large part of western Europe under Pippin and Charlemagne, this spiritual leadership could begin to find practical expression. To these developments the work of Boniface made a substantial contribution. It is in this sense that Boniface helped to lay 'the Christian foundations of Europe', and in this sense that a title like 'Boniface and Europe' can be justified.

NOTES

1. T. Schieffer, *Winfrid-Bonifatius und die christliche Grundlegung Europas* (Freiburg, 1954; reprint with bibliographical postscript Darmstadt, 1972), based on his earlier *Angelsachsen und Franken* (Mainzer Akademie der Wissenschaften und Literatur, Abhandlungen der geistes- und sozialwissenschaftlichen Klasse, 1950 Nr. 20); references are to the later work unless otherwise stated. The other major production of the 1954 centenary was *Sankt Bonifatius. Gedenkgabe zum zwölfhundertsten Todestag* (Fulda, 1954), a collection of essays. There has been little in English since W. Levison, *England and the Continent in the Eighth Century* (Oxford, 1946), except for G. W. Greenaway, *Saint Boniface* (London, 1955) and J. M. Wallace-Hadrill, 'A Background to St. Boniface's Mission', first published in 1970 and reprinted in his *Early Medieval*

History (Oxford, 1975), 138–154, a brilliant if allusive essay to which I am much indebted in what follows. I have tried to give some indication of the results of recent German scholarship in the notes which follow, which I hope will excuse their considerable length.

2. See W. H. Fritze, 'Zur Entstehungsgeschichte des Bistums Utrecht. Franken und Friesen, 690–734', *Rheinische Vierteljahrsblätter* 35 (1971), 107–151: Greater Frisia extended southwards to the Scheldt, though by 722 the boundary with the Franks was the Vlie and Ijssel, and by 735 the Lauwers.

3. The church in Aquitaine and Burgundy was being brought under Carolingian control only late in Boniface's career: see E. Ewig, 'Milo at eiusmodi similes', in *Sankt Bonifatius* (as note 1), 412–440, here 426–9. Boniface seems to have hoped to extend his work to Alemannia at the time of his reform of the Bavarian church in 739; he brought a letter from Gregory III addressed to five named bishops *in provincia Baioariorum et Alamannia* back from this third visit to Rome in 738 (*ep*. 44, p. 70). The identification of these bishops is controversial and uncertain, but even if some were Alemannic bishops it is clear that Boniface had no effect in Alemannia. It was the province of Pirmin, on whom see H. Löwe, 'Pirmin, Willibrord und Bonifatius. Ihre Bedeutung für die Missionsgeschichte ihrer Zeit', in *La conversione al cristianesimo nell'Europa dell'alto Medioevo* (Settimane di Studio . . . sull'alto medioevo 14, 1967), 217–261, here 219–227, and A. Angenendt, 'Pirmin und Bonifatius. Ihr Verhältnis zu Mönchtum, Bischofsamt und Adel', in *Mönchtum Episkopat und Adel zur Gründungszeit der Abtei Reichenau*, ed. A. Borst (Vorträge und Forschungen . . . 20, 1974), 251–304: the two men never met, but several others, notably Heddo of Strasbourg, were closely linked with both, and their views were in most respects very similar. Boniface's exclusion from Alemannia was probably due rather to the lack of Frankish control over the area until the late 740s; as the Carolingians' man he was unwelcome to the Alemannic leaders.

4. See J. M. Wallace-Hadrill, 'The Long-Haired Kings', in *The Long-Haired Kings* (London, 1962), 148–248, here 148–185, and L. Musset, *The Germanic Invasions* (London, 1975), 68–83, on early Frankish history; for the Alemanni and Frankish expansion into the Mainland in the early sixth century or before see W. Schlesinger, 'Zur politischen Geschichte der fränkischen Ostbewegung vor Karl dem Grossen', in *Althessen im Frankenreich*, ed. W. Schlesinger (Sigmaringen, 1975), 9–61, here 13–17, 19–20.

5. M. Lintzel, 'Die Tributzahlungen der Sachsen und die Franken zur Zeit der Merowinger und König Pippins', *Sachsen und Anhalt* 4 (1928), 13–28; W. Schlesinger, 'Das Frühmittelalter', in *Geschichte Thüringens*, edd. H. Patze and W. Schlesinger (Cologne, 1968), i, 317–380, here 320–4, 334–6.

6. On Bavaria and the Alemanni see Musset (as note 4), 81–84, and K. F. Werner, 'Les principautés périphériques dans le monde Franc', in *I problemi dell' Occidente nel secolo VIII* (Settimane di studio . . . sull'alto medioevo 20, 1973), 483–514, here 503–9. The Frankish rulers generally controlled the appointment of the *dux* in Bavaria; this is usually assumed of the Alemanni as well, but B. Behr, *Das alemannische Herzogtum bis 750* (Berne, 1975), has argued, convincingly in my opinion, that the Alemanni had no central institutions either before or after their defeat by Clovis and existed in a loose dependency on the Frankish kingdom under a number of *duces* until the Frankish conquest of 709–746.

7. R. Holtzmann, *Die Italienpolitik der Merowinger und des Königs Pippin* (Darmstadt, 1962; first published 1940).

8. A. Lohaus, *Die Merowinger und England* (Munich, 1974), 1–16, 144–151.

9. See the account of Clovis' reign in Gregory of Tours, *Historia Francorum*

(MGH SRM 1.1 edd. B. Krusch and W. Levison), ii, 40–42; Wallace-Hadrill (as note 4), 184.

10. Wallace-Hadrill (as note 4), 202–3.

11. The essential work on the divisions is by E. Ewig: *Die fränkische Teilungen und Teilreiche (511–613)*, (Mainzer Akademie der Wissenschaften und Literatur, Abhandlungen der geistes– und sozialwissenschaftlichen Klasse, 1952 Nr. 9); 'Die fränkischen Teilreiche im 7. Jahrhundert (613–714)', *Trierer Zeitschrift* 22 (1954), 85–144. See also Werner (as note 6), especially on Aquitaine.

12. K. F. Stroheker, *Der senatorische Adel im spätantiken Gallien* (Tübingen, 1948); F. Prinz, 'Die bischöfliche Stadtherrschaft im Frankenreich vom 5. bis zum 7. Jahrhundert', *Historische Zeitschrift* 217 (1974), 1–35, especially 3–9; K. F. Werner, 'Important noble families in the reign of Charlemagne', in *The Medieval Nobility*, ed. T. Reuter (Amsterdam, 1978), 137–202, here 142–6. I have not yet seen M. Heinzelmann, *Bischofsherrschaft in Gallien* (Munich, 1976).

13. Werner (as note 12), 155 and note 23.

14. Wallace-Hadrill (as note 4), 169–173.

15. J. Imbert, 'L'influence du christianisme sur la législation des peuples francs et germains', in *La conversione . . .* (as note 3), 365–396, here 369. See also the assembly of examples of Frankish pagan survivals in O. M. Dalton, *The History of the Franks by Gregory of Tours* (Oxford, 1927), i, 245–249.

16. On the distinction see H. Kuhn, 'Das Fortleben des germanischen Heidentums nach der Christianisierung', in *La conversione . . .* (as note 3), 743–757, here 743–4. It was important for Boniface, who did not have to deal with fully-fledged pagan religion except perhaps in Frisia: see A. Mayer, 'Religions- und kultgeschichtliche Züge in bonifatianischen Quellen', in *Sankt Bonifatius* (as note 1), 291–319, here 302, 316–19, and below, note 38.

17. D. Baker (ed.) *The Church in Town and Countryside* (Studies in Church History 16, 1979), which has several articles on the problem of Christianity in the countryside at this period, appeared too late for me to make use of it.

18. *Ep.*24 (Gregory II to Boniface, 724), p. 42. the reference is usually taken to be Gerold of Mainz, but this is not certain. Here, as frequently in the Boniface correspondence, Boniface's complaint is only known from the papal reply; as the popes normally seem to quote Boniface's own words, I shall in future cite them without comment. The complaint of negligence was not a new one: see Ionas, *Vita Columbani* (*MGH SRG,* ed. B. Krusch) i, 5, p. 161: *negligentia prasesulum religionis virtus pene abolita habebatur,* referring to Francia at the end of the sixty century.

19. Except where other references are given the section which follows is based on H. Büttner, 'Mission und Kirchenorganization des Frankenreiches bis zum Tode Karls des Grossen', in *Karl der Grosse, Lebenswerk und Nachleben: 1, Persönlichkeit und Geschichte,* ed. H. Beumann, (Düsseldorf, 1965), 454–487. See also Wallace-Hadrill (as note 1), 142–6.

20. See most recently K-U. Jäschke, 'Kolumban von Luxeuil und sein Wirken im alemannischen Raum', in *Mönchtum . . .* (as note 3), 77–130, with references to earlier literature.

21. *Ep.* 109 (Boniface to Pope Stephen II, 753); see Schieffer (as note 1), 270–1.

22. I use Westfalia as a geographical expression here; much of it was under Frankish control until the Saxon advance at the end of the seventh century.

23. H. Büttner, 'Christentum and Kirche zwischen Neckar und Main im 7. und frühen 8. Jahrhundert', in *Sankt Bonifatius* (as note 1), 362–387, here 372–9. Büttner's suggestion in 'Die Franken und die Ausbreitung des Christentums bis zu den Tagen von Bonifatius', *Hessisches Jarhbuch für Landesges-*

chichte 1 (1951), 9–24, here 22, that the bishops of Speyer were active also in Thuringia through the connexions between the monastery of Weissenburg and the monastery of St. Peter's, Erfurt, must be abandoned: see M. Werner, *Die Gründungstradition des Erfurter Petersklosters* (Sigmaringen, 1973).

24. M. Gockel, *Karolingische Königshöfe am Mittelrhein* (Göttingen, 1970), 301, has produced fresh arguments to support the old view that Rupert not only came from Worms but was bishop there.

25. On the obscure early history of the bishopric of Augsburg see F. Zoepfl, *Das Bistum Augsburg und seine Bischöfe im Mittelalter* (Augsburg, 1955) chapters 1–3, especially pp. 6–11, 21, 26–35. F. Prinz, 'Frühes Mönchtum in Südwestdeutschland und die Anfänge der Reichenau', in *Mönchtum . . .* (as note 3), 37–76, here 46–8, refers to an article by E. Klebel which I have not been able to see and to as yet unpublished excavations at St. Afra in Augsburg. He follows Klebel in dating the beginnings of the to the reign of Dagobert I, probably the 630s.

26. On Constance see H. Büttner, 'Die Entstehung der Konstanzer Diözesangrenzen', *Zeitschrift für schweizerische Kirchengeschichte* 48 (1954), 225–274; O. Feger, 'Zur Geschichte des alemannischen Herzogtums', in *Zur Geschichte der Alemannen*, ed. W. Müller (Darmstadt, 1975; article first published 1957), 151–223, here 193–219. The roles of the Roman bishopric of Chur, the Franco-Burgundian nobility, the Merovingian king and the Alemannic *dux* (but see above, note 6) in the foundation of Constance have still not been finally resolved, though it is fairly clear that the Merovingians had a hand in it.

27. Büttner, 'Christentum' (as note 23), 370. The Alemanni in Alsace were more accessible to Christianization. See also above, note 3.

28. K. Reindel, in *Handbuch der bayerischen Geschichte*, ed. M. Spindler (Munich 1967), i, 99–101, 134–143, sifts the evidence for the survival of Roman Christianity in Bavaria. See also above, note 25.

29. Reindel (as note 28), 104–5, 143. The origins of the Agilolfings have been variously claimed to have been Thuringian, Lombard, Burgundian and Frankish, but the Frankish connexions of the family are not in dispute.

30. E. Klebel, 'Zur Geschichte des Christentums in Bayern vor Bonifatius', in *Sankt Bonifatius* (as note 1), 388–411.

31. See Reindel (as note 28), 144–152, with further literature. The three came to be regarded as the 'founders' of the later bishoprics of Regensburg, Freising and Salzburg, respectively.

32. Reindel (as note 28), 151.

33. Charles relied heavily on monasteries which had been commended to him: see J. Semmler, 'Karl der Grosse und das fränkische Mönchtum', in *Karl der Grosse, Lebenswerk und Nachleben: 2, Das geistige Leben,* ed. B. Bischoff (Düsseldorf 1965), 253–289, here 261–2, 270–2, 281–7.

34. Apart from the obligation to pay tithes, made general by Charlemagne in 779, the Saxons also had to contribute land and slaves for the newly-built churches; see *MGH Cap.*, i, no. 20 c. 7, p. 48; no. 26 c. 15, p. 69. The bishoprics also required fiscal lands from the king for their foundation; on this general principle see R. Schieffer, 'Über Bischofssitz und Fiskalgut im 8. Jahrhundert', *Historisches Jahrbuch* 95 (1975), 18–32.

35. See previous note; it is assumed that the tithes referred to in the Boniface correspondence on occasions (in *Ep*. 83 of 748 from Pope Zachary to sixteen Frankish magnates, for example) were voluntary offerings. The canonical division of church revenues (see *Ep*. 18, Gregory II for Boniface, December 1, 722) made no specific provision for missionary work, though the two quarters reserved for the bishop and for his clergy could no doubt have been used to support missionaries.

36. See Schieffer (as note 1), 152, 165–6, 222–5, for Boniface's use of monasteries, and the contribution by Christopher Holdsworth to this volume.

37. *MGH Cap.*, i, no. 107 p. 222; the words translated in brackets are possibly a later addition to the text.

38. For example, feasts held in honour of the dead helped to strengthen the solidarity of kin-groups. Gregory the Great had advised Augustine of Canterbury to try to Christianize pagan practices as far as possible; H. Nottarp, 'Sachkomplex und Geist des kirchlichen Rechtsdenkens bei Bonifatius', in *Sankt Bonifatius* (as note 1), 173–196, here 196, argues, I think rightly, that Boniface had seen the undesirable consequences such a policy had had in Anglo-Saxon England, and was both much firmer and much more anxious about pagan survivals.

39. See Prinz and Heinzelmann (as note 12), and Ewig, (as note 3).

40. The phrase is that of Ewig (as note 3), 434.

41. There is as yet no modern history of the Frankish empire between 638 and 768, though one is badly needed. On the events of 714 and after see now J. Semmler, 'Zur pippinidisch-karolingischen Sukzessionskrise 714–723', *Deutsches Archiv für Erforschung des Mittelalters* 33 (1977), 1–36, who shows that Charles Martel was not fully secure even after his victories at Vincy (717) and Soissons (718).

42. Schieffer (as note 1) constantly emphasizes the hopelessness of attempts to conduct missionary work outside the Franks' sphere of influence; see for example his remarks on the early Anglo-Saxon mission, pp. 96–102.

43. On Trier see Ewig (as note 3), 413–421, 439–40.

44. Besides Ewig (as note 3) and Semmler (as note 41), see the discussion in Wallace-Hadrill (as note 1), 149.

45. This was fortuitous; the Austrasians happened to win in 687 and 718. It was not done to protect bishoprics nearest to the field of mission.

46. Ewig (as note 3), 419.

47. On Willibrord's mission see Löwe (as note 3), 227–238; Fritze (as note 2); and A. Angenendt, 'Willibrord im Dienste der Karolinger', *Annalen des historischen Vereins für den Niederrhein* 175(1973), 63–113, who shows that Willibrord was in many respects (as in his attitude to diocesan organization and monastic discipline) a more traditional figure than has been supposed; he was closely bound to the Carolingians, and was not a precursor of Boniface as a Rome-orientated church reformer.

48. Reindel (as note 28), 164–7.

49. See above, p. 81, and below, notes 65, 67.

50. See below, note 73.

51. This is the generally accepted conclusion of W. H. Fritze, 'Bonifatius und die Einbeziehung von Hessen und Thüringen in die Mainzer Diözese', *Hessisches Jahrbuch für Landesgeschichte* 4 (1954), 37–63, based on a careful re-examination of the obscure wording of *Vita*, c. 8, p. 44, on the subject.

52. The Anglo-Saxon inspiration is clear; see Levison (as note 1), 38, 82. The motivation is not. One contemporary tradition ascribes it to Carloman's remorse for his part in the butchery of the Alemanni at Cannstatt in 746. Recently the sources have been re-examined by D. Riesenberger, 'Zur Geschichte des Hausmaiers Karlmann', *Westfälische Zeitschrift* 120 (1970), 271—285, who argues that Carloman's abdication was more or less forced on him by his brother Pippin, who exploited the opposition which Carloman's support for church reform had aroused. This is not impossible, but it seems to me to overestimate the degree of opposition to reform; see above, pp. 81–4.

53. Boniface's participation in the ceremony is mentioned only in accounts of two generations later, and is therefore uncertain. The most recent discus-

sion is K-U. Jäschke, 'Bonifatius und die Königssalbung Pippins des Jüngeren', *Archiv für Diplomatik* 23 (1977), 25–54, who argues against it, and, less convincingly in my view, that Boniface was not connected with the transfer of power at all. Jäschke also gives references to the very extensive literature on the unction and change of dynasty; the best discussion is still H. Büttner, 'Aus den Anfängen des abendländischen Staatsdenkens. Die Königserhebung Pippins', *Historisches Jahrbuch* 71 (1951), 77–90.

54. The year of the martyrdom is certainly 754, as the Fulda charters show; I would accept the chronology proposed for the events of these years by L. Levillain, 'L'avènement de la dynastie Carolingienne et les origines de l'état pontifical (749–757)', *Bibliothèque de l'École des Chartes* 94 (1933), 225–295 except in this respect. In fact it is not necessary for his other arguments, as he seems to think, that the Mainz tradition of 755 for the martyrdom should be accepted.

55. Levison 78.

56. See *ep*. 63 (742–746) to his friend Bishop Daniel of Winchester, where the unreformed Frankish bishops are mentioned in the same breath as the pagans, *talibus et cum paganis* (p. 130).

57. Compare *Vita* c. 6 p. 33, c. 7 pp. 37, 40.

58. *Vita*, c. 8 p. 43.

59. See in general Nottarp (as note 38). Boniface's general concern is shown in his lists of questions sent to the papacy for definitive answers (some of these are only known from the papal answers). The 'missionary' and 'organizational' questions are mixed together with no attempt at separation or classification.

60. For Gewilib of Mainz see Wallace-Hadrill (as note 1), 145. On *praedicatio* see for example *ep*. 63, p. 130: . . . *timeo magis damnum de predicatione, quam populis inpendere debeo, si ad principem Francorum non venero; Vita*, c.7 p. 37, where Boniface's praching in Bavaria and reform of the Bavarian church in 739 are summed up as *praedicans et evangelizans verbum Dei*.

61 This is the contention of F. Flaskamp, most notably in 'Wilbrord-Clemens und Wynfrith-Bonifatius', *Sankt Bonifatius* (as note 1), 157–172, especially 164, 166–9, and more recently in 'Die frühe Friesen- und Sachsenmission aus northumbrischer Sicht. Das Zeugnis des Baeda', *Archiv für Kulturgeschichte* 51 (1969), 183–209, here 209. It rests essentially on the assumption that Boniface's attempts to lay down his office in 738 and to have a successor chosen at Mainz during his own lifetime were governed by his desire to return to Frisia; this is unprovable and seems improbable.

62. *Vita*, c.8 p. 46.

63. The fact that Bede, who had good contacts with the Frisian mission (see Flaskamp, 'Friesen- und Sachsenmission' [as note 61]), does not mention Boniface is suggestive. Dadanus, perhaps Willibrord's successor at Utrecht, attended the Concilium Germanicum, and the original plan for an Austrasian church province put Utrecht under Cologne, but the only other evidence for contact in the 740s between Boniface and the Frisian mission is *Ep*. 79 of early 748 which refers to the sending of clothes from Frisia.

64. See note 21.

65. *Ep*. 46 (c. 738) to all Anglo-Saxons asks for prayers and mentions his discussions with Gregory II and Gregory III. Ep. 21 from a Pope Gregory to the 'Old Saxons' calling for their conversion is usually dated to this period as well, and I am not convinced by the attempt of R. Rau in his bilingual edition of the Boniface sources *(Briefe des Bonifatius. Willibalds Leben des Bonifatius*, Ausgewählte Quellen zur deutschen Geschichte des Mittelalters IVb, Darmstadt, 1968), 21 note 1 to argue that it belongs to the time of Boniface's second journey to Rome in 722. The only other pieces of possible

evidence for Boniface's activity among the Saxons are *epp*. 43 (c. 738, Gregory III to the nobles and people of six named tribes) and 86 (751, Boniface to Pope Zachary). Some of the tribes mentioned in *ep*. 43 *may* have been Saxon or under Saxon rule, though as *ep*. 21 of the same time is addressed to the Saxons this seems improbable (on the interpretation of the names of the tribes see D. Grossmann, 'Wesen und Wirken des Bonifatius, besonders in Hessen und Thüringen', *Hessisches Jahrbuch für Landesgeschichte* 6[1956], 232–253, here 236–9). The four peoples mentioned in *ep*. 86 as being the subject of Boniface's missionary work are more likely to have been tribes around Fulda than Saxons, Hessians, Thuringians and Bavarians (so Rau, 290 note 5). Other attempts to show Boniface's connexion with Saxony, either through 'proving' the genuineness of bogus papal letters or through accepting the historicity of 'local traditions', have not inspired confidence; see the harsh but just comments of F. Flaskamp, 'Der Bonifatiusbrief von Herford', *Archiv für Kulturgeschichte* 44 (1962), 315–334, especially 321–2, 326–8.

66. *Ep*. 63, p. 130.

67. There were campaigns in 718, 720, 722(?), 724, 729(?), 738, 743, 744, 748 and 753; the chronology is frequently uncertain and needs a fresh investigation. Baptisms are mentioned by the continuator of Fredegar in connexion with the campaigns of 744, 748 and 753, but this seems unlikely; mass baptisms were used by Charlemagne in the 770s and 782s, but are not reported of earlier Carolingians in their campaigns against the Alemanni or Frisians. We would also expect to find traces of such events in Boniface's correspondence, but there are none, nor is there archeological evidence for Saxon conversions before the second half of the eight century (cf. K. Weidemann, 'Die frühe Christianisierung zwischen Schelde und Elbe im Spiegel der Grabsitten des 7. bis 9. Jahrhunderts', in *Die Eingliederung der Sachsen in das Frankenreich*, ed. W. Lammers [Darmstadt, 1970: article first published in 1966], 389–415).

68. I have not dealt with the various 'heretics' who appear in Boniface's correspondence. J. B. Russell, 'Saint Boniface and the Eccentrics', *Church History* 33 (1964), 235–247 gives an account which makes them out to be perhaps too harmless; I agree with S. Epperlein, *Herrschaft und Volk im karolingischen Imperium* (E. Berlin, 1969), 179–84, that they and their doctrines were a serious threat to Boniface and the Frankish church.

69. Above, p. 79.

70. *Ep*. 22 (723); see Wallace-Hadrill (as note 1), 147.

71. See c. 4 of the council of Les Estinnes (*MGH Cap*., i, no. 11 p. 28) and above, note 12.

72. *Ep*. 28, p. 50 (Gregory III to Boniface): *precipimus, ut iuxta sacrorum canonum statuta, ubi multitudo excrevit fidelium, ex vigore apostolicae sedis debeas ordinare episcopos, pia tamen contemplatione, ut non vilescat dignitas episcopatus*. The reference is to an old canonical provision, appropriate for Mediterranean Christianity, that bishoprics should only be erected in cities, not in villages. On the trouble it caused Boniface in the very different conditions of Hesse and Thuringia see Nottarp (as note 38), 174, 184.

73. The problem lies in the date of consecration of the three new bishops and the date of the Concilium Germanicum, which at least two of them attended. The date of consecration of Willibald can be worked out from his life as October 21, 741, and the Concilium Germanicum is dated April 21, 742. This seems straightforward, but accepting it leads to difficulties in the dating of Boniface's correspondence with Zachary, and also means that we have to assume that Charles Martel, who died in October 741, gave his consent to the new foundations. Schieffer, *Angelsachsen* (as note 1), 1463–71, argued therefore that the new bishoprics were founded under Carloman in

742 and that the Concilium Germanicum took place in 743. H. Löwe, 'Bonifatius und die bayerisch-fränkische Spannung', *Jahrbuch für fränkische Landesforschung* 15 (1955), 85–127, here 110–120, argued for the traditional dating, and for a 'change of course' by Charles Martel, perhaps under the influence of his Bavarian wife Swanahild. Recently K-U. Jäschke, 'Die Gründung der mitteldeutschen Bistümer und das Jahr des Concilium Germanicum', in *Festschrift für Walter Schlesinger* (Cologne, 1974), ii, 71–136, argued for 741 for the foundations and 743 for the Concilium Germanicum. These are the three possibilities; none is without chronological difficulties. They can be defended on a variety of different grounds, however, and almost all writers on the subject have assumed in their arguments that we know far more about Charles Martel's attitudes than we do. In fact we know nothing, unless the foundations of the bishoprics can be definitely shown to have taken place in either 741 or 742 without the use of arguments based on what Charles Martel is supposed to have done or thought. No-one has yet succeeded in doing this.

74. See R. Schieffer (as note 34), especially p. 30.

75. Charles Martel's expedition against the Saxons in 738 was of great importance for the mission in Thuringia and Hesse: see *ep*. 45 (Gregory III to Boniface, October 29, 739), p. 72, and M. Lintzel, 'Karl Martells Sachsenkrieg im Jahre 738 und die Missionstätigkeit des Bonifatius', *Sachsen und Anhalt* 13 (1937), 59–65. It is worth noting that the gap between the initial period of missionary work and the erection of bishoprics was about the same in Saxony at the end of the eighth century as it was for Boniface in Hesse and Thuringia; such things took time.

76. See note 51. Büttner, 'Christentum' (as note 7), 386, argues that the bishops of Worms and Speyer did not take part in the Concilium Germanicum because of their hostility to the newly-founded bishopric of Würzburg, which cut across their interests. This is possible.

77. Levison 18–22.

78. The history of the proposals can be found in *epp*. 57 (Zachary to Boniface, June 22, 744), pp. 102–3; 58 (Zachary to Boniface, November 5, 744), p. 106; and 86 (Boniface to Zachary, summer 751), p. 193. See Levison 87–8.

79. Levison 87, 234–5.

80. Zachary to Pippin (January 5, 747), *MGH Epp*., iii, 480.

81. The first proposal and the compromise are in *MGH Cap*., i, no. 10 c. 1, p. 25 (Concilium Germanicum); no. 11 c. 2, p. 28 (council of Les Estinnes). See also the Neustrian version of the compromise in Pippin's council of Soissons in 744 *(MGH Cap.,* i, no. 12 c. 3, p. 29). Zachary's comment is *ep*. 60 (October 31, 745), p. 123. How far even the compromise was effective is a question which needs further investigation: see Wallace-Hadrill (as note 1), 149 note 70.

82. See Zachary's reply, *ep*. 87, p. 198; on Milo see Ewig (as note 3), 413–21. The statement by Wallace-Hadrill (as note 1), 143, that 'it was [Milo's] hunting that annoyed Boniface' seems to rest on Boniface's complaint about (unnamed) bishops in *ep*. 50 to Zachary (742), p. 83; but Zachary's words in *ep*. 87 'they do much harm to the churches of God' could well mean other (and worse) things.

83. *Ep*.16, p. 29; see M. Tangl, 'Studien zur Neuausgabe der Bonifatiusbriefe, I', *Neues Archiv der Gesellschaft für ältere Geschichtskunde* 40 (1916), 639–790, here 742.

84. See *epp*. 24, p. 42; 26, p. 47; 50, pp. 82–3; 60, pp. 121–2; 63, pp. 129–30; 80, pp. 175–6; 86, pp. 192–3 (nos. 24, 26, 60 and 80 are papal replies to letters by Boniface).

85. On Agilolf see W. Levison, 'Bischof Agilolf von Köln und seine Passio', in *Aus rheinischer und fränkischer Frühzeit* (Düsseldorf, 1948; article first published in 1929), 76–95, here 77–8. For the name see Gockel (as note 24), 238–242, 278 and note 562, 308 (on the connexion between Agilolf's probable family and Gerold and Gewilib of Mainz). I know of no evidence to support the statement by Schieffer (as note 1), 223, that Boniface's followers resented Agilolf.

86. Gockel (as note 24), 298 and note 739.

87. *Ep*.87 (Zachary to Boniface, November 4, 751) refers to two bishops without naming them. These cannot both be Gewilib of Mainz, though one of them probably is.

88. The last case before that of Gewilib is probably that of Salonius of Embrun and Sagittarius of Gap, who were deposed at the council of Chalon-sur-Saône in 579; even here political charges and the king's intervention were needed to finish them off. See Gregory of Tours, *Historia Francorum (MGH SRM* 1.1, edd. B. Krusch and W. Levison) v, 20, 27.

89. See *Vita*, c.8, p. 45: *quia sanctus vir, infirmitate corporis praegravatus, synodalia conciliorum conventicula per omnia adire non poterat . . .*, which need not just refer to the synod of 747.

90. For Fulrad see *ep*. 93 of 752; for Chrodegang see Schieffer, *Angelsachsen* (as note 1), 1456–9, who seems to me to infer a distance between the two men which need not have existed.

91. See note 53 for the change of dynasty, and Wallace-Hadrill (as note 1), 145–6, for the translation of St Kilian.

92. J. Haller, *Das Papsttum: Idee und Wirklichkeit, I: Die Grundlagen* (Third edn., Munich, 1965), 339–40; see also 283–299 for his account of the Anglo-Saxon mission.

93. K. Hallinger, 'Römische Voraussetzungen der bonifatianischen Wirksamkeit im Frankenreich', in *Sankt Bonifatius* (as note 1), 320–361; see 320–3 for his discussion of Haller; E. Ewig, 'Der Petrus- und Apostelkult im spätrömischen und fränkischen Gallien', *Zeitschrift für Kirchengeschichte* 71 (1960), 215–251.

94. Wallace-Hadrill (as note 1), 141; cf. Haller (as note 92), 271–9.

95. Effectively demolished by Schieffer, *Angelsachsen* (as note 1), 1435–1443, who argued that this was the result of projecting the attitudes of the Investiture Contest back into eighth-century history.

96. W. H. Fritze, 'Universalis gentium confessio', *Frühmittelalterliche Studien* 3 (1969), 78–130, has argued that from the seventh century onwards the papacy did indeed actively propagate the idea of mission to all peoples as a general task for the church, and contrasts this with the ties of common origin which are supposed to have motivated the Anglo-Saxon missionaries in particular. I think he overstates his case; but in any case, the history of Boniface's mission shows that the popes, whatever views they may have held about the desirability of mission, knew little about the practical difficulties involved (see for example above, note 72), and could do not more than give help when it was asked for. This they did freely, but they could not initiate.

97. Grimoald: E. Ewig, 'Noch einmal zum "Staatsstreich" Grimoalds', in *Speculum Historiale. Festschrift für Johannes Spörl* (Freiburg, 1965), 454–7; R. Schneider, *Königswahl und Königserhebung im Frühmittelalter* (Stuttgart, 1972), 151–3. The intention is clear, even if the precise sequence of events is not. Pippin and Liutprand: Löwe (as note 73) 105 and note 101.

THE CHURCH IN CREDITON FROM SAINT BONIFACE TO THE REFORMATION

Nicholas Orme

CHAPTER 5

The Church in Crediton from Saint Boniface to the Reformation

The history of Crediton Church is one of the oldest in Devon. It can be traced continuously in written records back to at least the tenth century: something that is not surpassed by any other religious institution in the county, with the possible exception of Exeter Cathedral. During its history the church has had three different constitutional bases. It was a cathedral from about 910 to 1050, a collegiate and parish church from 1050 to 1545, and since 1545 it has been a parish church alone. The present study is concerned with the first and second of these periods, and with the beginning of the third. The first, in which Crediton was the seat of a bishop, is undoubtedly the time for which it is most famous and when it achieved its greatest importance. Unfortunately, this is also the least recorded phase of its history. The relevant sources are scarce and their authenticity is open to question. The indisputable facts which they contain are few and simple.[1]

The earliest event of Church history usually associated with Crediton is the birth of St Boniface in about the year 675 or 680. The association, however, is not based on any contemporary information. The tradition that Boniface was born in Crediton is not recorded until the 1330s, nearly six hundred years after the death of the saint.[2] Even if it is true, it tells us nothing about religion in Crediton in the late seventh century, except that Christian Saxons already lived there, since Boniface was educated in a monastery at Exeter and passed the rest of his life away from Devon.[3] He has come to exercise a profound influence on the Church in Crediton since the fourteenth century, but in his own time, as far as we know, he had none. Next and more tangible is the evidence of a charter of 739 in which Aethelheard, king of the West Saxons, granted twenty hides of land at Crediton to Bishop Forthhere of Sherborne 'to build a monastery'.[4] The surviving text of the charter was not written until about 1069, however, and its reliability is not certain in all respects. There is nothing improbable about the grant of land, but there is no evidence that the monastery was ever founded. We have to wait until the tenth century for positive proof of a church in Crediton. In 909, or thereabouts, Devon and Cornwall, which had hitherto formed part of the large diocese of Sherborne, were separated from it and given a bishop of their own. Crediton was chosen as his seat soon afterwards. It may have been selected, if the charter of 739 is authentic, because it was already the centre of a large episcopal estate, which presumably became transferred from the bishop of Sherborne to the new bishop of Devon. The site was certainly a good geographical one. It lay close to the centre of Devon, with access to the Exeter region, to the north of the county, and to Cornwall. An old Roman route stretches westwards from Crediton through Okehampton to Launceston, and this was probably still in use.

Ten bishops ruled at Crediton between 909 and 1050,[5] for most of which time their jurisdiction stretched over both Devon and Cornwall. Although a series of bishops of Cornwall began to be appointed in about 926, these at first were only *chorepiscopi* or suffragans of the bishop of Crediton. A separate diocese of Cornwall was formed in 994 but it remained fully independent for only a short time. In the 1020s the bishop of Crediton was also appointed to Cornwall, and thereafter the two sees were held in plurality. The bishop's seat at Crediton in the tenth and eleventh centuries lay in the middle of the large episcopal estate already mentioned, with a population both of free tenants and slaves. The bishops had a house or palace there, which was their principal but not their permanent residence, and which they visited frequently with their travelling household of clergy and lay servants. Near the palace was the church, in which the bishop worshipped and held ecclesiastical ceremonies. As time went on this church acquired its own resident staff of clergy, distinct from the bishop's household, and its own endowments, separate from his. This was the case by 1012 when Bishop Aelfwold of Crediton died leaving land at Sandford to the church, together with three service books and a mass vestment.[6] The clergy were of the kind later to be known as 'secular canons'. We do not possess any direct evidence about their way of life, but it was certainly looser and less organised than that of monks. They were able to move freely about the world and to own private property. Under Bishop Lyfing (1027–1046), who was also bishop of Worcester and must have been frequently absent, it is likely that the Crediton clergy acquired a good deal of autonomy.

Some of them may well have lived in private houses and even have married.

This state of affairs did not please Leofric, who succeeded Lyfing as bishop of Devon and Cornwall in 1046. Leofric was a well-educated, widely travelled man, and an active supporter of Church reform. He soon conceived the idea of creating an entirely new cathedral by moving his seat from Crediton into the monastery of St Peter in Exeter, and establishing there a reformed body of canons. In about 1049 Leofric wrote to the pope, Leo IX, requesting approval for the change, asserting that Crediton was a mere village, unsuitable for the seat of a bishop, whereas Exeter was a walled city. The pope agreed and wrote to the English king, Edward the Confessor, requesting him to carry out the project. In 1050 Edward came in person to Exeter, attended the enthronement of Leofric in the new cathedral, and issued a charter approving the translation of the see.[7] The charter contains a second reason for the change. Exeter, it avers, would provide better protection for the bishop against pirates who had devastated the church at Crediton. A third unstated reason was probably that Leofric, who wished his cathedral to be staffed by a well-regulated body of clergy living under strict rules, realised that he could not mould the canons of Crediton to this end. There is no evidence that Leofric moved them to Exeter into his new foundation; on the contrary, he is likely to have made a fresh start with new personnel. The church and community at Crediton were left there, and probably continued to function along traditional lines.

The removal of the see to Exeter deprived Crediton of its chief distinction. Henceforward it became what it remains: only one among the lesser towns of Devon. The period of the bishopric was never forgotten and came in later times to be seen, perhaps mistakenly, as a golden age. Bishops especially, when dealing with the affairs of the church in Crediton, lamented what they asserted to be its sad decline from earlier splendour. Yet apart from the loss of the see, most of the other local institutions remained after 1050 much as they had done before. The bishops kept their estate which, after the Conquest, came to be known as the manor of Crediton. They also retained their palace on the north-east side of the church, which they went on visiting frequently until the Reformation, as they travelled between their various dwelling places in the diocese. The church survived as well, and so did its college of canons, the existence of whom is mentioned under each of Leofric's two successors: Osbern (1072–1107) and William Warelwast

(1107–1137).[8] At first the church was known by the name of St Mary, the present dedication to the Holy Cross coming into use only after the 1230s. As a parochial system grew up in England during the twelfth century, it became a parish church as well as a house of clergy. A parish of Crediton emerged, based on the manor, whose inhabitants became entitled to worship in the church and obliged to contribute to its support. Like the manor the parish enjoyed a direct relationship with the bishop. It was not associated with the other parishes in the neighbourhood, but constituted a peculiar jurisdiction outside the control of the diocesan consistory court and the local archdeacon, having its own church court and its own rural dean.[9] The revenues of the manor and parish came to be shared between the bishop and the college of canons. The bishop received most of the temporal rents and dues from the manor, as well as certain tithes of hay and of mills in the parish. The college enjoyed the majority of the tithes and all the other religious dues and offerings. In 1535 on the eve of the Reformation, when comprehensive information first survives, the bishop's revenues from Crediton were valued at just over £146 gross and those of the college at about £225 gross.[10]

By about 1100 the staff of the college consisted of eighteen canons who were probably appointed by the bishop, as was certainly the case from the thirteenth century onwards. The canons were a community of equals, electing their own presiding officer or 'provost' whom the bishop then confirmed in office. Bishop William Warelwast (1107–1137), who approved these customs, also permitted the number of canons to be reduced to twelve, on the grounds that the church had become too poor to support eighteen.[11] After this reduction and likely during the twelfth century, the twelve canons followed the usual practice in English collegiate churches and secular cathedrals of dividing up the revenues of the foundation into prebends of unequal value. This differed from the system at Exeter Cathedral where, under the influence of Leofric's reforms, the revenues were shared between the canons on an equal basis.[12] Each of the Crediton prebends consisted of the tithes of a particular district within the parish, and eventually the prebends came to be known by the name of the chief farm or estate within these districts. The names of the twelve prebends, in their modern forms, were Aller, Creedy, Cross, Henstill, Kerswell, Pool, Priestcombe, Rudge, Stowford, West Sandford, Woodland, and Woolsgrove. There once existed in the archives of the college a register called the 'Red Book', in which the endowments of the prebends were all carefully written down.[13]

Unfortunately, this book is no longer extant and all that survive are the entries relating to the prebends of Cross and Priestcombe, which were copied out in 1443 during the adjudication of a dispute. They read like a roll-call of the local farms and hamlets, some of them lost but others still inhabited today. The prebendary of Cross, we are told, received all the greater and lesser tithes of the tenants of East Neopardy, West Neopardy, Yeoford, Keymelford, *Northebykemore*, a ferling of land in Uton formerly held by Luke of Uton, and of all the tenants of the prebend in West Sandford and Crediton. The prebendary of Priestcombe had the greater and lesser tithes of all of his own tenants in Sandford and Crediton, and of all the tenants of Hollacombe, Yeo, Uton (excepting the land of Luke of Uton), *Sothbykemore*, Curtlake, *Westebeakelegh*, and *Westera*. He also enjoyed the tithes of a close of land at Moor called *Dogetysperk* and of a certain hill in the western part of the waterland of Winstode. The value of these and the other prebendal endowments is first recorded in the papal taxation assessment of 1291.[14] This estimated the wealthiest (Woolsgrove) to be worth £4 a year and the poorest (Creedy and West Sandford) each £2. The rest all lay between.

Each canon-prebendary (if he were resident) lived in a separate dwelling house beside the church in Crediton, and might possess other buildings such as barns for the storage of his tithe produce. He was expected to keep these structures in repair, and in later centuries we find the bishops intervening to impose the duty on those who neglected it.[15] By the second half of the thirteenth century, however, it is manifest that most of the prebendaries had ceased to be resident. They stayed away from Crediton and 'farmed' or leased their tithes to local laymen who paid them an agreed annual sum and then collected the tithes at a profit. This situation probably arose in the twelfth century and lasted throughout the rest of the college's history down to the Reformation. It arose for three reasons. First, the location of Crediton, after the see was moved, became peripheral and unattractive. Second, each prebendary was allowed to receive his income whether or not he was present, and the revenues of the college were so fully divided between the prebendaries that little or nothing remained as a surplus to be given to those who resided. Third, the duty of residence was not enforced by the bishops. They found the prebends, which lay in their gift and carried minimal duties, a valuable means of rewarding their relatives and servants, or those of the king and other great magnates. For all these reasons the college at Crediton developed at an early date into a fund of stipends for non-resident canons, rather than a community of canons who resided.

The departure of most of the canons was no less important for the college's history than that of the bishop. One of its effects was probably the decline of the office of provost, which is last mentioned in 1250.[16] Instead, the college evolved or acquired two new officers: a precentor, responsible for organising the choral services, and a treasurer in charge of the goods of the church.[17] Both the precentor and the treasurer were canons appointed by the bishop, and each office was attached to a prebend, the precentor occupying the wealthiest one (Woolsgrove) and the treasurer the third wealthiest (Kerswell). By the end of the thirteenth century the precentor had become the titular head of the college. The replacement of an elected provost by a precentor whom the bishop appointed is a clear sign of the decreasing involvement of the canons in the college's affairs. They had little interest in electing the head of an organisation from which they merely drew their stipends. Nor did they suffer from the demise of the provostship, since the new precentor held little authority over them. He remained the titular senior and presided at chapter meetings (unless he too were non-resident), but that was all. Another result of the canons' absence was to cause difficulty in maintaining the church buildings, since nothing was allocated from the college revenues for this purpose. This was met, by the 1220s, by the imposition of a tax on each incoming canon for the benefit of the fabric, equal to the whole of the first year's income of his prebend.[18] In 1253 Bishop Blondy permitted, by way of recompense, that every canon who died in office should receive the revenues of his prebend for one year after his death.[19] This latter arrangement copied a similar one in use at Exeter Cathedral. Henceforward the successor of every dead canon faced the loss of two years' revenues: one to his predecessor's executors and one to the fabric. Only when these had been paid could he lawfully enjoy the full benefits of his prebend.

In place of the absent canons a body of deputy clergy came into existence, probably during the twelfth century, in order to carry out the daily round of services in the choir of the college. These were the vicars choral.[20] No doubt they would have evolved even if the canons had resided, as happened at Exeter Cathedral, since most English secular canons were ceasing to attend the whole of the daily worship in their churches by the end of the twelfth century, and were hiring vicars to do so instead. By the middle of the thirteenth, when they are first mentioned in records, the Crediton vicars were twelve in number: one for each canon.[21] They were not statutorily bound to be priests, but it is probable that most were of this grade by at least the fourteenth century.[22] Who appointed them is obscure, but seems likely to have been the precentor or the resident canons. All the vicars had to participate in the whole round of daily services in the church. At first they lived dispersedly in separate houses or chambers in the neighbourhood, wherever they pleased. Their stipends probably came from the minor ecclesiastical revenues of the college: the offerings made in the church, the mortuary goods of dead parishioners, and some of the lesser tithes of the parish.[23] In 1272 the value of their stipends was 20s. each.[24] One of the vicars also acted as curate of the parish, with the responsibility for providing such services as baptisms, weddings, and funerals. He received by 1334 a double stipend in return for these extra duties, and was assisted in his ministrations by two parish clerks.[25] The clerks are mentioned throughout the later middle ages.

The institutions which we have just surveyed evolved between the beginning of the twelfth century and the middle of the thirteenth. By the latter period the college had acquired several of its permanent later features. Most of the canons were absentees, most of the revenues of the college consequently passed out of the parish, and the resident clergy were chiefly made up of poorly paid vicars. In turn this situation stimulated attempts to reform the college and to increase the size and quality of the resident community. As early as the late twelfth century Bishop John (1186–1191) gave the college his tithes of hay and of mills in Crediton '*ad panem communem*' – presumably to support a common table or to distribute food to those who resided.[26] The most ambitious scheme of improvement, however, was carried out by Bishop Walter Branscombe between about 1269 and 1272. He began, before 1269, by appropriating to the college the revenues of the rectory of Egloshayle in Cornwall; next, in 1269 he appropriated the rectory of Coldridge in Devon for the support of the vicars; finally in 1272, discovering the revenues of Egloshayle to be insufficient, he replaced them by the revenues of a wealthier Cornish church: Lelant.[27] Branscombe's objectives, by means of these endowments, were fourfold. First, he restored the number of canons to the original total of eighteen by instituting six new bursal prebends, each holder of which received a cash stipend of £4 a year from the revenues of Lelant. Second, he increased the vicars to the same number by six additional appointments with stipends of 20s., also out of Lelant. Third, he tried to encourage more of the canons to visit Crediton by ordering the remaining income from Lelant to be distributed in small daily portions to those who were resident. Fourth, he increased the stipends of all the vicars by dividing the revenues of Coldridge equally among them. Since Coldridge was estimated to be worth £6.13s.4d. in 1291,[28] this would have benefited each vicar by about a further 6s. 8d.

The success of Branscombe's reforms, unfortunately, was limited. The six bursal prebends remained in existence until the Reformation, and the six extra vicars probably did so down to the Black Death. But Branscombe's inducements failed to persuade the absent canons to return. This is apparent from the actions of Thomas Bitton, the next bishop of Exeter to involve himself with the college on a large scale. In 1304 Bitton drew up a set of statutes for its government, not introducing new principles but codifying the customs of earlier years.[29] In particular he tried to bring order into the daily distributions of money which Branscombe had provided. Each canon was to be entitled to 4d. for each day on which he attended at least one of the choral services. Bitton especially urged the precentor to reside, and gave him the duty of supervising the distributions if he were present. He also regulated the holding of chapter meetings and laid down procedures for informing the absent canons about forthcoming business. Yet Bitton, like Branscombe, shrank from imposing residence by force. No doubt he perceived that the custom of absence was too well established to be changed, and would weaken his fund of patronage even if change were possible. Indeed, his statutes assumed that very few canons would reside. If the precentor were not available to supervise the daily distributions, two resident canons must do so. If no canon were resident, two trustworthy vicars must be chosen instead. Vicars were also to be appointed to administer the money contributed by the canons towards the church fabric. The latter was evidently causing problems. The absent canons were neglecting to hand over their first years' income for the purpose, and had sometimes failed to do so even when they died. As a counter measure, the bishop ordered that when a canon failed to pay his quota in his lifetime, a double rate should be charged upon his executors.

The successor of Bitton, Bishop Stapledon (1307–1326), scarcely involved himself in the affairs of Crediton Church except to give it a small endowment to pray for his soul.[30] It was not until the episcopate of Bishop Grandisson (1327–1369) that major new attempts were made to reform the college. By this stage the bishop's objectives had undergone change. Grandisson did not concern himself with the residence of the canons in general, which he evidently regarded as a lost cause. Instead, he concentrated his efforts on making two of them reside – the precentor and treasurer – and on increasing the efficiency of the lesser clergy, whose residence could be taken for granted. Grandisson issued two reforming statutes for the college, with a wide interval between them. The first, in 1334, set out to improve the standard of worship in the college and the pastoral care of the parishioners.[31] Hitherto the choir of the college had been chiefly staffed by the vicars and the music of the services must have been mainly confined to plainsong. Grandisson now enlarged the resources of the choir by the addition of four secondary clerks – young men with adult voices – and four choristers. This made it possible for the choir to tackle polyphonic music in several parts, and brought the college into line with the cathedral and with the bishop's own foundation at Ottery St Mary which also had the threefold orders of vicars, secondaries, and boys. Each clerk possessed a further special duty: one to be sacrist in charge of the church's books and ornaments, one to ring the bells, one to look after the offerings of money and wax at the high altar, and one to teach song to the choristers. They each received 26s. 8d. a year, and the boys each 17s. 4d. These sums, together with the other costs of worship, were found by instituting a new tax on each of the prebendaries, thereby increasing the proportion of the church's revenues that stayed in Crediton. Henceforward each prebend had to pay a graduated contribution of between 2s. and 16s. per annum, according to its wealth. Next, Grandisson improved the status of the vicar who acted as curate of the parish. He took the appointment into his own hands, and for the rest of the middle ages the office was filled by the bishop.[32] The parochial vicar was allowed to be absent from the choral services when this was made necessary by his pastoral duties, except on solemn festivals. His emoluments were also increased.[33] Hitherto he had received the profits of two vicarships and a little besides: perhaps about £6.13s.8d in all. Grandisson took away the vicarships, which he applied to the maintenance of the clerks and boys, and compensated the parochial vicar with a miscellaneous group of lesser tithes, offerings and monetary dues which in 1535 brought in the considerable total of £29.5s.4d.[34] This made the parochial vicarship into a very attractive benefice. Its status rose, and by 1409 the occupant was retaining a parish chaplain to assist him with his work.[35] During the fourteenth century the term 'parochial vicar' came to be supplemented by the title 'dean' of Crediton. This was not by analogy with the dean of a cathedral, but referred to another of the parochial vicar's functions: that of acting as rural dean of the parish. It nevertheless conferred a certain distinction upon its holders, and they were careful to use the title.

In 1349 Crediton, like the rest of England, was stricken by the Black Death with serious results. Contemporary evidence about the impact of the plague on the college is not available, but later documents suggest that it had profound and lasting consequences which endured throughout the rest of the medieval period. The effect on the prebends, it is true, does not appear to have been very great. They remained in their original numbers, with similar stipends, and so did the customary absence of their holders. The chief impact of the plague was borne by the resident community of vicars and clerks. Until the Black Death there had been a plentiful supply of clergy in the diocese of Exeter, as elsewhere in England. In 1308, for example, when Bishop Stapledon held the first ordination of his reign, in Crediton itself, he ordained over a thousand males to the five grades of holy orders on one single occasion.[36] All these clergy wanted posts, even with the small stipends offered at places like Crediton where it is likely that each vicar was being paid about £2.14s.2d. in 1334: twice as much as the clerks.[37] It is reasonable to suppose that the full complement of eighteen vicars (sixteen after 1334) was fully maintained in the early fourteenth century, as well as that of Grandisson's four new clerkships. After 1349, however, all this changed. The large number of clerical deaths created a surplus of benefices, many of them rectories and parochial vicarages with greater emoluments and better status than choral vicarships and clerkships, and candidates for these inferior posts became difficult to find. It is therefore likely that the plague first caused deaths among the resident clergy at Crediton and then made it difficult to fill the vacancies. By 1361 Grandisson was complaining that the surviving vicars were actively resisting the filling of the empty places, so that they could each receive a larger share of the common revenues.[38] Interpreted more charitably, this shows that the vicars were trying to raise their standard of living nearer to the level enjoyed by clergy elsewhere. It looks as though by 1361 the number of vicars had fallen from sixteen to ten or less, and that the pre-plague total was never again achieved.[39] As for the clerks, we never hear of more than two after 1334, and it is probable that here too the stipends attracted few applicants after 1349.

It was against this background that Grandisson issued his second set of statutes for the college in 1361.[40] He began by extending his reforms to the major clergy of the college, with an order that the two dignitaries – the precentor and the treasurer should both keep residence. Branscombe and Bitton had urged the precentor to do so, but they had stopped short of an absolute commandment and they had not included the treasurer in this connection. Grandisson therefore established a new principle by insisting that both dignitaries should reside in person, though he allowed them sixteen days of absence every quarter provided they were not away together. The precentor, as well as supervising the choir, was given disciplinary powers over the vicars and other minor clergy. The treasurer's traditional duty of looking after the goods of the church was restated, and he was awarded an extra stipend of £4 as a palliative for having to live in Crediton. The rest of the statutes were concerned with the minor clergy and with the consequences of the plague. Although Grandisson grumbled that the surviving vicars were greedy and dishonest, he was nevertheless aware that they had to be offered a higher standard of living, given the better rewards available to clergy in general. He therefore laid down that they should each receive £4 a year paid quarterly, which seems to have been a definite improvement on their previous stipends. In addition, whereas they had hitherto lived separately and by themselves, 'to the occasion of many scandals', he now provided – apparently at his own expense – a common dwelling in which they could live and eat together. This reflected a general movement at cathedrals and collegiate churches in the fourteenth century to gather the lesser clergy into special accommodation where they could be better housed under closer supervision.[41] A similar community was also established for the vicars choral of Exeter, but not until twenty-two years later in 1387.[42]

One other respect remains to be mentioned in which Grandisson reshaped the Church in Crediton for the future. This was his introduction or revival of the cult of St Boniface. In about the 1330s Grandisson compiled his *Legenda*: a collection of lessons to be read at mattins in Exeter Cathedral throughout the year. It is here, in the first lesson for 5 June, that we find the earliest statement that Boniface was born in Crediton.[43] Where, may we ask, did Grandisson discover this information? Did he read about it in a life of St Boniface? Was it a living memory in Crediton? Or did he conceive the idea himself, on the basis of his knowledge of Church history? The evidence is slender, but inclines to the third interpretation. We do not find references to Boniface's birthplace in any of the early lives of him which survive today, and it seems unlikely that any such reference was available to Grandisson. Nor is there any sign of a cult of Boniface in Crediton before the bishop's reign. The earliest evidence of the cult comes from 1334 in Grandisson's document reforming the office of dean, which mentions an altar in the church dedicated to St Boniface.[44] It is significant that this altar is never again recorded, although we possess several later references to the altars in Crediton church. This suggests that the cult was not based on a living local tradition, but was introduced to Crediton by Grandisson and did not at first attract much local interest. There were probably no relics of Boniface to accompany it, and there was nothing to commend the cult to unfamiliar people above those of the better-known bishops and martyrs. Nevertheless, since Grandisson's time, a slowly developing interest in Boniface can be traced in Devon. The story of the saint's birth at Crediton is likely to have been read each year at Exeter Cathedral on his feast day, down to the Reformation. It is recorded by the early Devon antiquaries, Thomas Westcote and Tristram Risdon, in the 1630s,[45] and they transmitted it to later local historians. Since the middle of the nineteenth century, the cult of St Boniface in Crediton has grown steadily. His feast has been revived, centenary celebrations have been held in his honour, and a Catholic church has been dedicated to him. The tradition of his association with Crediton, whatever the truth on which it was based, has itself become a truth and is now widely accepted. The connection of many more famous saints with their shrines rests on no firmer foundations.

Grandisson's reforms established the framework in which Crediton collegiate church functioned for the remaining 200 years of its history. Further statutes were indeed issued for it by at least three later bishops, but these merely repeated the earlier customs and ordinances, or made a few alterations of detail; they introduced no changes of principle. The major clergy of the college, down to the Reformation, went on consisting of eighteen prebendaries, of whom only the precentor, the treasurer, and possibly one or two others were resident.[46] The minor clergy included a small number of vicars, clerks and choristers, totalling about a dozen. In 1409 Nicholas Bubwith, bishop of Bath and Wells, and four other persons granted properties to the college to maintain two extra choristers, which accounts for the number of boys in later times being sometimes reckoned as four and sometimes as six.[47] In 1438 Bishop Lacy, concerned by the poor attendance of some of the minor clergy at services, issued a statute reiterating Grandisson's reforms and laying down a detailed list of fines for absences.[48] In 1492, at the metropolitical visitation of Exeter diocese by Archbishop John Morton, the deputy visitor who came to Crediton found the precentor, the treasurer and the dean all residing, but the complement of vicars, which ought to have been sixteen, reduced to only six.[49] A few years later in 1511 Bishop Oldham characterised the college as being ruined and deformed, equally with regard to the conduct of services, the provision of ornaments for carrying them out, and the condition of the church roof.[50] He ordered that more care should be taken to see that the prebendaries paid their contributions to the fabric, that the two resident dignitaries should lose part of their emoluments if they were absent, and that the minor clergy should include at least six vicars, two secondary clerks, and four boys. One of the clerks was to teach the choristers and look after the organs, while the other rang the bells and cared for the clock. Oldham's commands do not seem to have been very effective. Only eleven years later the next bishop, John Veysey, found the vicars reduced to four, the clerks to one, and the boys to two. This caused him to issue the last pre-Reformation statutes for the college in 1523, in which he edited all the enactments of previous bishops into one harmonious code.[51] He enumerated the duties of the precentor and treasurer, the contributions to be made by the prebendaries, and the numbers and stipends of the minor clergy. The latter were to consist of six vicars with £7.6s.8d. each, two secondaries (the teacher of the choristers with £6.13s.4d. and the bell-ringer with £6), and six boys with £1.6s.8d. each. Veysey concluded with a reiteration of the tasks and emoluments of the dean. The college continued to be governed by this code, in theory at least, until the dissolution in 1545.

The people who staffed the college during the fourteenth, fifteenth and early sixteenth centuries can be separated into three categories: the non-resident canons or prebendaries, the resident dignitaries, and the minor clergy. The prebends, as we have seen, were filled by the bishop who found them suitable posts for his servants and kinsfolk, and for the protégés of other important people who asked him for favours and promotions. The prebendaries of the later middle ages were consequently a mixture of diocesan officials, royal clerks, and wealthy clergy of noble birth or good connections. Nearly all of them occupied other benefices besides their prebends, and they spent their lives in Exeter, London, or elsewhere. A few of them were men of national importance. One such in the early fourteenth century was Adam Murimuth, the diplomatist and chronicler, and the end of the middle ages saw prebendaries as notable as John Gunthorpe, keeper of the privy seal, the early humanist scholar; two future bishops of Exeter, Oldham and Veysey; and the well-known Tudor courtier and diplomatist, Sir John Mason,[52] Their connections with Crediton, however, were no stronger than those of eighteenth-century politicians with their rotten boroughs. They need never have seen the place from which their income came, and they often remembered it only when making their wills, if then. The resident dignitaries are more interesting because their careers were necessarily involved with Crediton itself. Most of the precentors and treasurers after 1400 were graduates: chiefly bachelors of canon or civil law, together with a few masters of arts and one or two doctors of theology. Some died at Crediton, but the majority, after a few years of service there, were promoted by the bishop to canonries of the cathedral or archdeaconries of the diocese. The presence of men with these qualifications and prospects must have enhanced the local community, both of clergy and laity. The same was true of the office of dean which, as has been stated, became a desirable benefice after Grandisson's reforms. Of its nine known holders between 1412 and 1545, at least eight were graduates of arts or law, and three became dignitaries of the cathedral. The cure of the parish accordingly belonged to men of good standing, probably as good as could be found anywhere else in England at that time.

The minor clergy, on the other hand, seem to have been ordinary folk, typical of the lower ranks of the medieval Church. We are best informed about the vicars. Of the fifteen or so whose names survive between 1300 and 1545, one was a previous curate of Plymtree, two others became rectors of parishes near Crediton, and a fourth, after serving as a vicar choral of the cathedral, ended his life as rector of one of the small city churches in Exeter.[53] This probably fixes the status of a Crediton vicarship in the local hierarchy of benefices. It was better than a parochial curacy with a minimal salary and no security of tenure, but inferior to the better-paid and more prestigious vicarships of the cathedral and to the incumbency of a parish, even one of moderate value. We know very little about the vicars' individual capabilities. All, from the nature of their work, ought to have been able to pronounce the words of the Latin texts they had to read in the choir, but how well they understood the Latin is not clear. None, as far as we know, was a graduate, though one in the thirteenth century was bequeathed a volume containing part of the New Testament,[54] and the bishop's insistence that the vicars should help administer the funds of the college and its fabric suggests that some of them could handle Latin well enough to draw up a financial account.[55] They certainly got involved in the types of misdemeanours common among the rank-and-file clergy of the later middle ages. In 1312 three vicars were convicted of fornication with women, one with his cousin; the first resigned and the others agreed to do so if they should ever be found guilty with the same women in future.[56] In 1414 Vicar John Lyghfote came to blows with the treasurer, and twelve years later he had another fight in the churchyard at Honiton where he had become a chaplain.[57] Wandering at night and visiting taverns were other peccadilloes of the Crediton vicars, as they were of their colleagues at Exeter, and in 1361 Bishop Grandisson strictly forbade them to enter taverns at any time or to leave the close around the church after curfew.[58] Fines were imposed for breaches of this rule, and deprivation for a fourth offence.

The church of the Holy Cross at Crediton, in which these clergy served, seems to have been a cruciform building as early as the mid-twelfth century, with choir, nave, and transepts, crowned by a central tower.[59] The massive Norman work of the lower stages of the tower is still visible, but the dimensions of the buildings which originally surrounded it are not known. The Lady chapel seems to have been added in the late thirteenth or early fourteenth centuries. Soon afterwards the main structure of the church was considered to need rebuilding. The prospect of this is first mentioned by Bishop Grandisson in 1334,[60] but the work does not seem to have begun until the episcopate of Thomas Brantingham (1370–1394), who instituted a tax on the prebendaries to provide the necessary funds.[61] The rebuilding probably began in about the 1380s or early 90s, commencing with the east end of the choir. In 1399, however, Bishop Stafford reported that the work, though laudably begun, was currently languishing for lack of funds.[62] He ordered the accounts of money collected and spent on the project to be investigated, the prebendaries to provide further modest contributions, and the work on the choir and ambulatories to be completed. Several bequests in wills suggest that steady progress in the matter was made after 1400. The choir, ambulatories and south transept seem to have been finished by 1415 when Thomas Barton, canon of Exeter, bequeathed £20 to heighten the walls of the north transept and to build a new window and roof to make it like the south transept; if not, the money was to be used to enclose and beautify the presbytery.[63] The nave was also taken in hand at this time. In 1414 William

Langton, one of the non-resident canons, called it 'almost prostrate to the ground' and allocated part of the profits of his prebend for repairs;[64] four years later another non-resident, Richard Penels, left £20 for the same purpose.[65] In this way the present church in the perpendicular style was probably erected between about the 1380s and the 1420s, consisting of choir, ambulatories or choir aisles, transepts, nave and nave aisles. The windows of the Lady chapel were also rebuilt in the style of the rest of the church. There are two brief descriptions of the building by antiquaries before the Reformation. William Worcester, who visited Crediton in 1478, was favourably impressed.[66] He measured the dimensions by pacing them, counted the arches of the piers in the nave, and admired the 'beautiful clerestory'. John Leland, on the other hand, who came in about 1540, made no observations upon the size or features of the building and seems to have found it uninspiring; he merely recorded that 'the church now standing hath no manner or token of antiquity'.[67]

Inside, the building was divided into two parts: those of the college and of the parish. The college area included the choir, the ambulatories, the transepts and the Lady chapel; the parochial area was the nave and may have been separated from the rest of the church by a screen. The heart of the church, in which the chief of the daily worship took place, was the choir. This consisted of the sanctuary at the east end with the high altar in honour of the Holy Cross, and the choir proper on the west containing the stalls of the clergy. The stalls would have run east to west, in the usual fashion, and consisted after 1334 of at least two rows or levels on each side.[68] The canons and vicars would have occupied the stalls of the back row, with the secondaries in front of them perhaps accompanied by the parish clerks and other miscellaneous clergy. The choristers were either placed on the same level or had small forms of their own in front of the secondaries, as they did at Exeter Cathedral. A reference of 1508 to the precentor's stall as lying on the right-hand side of the choir suggests that it lay at the south-west end, analogous to the dean's stall in a cathedral.[69] If so, the treasurer probably took the end at the north-west, opposite. The rest of the church provided space for the congregation in the nave, for processions around the aisles, and for the organisation of saint cults at altars and images placed along the walls. Six lesser altars are mentioned in 1334,[70] and after the rebuilding of the church there were probably eight: one in the Lady chapel, one at the east end of each choir aisle, one in each transept, and two parochial altars standing side by side at the east end of the nave.[71] The eighth would have been in the chapter-house adjoining the south choir aisle, where mass was also sometimes celebrated.[72] Six of the altar dedications are known, the locations of which are likely to have been as follows: the Virgin (Lady chapel), St Nicholas (north choir aisle), St John (south choir aisle), St Katherine (north transept), St Michael (south transept), and St Peter (nave altar, south side).[73] The dedication of the other nave altar – the parochial altar proper – is not known. Some of the altars were accompanied by images of their saints, and in the sixteenth century there were also images of St George, St Leonard and St Margaret.[74] It is possible that the windows, too, contained images of saints or scenes of Christian history, but the earliest description of the medieval glass by Thomas Westcote in 1630 mentions only armorial bearings.[75] These were of bishops of Exeter, earls of Devon, and local gentry families who may have contributed to rebuilding the fabric. The remaining feature of the church to be noted was its use as a burial place for important people who did not care to lie in the cemetery outside. At least a dozen interments are recorded inside the church before the 1540s, and there must have been many more. Canons and dignitaries were buried in the choir, ambulatories or Lady chapel, according to choice, either in tomb chests or under slabs with brasses or incised inscriptions.[76] The most notable lay burials, those of Sir John Sully who died in 1387 and his wife Isabel, were marked by monumental effigies on a tomb chest in the north transept; other layfolk were probably interred under slabs in the nave. The latter privilege had to be purchased, as was usual in medieval churches, the one recorded sum being 6s. 8d., paid by Simon Slader in 1537.[77]

Besides the church itself there were other buildings ancillary to its life or occupied by its clergy. The structure immediately adjoining the south choir aisle, which still survives in an altered form, probably included the vestry and the chapter-house in medieval times.[78] A mention of the archives in 1443 suggests the presence of a third room where muniments were kept, and maybe money and other valuables.[79] Further away and separated from the church by the cemetery were the houses of the clergy, possibly forming a close on all four sides. Their exact locations are not known, but they must have included dwellings for the two resident dignitaries, and the other prebendaries may also have owned premises, as has been mentioned. The dean had a special house and garden by 1334, and the vicars choral after 1361 inhabited the building provided for them by Grandisson. The latter, which is conjectured to have lain on the north side of the cemetery,[80] was referred to by Bishop Veysey in 1523 as 'Kalenderhey' (after the name of the college of vicars in Exeter), and described as a house (*hospicium*) containing enclosures (*septa*).[81] In 1547 it was called 'the vicars' house alias the common hall'.[82] These references suggest that the vicars occupied chambers within a single structure, rather than separate houses of their own like some cathedral vicars. They also had a hall and kitchen for their meals, and employed a cook whose salary in the 1520s was £1. 6s. 8d.[83] Other buildings mentioned in 1547 included the 'Plommehouse' – perhaps a lead-roofed structure – and the schoolhouse. The latter was either the song school where the clerk taught the choristers, or else the public grammar school which is also recorded in medieval times.

The cycle of daily worship in the church probably followed the pattern observed at Exeter Cathedral. This is made likely by the proximity of the two places, the presence of many of the same clerics on both foundations, and records of the same liturgical instructions being given to both by medieval bishops.[84] If the assumption is correct, the liturgical day at Crediton would begin with mattins in the choir, usually at or soon after midnight, except from Easter to Trinity when it was said at dawn or shortly beforehand.[85] Mattins was followed immediately by lauds, after which there would be an intermission of duty for two or three hours when most of the clergy could return to bed. Meanwhile the 'morrow mass' or first mass of the day would be celebrated at a subsidiary altar by one of the vicars, for the benefit of pious parishioners before they started work. After this, at about 6.00 or 7.00, private masses could be celebrated by the rest of the vicars at the other altars. At about 8.00 the mattins and hours of the Virgin would be said in the Lady chapel, followed by another mass there in her honour. At about 8.30 the clergy would all gather in the choir for the service of prime, after which they would go in procession to the chapter-house where notices of services for the next day would be read out and other business transacted. A 'capitular' mass would sometimes be celebrated at this point by some of the clergy in the chapter-house. Meanwhile the majority would return to the choir for the offices of terce and sext, followed by the high mass or chief mass of the day at the high altar and then by the office of none. This group of services would end at about 10.00, or an hour later in Lent when extra prayers had to be said. The clergy would then be free for three or four hours until the afternoon. They would return to the choir at about 2.00 or 3.00 to say the office for the dead (*placebo* and *dirige*), vespers and compline, ending about an hour or more later. The cycle would close with a recital of the vespers and compline of the Virgin in the Lady chapel. The main burden of attending these services fell on the minor clergy. The canons had only to come to one service each day, and only then if they wished to claim the daily distributions.[86] The vicars, secondaries, and choristers, however, had to be present at all the choir services and at the others by rotation.[87] Even the boys were allowed to be absent only in order to go to school, medieval people regarding children as young adults and expecting from them the full day's work of an adult.

Closely connected with worship were literacy and education. Medieval liturgical services had to be read from complicated books, and this was supposed to be done not merely with the lips but with understanding and devotion. The Church therefore encouraged the schooling of boys to prepare them for clerical careers, as well as the reading by adults of works on theology and law which would enable them better to understand the liturgy and their other duties as clerics. Like most religious communities in medieval England, Crediton supplies some evidence of the education of children. In 1334 Grandisson's appointment of a clerk responsible for teaching the choristers established what was effectively a small private song school, in which a few boys learnt plainsong and polyphony and in doing so practised the ability to read.[88] We know the name of only the last of these clerks, Philip Alcock, who gave up his post when the college was dissolved in 1545. Alcock was a former vicar choral of Lichfield Cathedral, whose setting of an antiphon to the Virgin, *Salve Regina mater misericordiae*, is still extant.[89] The work is for four voices and apparently dates from the 1530s, either from Lichfield or Crediton. It is a competent straightforward piece, typical of the everyday church music of the time, and probably gives a fair indication of Alcock's own abilities.[90] Besides the song school, a grammar school is also mentioned at Crediton in 1377 when Bishop Brantingham licensed Walter Cotel, vicar of Veryan in Cornwall, to be absent from his benefice for three years in order to teach it.[91] The school would have been a fee-paying one, open to anyone who could afford the charges. Its subsequent existence is likely, but the evidence for this is only indirect. A reference in Brantingham's licence to certain persons having the power to appoint the master seems to imply that appointments were often made, probably by the college authorities. The will of John Clifton of Crediton in 1449, requesting that twelve boys should read the psalter around his body before he was buried, suggests the presence of a school at that time in which such boys were taught.[92] Finally, the foundation of a new grammar school in 1547, so soon after the college was dissolved, also implies the existence of an earlier institution.[93] It is to be hoped that direct evidence about the matter will come to light in future.

The college was also a place of literacy and study for adult clergy. True, we must beware of overstatement: Crediton seems to have housed few books compared with its sister foundation at Ottery, and came well behind Exeter Cathedral, the chief centre of learning in the diocese. Nevertheless, liturgical texts, as we have seen, are mentioned as early as 1012,[94] and there were probably volumes of a scholarly kind after the 1220s when Bartholomew of St David, one of the canons, bequeathed several works of Latin theology to the college, including the *Sentences* of Peter Lombard, a versified Bible, and the books of Isaiah, Matthew and Mark accompanied with glosses.[95] In 1436 a copy of the *Pupilla Oculi* of John de Burgh, a handbook for priests, was given to be chained in the choir of the college for those who wished to use it.[96] Like Bartholomew's bequest, this was evidently to be read by the clergy; there is no evidence that the college possessed any books suitable for the laity. These resources were supplemented by the resident dignitaries themselves, several of whom we know to have owned private copies of scholarly Latin works during the fifteenth century. Here the best recorded example is that of John Lyndon, dean of the college from 1442 until his death exactly forty years later. Lyndon, who began life in about 1410, was a local boy who received the clerical tonsure from Bishop Lacy at Crediton itself in 1421.[97] He went to Exeter Cathedral to be a secondary clerk in 1428,[98] where he probably also studied grammar in the city high school, and from Exeter he passed in the early 1430s to Oxford. He became a fellow of Exeter College and a master of arts, and in 1442 when the deanship of Crediton fell vacant, Lacy appointed him to it.[99] This makes it look as though Lyndon was a protégé of the bishop or of one of the Exeter canons, who trained and maintained him for just such a purpose. He brought back to Crediton not only the experience of study at Oxford but a continuing interest in scholarly authors. He personally owned at least eight volumes of Latin theology, of which three – the *Works* of St Augustine, Robert Holcot's *Distincciones Theologie* and Haimo's commentary on St Paul's *Epistles* – still contain notes in his handwriting. On his death in 1482[100] he left all eight volumes to his successors as deans, jointly with the parishioners. They do not survive in the church today because when the college was dissolved the last dean, George Mason, gave them away to a friend. From him they eventually passed by obscure routes to three different libraries in Oxford, where they remain today.

It is now time to extend our view of the Church in medieval Crediton to the parish as distinct from the college. The church building, as we have seen, was also a parish church to which every inhabitant of Crediton was bound by means of rights and obligations. The rector of the parish, in this case the collegiate body, was entitled like rectors everywhere to three regular dues and payments from the parishioners. The first and greatest of these were tithes. Every holder of land had to pay predial tithes, consisting of one tenth of the produce of land each year, both of the crops and of the offspring of the livestock. Those who did not hold land, such as craftsmen, servants and labourers, paid personal tithes related to their earnings. Every conceivable produce of the land was tithed at Crediton. As well as the tithes of corn, hay and animals which went to the college, the dean received by Grandisson's ordinance of 1334 the tithes of all rushes that were gathered, all furze, broom and coppice woods that were cut, and also the tithes of 'cooking pots and cauldrons'.[101] The latter, which came to be known as 'garden money' after the Reformation,[102] were the tenth of all the vegetables and pot-herbs that grew in people's gardens. Second, every parishioner had to attend church on four days of the year to offer a small fixed sum of money, weekly collections of the modern kind being unknown. The four offering days in Crediton were Christmas, Candlemas, Easter and All Saints.[103] Third, every householder who died – and possibly every person – owed a mortuary to the church.[104] This consisted of his best animal, if he kept livestock, or his other best possession (such as a gown or a jewel) if he did not. In addition, all the parishioners were supposed to attend church frequently (though this could not necessarily be enforced, as we shall see). As elsewhere, they were probably expected to help maintain the nave, the parochial part of the church, through extra offerings or fund-raising activities. The office of churchwarden existed to organise this duty. Finally, every parishioner, when appropriate, had to be baptised, married, and purified after childbirth in the church, and to be buried in its cemetery. It was customary for offerings to be made on these occasions as well.[105]

It may seem strange that after the payment of all these necessary dues there was still interest and money in Crediton for extra religious activities of a voluntary nature. This was nevertheless the case; a pious section of the populace contributed more for spiritual purposes than they had to do by law. The college authorities, of course, encouraged lay people to visit the church, from inside and outside the parish, in order to worship and to make offerings. Those who did so were entitled to the benefit of indulgences. Crediton claimed to possess several of these, allegedly granted by various tenth– and eleventh–century popes and bishops, though the documents concerned are obvious forgeries of the twelfth or early thirteenth centuries.[106] They were nevertheless confirmed by Bishop Brewer in 1236[107] and were said to offer about 15,000 days or forty-one years relaxation of penance. This was not very far short of the fifty-four years claimed by Exeter Cathedral.[108] The church was also visited by the sick in search of cures. In 1315 Thomas Crey, a fuller of Keynsham in Somerset who had lost his sight, came to Crediton with his wife after being moved to do so in a dream, as he later asserted.[109] He arrived at the church on Wednesday 30 July and was still there on the following Friday when he claimed that his sight was restored while Bishop Stapledon was celebrating mass in the church in honour of the feast of St Peter ad Vincula. On hearing of the alleged miracle the bishop sent for Thomas and cross-examined him carefully. He was asked how he had lost his sight, why he had come to Crediton, and his vision was tested with questions about the bishop's ring and his finger. Witnesses from Crediton were also summoned to prove that he was blind at his arrival. Only when the bishop was thoroughly satisfied did he approve the miracle to be authentic, order the bells of the church to be rung, and the clergy to give thanks in the usual manner. This record is unique, but as late as the sixteenth century Crediton was a place of resort for pilgrims in search of health for their bodies or souls; in 1522–3 the college was paying a gratuity of 10s. a year to one of the two parish clerks for helping them to make their offerings.[110]

A very few wills of the lay parishioners survive from the later middle ages and throw a little more light on the voluntary devotions which centred upon the parish church.[111] All are the wills of prosperous people, however, and they must not be taken as guides to the resources or the piety of those who were poor. They show that some of the wealthy, nevertheless, retained an interest in the maintenance of the church and in its furnishings and cult objects. Maurice Burgh left £2 to glaze a window in 1405, and Thomas Bullok 20s. for the same purpose in 1409. Bullok gave a further 20s. to buy a chalice or other ornament, and bequeathed to the image of the Holy Cross a rosary of jet with gauds of gold. Money to repair the church was also given by Simon Slader in 1537. Prayers for their souls were another major objective of these testators. Joan Dyrwyn in 1391 and Thomas Reymound in 1413 both desired the clergy to say the office of the dead, the commendation, and a mass of requiem on the day of their death, and left money for the work. A few assigned sums large enough to find priests to celebrate daily masses for their souls over a long period. Thomas Bullok provided £10 for one chaplain to do so for two years, and Maurice Burgh £30 for two chaplains for three years. No doubt the 'annuellars' mentioned in Joan Dyrwyn's will were temporary chantry priests of this kind. Or, instead of a special priest, the money could be given to the vicars, as it was by Thomas Reymound who left £6. 6s. 8d. for one of them to say a daily mass for his soul for two years. For those who could not afford to endow prayers for the dead on such a grand scale, there was founded the parish guild of St Mary. This organisation, which is mentioned as newly established in 1405,[112] was a brotherhood of parishioners who joined together to pay a priest full time to celebrate a daily mass for all their souls together. The guild altar, at which the mass took place, was dedicated to St Peter and was one of the two parochial altars at the east end of the nave, probably that on the south side.[113] In 1448 the guild received a royal grant of incorporation, conferring the right to acquire property and to elect two wardens every year to manage its affairs.[114] It still existed in 1537, but appears to have been wound up by its members at about the time of the dissolution of the college in 1545.[115]

A good deal of voluntary religious activity also manifested itself outside the church and the town, in the surrounding countryside. Crediton was a parish of unusual size, the furthest parts of which lay up to five miles away from the church along indifferent lanes and tracks, almost impassable in winter. Not surprisingly, the gentry in some of these places and the lesser inhabitants in others were stimulated to build chapels of ease where services could be held, daily or weekly, for their greater convenience. There were eventually nine of these outlying chapels which, in the order that they first appear in records, were Yeo (early thirteenth century), Ruxford (1254), Trobridge (1329), Sandford, Kennerleigh and Uton (or Yeoton) (all 1334), Ash Bullayne (1407), Fulford now Shobrooke Park (1413), and Spencecombe (1415).[116] Each was maintained by a local gentleman or by the local inhabitants, and was served by the domestic chaplain of the former, by a priest hired by the latter, or by visiting clergy from Crediton. Two of the chapels – Sandford and Kennerleigh – eventually acquired full parochial status, but that was not until after the Reformation. During the middle ages they and the rest of the nine were kept strictly subordinate to the parish church. They were not normally allowed the right of baptism or burial, and all the offerings made in them had to be surrendered to the college. The inhabitants of Sandford, the largest of the outer communities, made specially strong efforts to acquire parochial rights for their chapel. In 1432 Bishop Lacy gave permission for divine services to be celebrated there by a suitable priest, [117] and one of the vicars of Crediton began to go out regularly on Sundays and festivals to say the divine office and apparently to celebrate mass. This led to the withdrawal of many local people from the services at Crediton, so that in 1437 the bishop revoked his licence and ordered them to return.[118] Sandford did not give up the struggle, however, and in 1524 the inhabitants approached Bishop Veysey, requesting permission for regular services and rights of burial.[119] They complained of the difficulties caused by the distance from Crediton, and rather speciously asserted that they had possessed a chapel and a cemetery time out of mind. The bishop, with the consent of the college authorities, gave a qualified approval. Sandford was given permission to have its own chaplain (paid for by the inhabitants), divine service, the sacraments, and burial rights. The dean of Crediton, on the other hand, received the power to appoint the chaplain, and his right was confirmed to receive all the offerings made in the chapel. Finally, the people of Sandford had also to promise to go on paying all their traditional dues and duties to the collegiate church.

A tenth chapel, that of St Laurence at the west end of Crediton itself, had a different and more varied history. It is first mentioned in 1242 as a chapel with an adjoining reclusory for an anchorite, [120] but by 1278 it had developed into a hospital with an endowment of land and a staff of brothers.[121] During the fourteenth century it was ruled by a series of rectors or wardens of the order of Trinitarian friars, appointed by the bishop on the recommendation of the minister and brethren of Hounslow, who belonged to this order.[122] The Trinitarians were an international religious order, able to own property and living under the Rule of St Augustine, who gave their time to relieving the poor and to ransoming Christian captives.[123] The function of St Laurence's Hospital was probably similar: to provide hospitality to travellers and a refuge for the sick and incapacitated. In view of the Hounslow connection, it seems that the hospital ought to be counted as a limb of the Trinitarian organisation during the fourteenth century, but it was not a full member since its head was never called a minister and it is not clear that there were any other brethren after 1278. The last warden nominated by Hounslow died in 1410, and the bishop then appointed a secular priest, John Matthew, to the office.[124] This appears to have been unpopular locally, and during the winter of 1410–11 the chapel was raided by unknown persons who carried off charters, vestments and offerings.[125] Matthew even felt it necessary to get the king's ratification of his right to be warden.[126] Perhaps for this reason the bishop, when Matthew left in 1417, restored the wardenship to a member of a religious order in the person of a Cistercian monk, John Huntyngdon.[127] Another Cistercian was appointed in 1443, who was still in charge in 1450.[128] Eventually, between 1450 and 1523, the hospital and its endowments were given to the vicars choral of Crediton, but the chapel remained and still enjoyed some local support. Its income in the latter year, besides £8 from its lands, included a sum of 8s. from monetary offerings.[129]

We should not assume from these examples of piety that all the people of Crediton were pious or that they exceeded other communities in this respect. The building of chapels was prompted by the size of the parish, as well as by popular devotion, and the records of bequests to the church by wealthy layfolk are paralleled in nearly every other English town. We know little about the spiritual life of any individual parish in the middle ages, and Crediton is no exception. The wide range of religious habits and attitudes which must have existed has perished almost unrecorded and is now impossible to reconstruct. It is nevertheless clear that the parish possessed its quota of problems as well as its fund of devotion. Its clergy had to contend not only with wealth and piety but poverty and death. In 1332 John de Leghe, the parochial vicar, was moved to ask the bishop what he should do with the bodies of his female parishioners who died in pregnancy, since his conscience troubled him lest they be buried while their unborn children were still alive.[130] The bishop ordered him to rely on the judgment of the surgeons or the midwives in the case, who would be able to establish the state of the child by probing the womb with a rod. There were others in the parish who strayed from the path of Christian duty or who failed to respect the institutions of Holy Church. Such were the women who fornicated with the vicars in 1312[131] and the man named Philip Persone who attacked Peter Bocher in the churchyard in 1387, causing blood to flow thereby polluting the consecrated ground.[132] There was even a sorceress in the early sixteenth century, Alice

Waren, who after abjuring her sorcery and other errors before Bishop Oldham was persuaded by the devil to return to her wickedness, causing her to be summoned afresh before Bishop Veysey in 1524.[133] No doubt between the extremes of piety and sin there was also some religious apathy. In 1523 Veysey noted with pain that the major part of the people of Crediton was scarcely present four times a year at the principal Sunday mass with musical accompaniment.[134] The reason, he was told, was that the service was too long, and he therefore laid down that the principal mass should end by ten o'clock. Even medieval laity could become bored with the complexities of worship beloved by their clergy.

In the middle of the sixteenth century the Church in Crediton suffered major changes of its institutions – changes so great that the medieval era with which we have been concerned can reasonably be terminated at this point. Not only was the parish involved in the general events of the Reformation, such as the imposition of royal supremacy upon the Church and the introduction of Protestant worship, but the collegiate body itself was dissolved, thus bringing to an end the religious community first founded in the tenth century. The dissolution of English collegiate churches by the crown began in about 1540, shortly after that of the monasteries, and lasted until 1548. The motives for it were the prejudice against religious houses of clergy, characteristic of the Reformation, and the yet unsated greed of the crown for seizing religious property. Crediton and Ottery, the two chief collegiate churches in Devon, were both dissolved in 1545, about halfway through the process as a whole. The income of Crediton at this date, as estimated by the 'Valor Ecclesiasticus' of 1535, was about £332: some £30 more than Ottery.[135] Of this the prebendaries enjoyed just over half, about £188, and the rest was appropriated to the lesser members of the college and the maintenance of its institutions. The wealthiest of the original twelve prebends was still Woolsgrove, worth £26. 6s. 9½d. net, and the least wealthy was West Sandford, worth £8. The six bursal prebends were still worth the original £4 each. Only three of the prebendaries were resident when the college was dissolved: the precentor, the treasurer, and the dean who was holding a prebend in plurality for the first time. The precentor, John Blaxton, and the treasurer, Walter Mugge, also held other benefices and must have been fairly wealthy men. Of the remaining prebendaries in 1545, seven were canons of Exeter Cathedral and belonged to the same élite of prosperous graduate clerical pluralists, while the rest were an assortment of persons, some of them obscure, who had a claim on the bishop's patronage.[136] Three of them are described as 'scholars' and were presumably young men undergoing education, whose prebends served them as scholarships. The condition of the minor clergy in 1545 is not known, and it is an open question whether the six vicars, two clerks and six choristers mentioned in 1523 were still being maintained.

In theory the collegiate churches, like the greater monasteries, terminated their own existence by surrendering themselves and their possessions to the crown; in practice the crown required them to do so. Royal commissioners to receive the surrenders of Crediton and Ottery were appointed on 17 May 1545.[137] The following Sunday, Whitsunday, was probably the last day on which the college of Crediton operated in full working order. If the sequence of events at Ottery can be taken as a guide, the commissioners arrived at Crediton on Whitmonday, 25 May, and took the surrender on that or the following day.[138] The act of surrender does not survive, but would have been signed in the chapter-house by the three resident canons in the commissioners' presence. During the following days the king's men would have examined the college muniments, perhaps removing rentals and title deeds. They would also have allocated pensions to the clergy and have paid off the servants. The dignitaries were well rewarded for their compliance. The precentor, the treasurer, and the dean (as prebendary of Henstill) received pensions equal in value to their old prebends.[139] The rest of the canons got sums ranging from £11 to £2 for each of the bursal prebendaries. Only one of the minor clergy is recorded being pensioned: Philip Alcock, the clerk in charge of the choristers, who received £4. How the vicars were treated is unknown. The final task of the commissioners was to take an inventory of all the church goods. This is still extant and was made on Wednesday 27 May.[140] It describes the whole of the furnishings of the collegiate part of the church, down to the white superfrontal for Pentecost which was still hanging upon the high altar. The commissioners left Crediton that evening or the following morning, and on Thursday 28 May they received the surrender of Ottery.

The fate of the parochial part of the church after the surrender is a rather obscure matter. The royal inventory did not list the furnishings and ornaments west of the transepts, and the nave was apparently left untouched. The parochial clergy: the dean, his chaplain and the two parish clerks, probably survived at their posts for a little, though the dean had left by April 1547.[141] Meanwhile, on 22 September 1545, the king granted all the possessions of the college to Sir Thomas Darcy, gentleman of the Privy Chamber, except for the church buildings and the house and revenues of the dean, now only called the vicar.[142] This reservation makes it look as though the conversion of the whole church into a parochial building was already forseen. Darcy did not hold the college possessions for long, since on 20 August 1546 he returned them to the crown in return for lands in other parts of the country.[143] Shortly afterwards, the parishioners of Crediton entered into negotiations with the crown for the purchase of the collegiate church, and these were successfully completed in the following spring. On 2 April 1547 the government of the new king, Edward VI, created a new parochial organisation to replace the college.[144] It established a corporation of twelve governors, nine from Crediton and three from Sandford, to administer the parish church and its endowments. The governors received a grant of the church and its adjoining buildings, the vicars' house and schoolhouse, the chapel of Sandford, and all the other chapels in the parish. They also acquired the advowson of the vicarage of Crediton, with the right and duty of appointing a vicar with £20 a year, two assistant curates, and a chaplain of Sandford with £6. 13s. 4d. A new free grammar school was established too, the master of which was also to be appointed by the governors and to receive £10. Much of the property transferred to the governors consisted of the former endowments of the deanery, and the parishioners had to pay the crown £200 in return for the church buildings. All that the crown added by way of an extra was the revenues of the vicarage of Exminster. With this exception, the scheme of 1547 should not be seen as a benefaction by the crown, but rather as a reorganisation of existing local institiutions after the dissolution of the college.

The Edwardian reforms inaugurated a new era for the Church in Crediton. The ancient power of the clergy over the parish and town was broken. The control of all the ecclesiastical patronage and buildings passed from their hands into that of the lay governors, and this process was carried further in the following year, 1548, when the bishop was forced to surrender the lordship of the manor and town to Sir Thomas Darcy.[145] There were also far fewer clergy in the parish after these changes. The accounts of the churchwardens of Crediton, which begin to survive in 1550, show that there only remained the parochial vicar, two assistant chaplains (with stipends of £10 and £8), the chaplain of Sandford, the two parish clerks (both of whom had disappeared by 1553), and a sexton.[146] This extremity of change was modified, however, when Queen

Mary succeeded in 1553. During her reign attempts were made both to re-establish Catholic worship in Crediton and to restore some of the former wealth and power of the clergy into their hands. Catholic services were probably resumed in the church soon after Mary's accession in July; the old furnishings were gradually re-established during the following years, and at Midsummer 1555 the governors appointed Hugh Deane, a former secondary clerk of Exeter Cathedral, as 'chapel clerk' in the church with a stipend of £8 a year.[147] This seems to imply the revival of elaborate worship, probably with music, either in the Lady chapel or in the choir, and it is possible that the choristers were also restored at about this time. Soon afterwards the bishop re-asserted his claim to appoint the incumbent of the parish, and on 23 March 1557 he collated John Nicolles to the office with the title of rector.[148] Nicolles was probably a strong Catholic, since he was chosen by the bishop when the Catholic revival was well advanced, and he seems to have left Crediton soon after Mary's death and the fall of her régime.

On 12 November 1557 Cardinal Pole restored to the ownership of Nicolles, not that of the governors, all the tithes and offerings of the late college which were still in the hands of the crown, worth £122. 7s. 10½d. per annum.[149] What appears to be a draft scheme for using this money, dated between 1557 and 1559, envisaged the personnel of the parish as consisting of the rector with £52, two curates of Crediton and one of Sandford with £10 each, a schoolmaster with £13. 6s. 8d., a chapel clerk with £10, two parish clerks and a sexton sharing £10, four grammar scholars sharing £10. 13s. 4d., and four poor men sharing £8.[150] This never became fully effective, owing to Mary's death in 1558, but under Elizabeth a compromise was reached with regard to the Church in Crediton, as in the Church of England as a whole. On 5 July 1560 a new royal charter was issued for the parish.[151] It followed the lines of its Edwardian predecessor in confirming the existence of the twelve governors and restoring to them all ecclesiastical patronage. Some aspects of the Marian 'reaction', however, were allowed to remain. The governors were permitted to keep the tithes restored by Cardinal Pole, though they had to pay an annual rent of £100 to the crown for the privilege. The staff of the church was fixed to include an incumbent (now again called the vicar) with £30, one curate of Crediton and one of Sandford with £10 each, four grammar scholars who also acted as choristers sharing £8, and four poor almsmen sharing a similar sum. The office of chapel clerk was not continued, but the churchwardens retained the services of Hugh Deane in an unknown post, possibly that of organist, and continued to pay him £10 a year until his death in 1583.[152]

What judgment should we make about the history of the Church in Crediton during the collegiate era? It is hard to resist the feeling that the collegiate organisation was a rather unsatisfactory one, at least after about 1200. That something was amiss with the college was perceived by each of the bishops who tried to improve its effectiveness. Branscombe, Bitton, Grandisson, Lacy, Oldham and Veysey all contrasted the splendour of Crediton in the days of the see, which no doubt they exaggerated, with its apparent decline in their own days. Yet none of them found a truly satisfactory solution to the problem. With the detachment possible today, four hundred years after the Reformation, we can see what was wrong. Too much of the college's income went to the absent canons, and too little to maintain the resident community. The latter contained too many clergy of low degree; it was not balanced by a strong enough body of learned and important men, even after Grandisson's reforms. From these arose other problems: the difficulty of maintaining the church fabric, the breaches of clerical discipline, and the college's lack of distinction as a centre of worship and learning. The bishops never succeeded in dealing effectively with the question of the non-resident canons; antiquity, social convention, and their own need for patronage all hampered them from doing so. The Reformation also failed to reform the college in a positive way and ended, here as elsewhere, by simply destroying the institution. Still, the collegiate period was by no means lacking in achievement. It gave the parish a large church building and a more elaborate worship, it brought to the town some learned and literate clerics, and it provided a good series of pastors in the persons of the deans. Whether medieval Creditonians got value for their tithes and offerings is debatable but, like so many creations of the past, the buildings and history which were once purchased at so high a price are now freely available. They remain objects in which anyone who wishes may take a pride and an interest.

NOTES

1. The best recent surveys of the subject are by H. P. R. Finberg, 'Sherborne, Glastonbury and the Expansion of Wessex', *Transactions of the Royal Historical Society*, 5th series, 3 (1953), 101–24; F. Barlow, *The English Church, 1000–1066* (London, 1963), 211–15; P. Chaplais, 'The Authenticity of the Royal Anglo-Saxon Diplomas of Exeter', *Bulletin of the Institute of Historical*

Research 39 (1966), 1–34, and F. Barlow & others, *Leofric of Exeter* (Exeter, 1972), 1–16.

2. See below, pp. 107–8.

3. For a brief life and bibliography of St Boniface see D. H. Farmer, *The Oxford Dictionary of Saints* (Oxford, 1978), 46–8.

4. Chaplais (as note 1), 10–11.

5. For the list see F. M. Powicke & E. B. Fryde, *Handbook of British Chronology* (Second edn. London, 1961), 219.

6. *The Crawford Collection of Early Charters & Documents now in the Bodleian Library*, edd. A. S. Napier & W. H. Stevenson (Oxford, 1895), 23–4, 125–33.

7. Chaplais (as note 1), 28–31.

8. *The Crawford Collection of Early Charters* (as note 6), 29–31.

9. *The Register of John Grandisson, Bishop of Exeter, 1327–1369*, ed. F. C. Hingeston-Randolph, 3 vols. (London & Exeter, 1874–9), i, 535–6; ii, 723–4.

10. *Valor Ecclesiasticus tempore Henrici VIII*, ed. J. Caley, 6 vols. (London, Record Commission, 1810–24), ii, 289–90, 324–5. The total for the college excludes income which did not come from the original endowments.

11. *The Crawford Collection of Early Charters* (as note 6). 29–31.

12. Audrey M. Erskine, 'The Medieval Financial Records of the Cathedral Church of Exeter', *Journal of the Society of Archivists* 2 (1962), 255–6.

13. *The Register of Edmund Lacy, Bishop of Exeter, 1420–1455: Registrum Commune*, ed. G. R. Dunstan, 5 vols. (Devon & Cornwall Record Soc., new series, vii, x, xiii, xvi, xviii, 1963–71), iii, 287–96.

14. *Taxatio Ecclesiastica Angliae et Walliae Auctoritate P. Nicholai IV* (London, Record Commission, 1802), 145. For the identification of the prebends see G. Oliver, *Monasticon Dioecesis Exoniensis* (London & Exeter, 1846), 416.

15. *The Register of Walter Bronescombe, 1257–1280*, ed. F. C. Hingeston-Randolph (London & Exeter, 1889), 322; *Reg. Grandisson*, i, 412; Devon Record Office, The Register of Edmund Stafford, i, fo 5v.

16. J. B. Davidson, 'On Some Further Documents Relating to Crediton Minster', *Transactions of the Devonshire Association* 14 (1882), 256.

17. The precentor is mentioned in 1239 (Exeter Cathedral Archives, henceforward D&C, 1502) and the treasurer in 1261 (*Reg. Bronescombe*, 128).

18. Davidson (as note 16), 256–7; Oliver (as note 14), 416.

19. *Reg. Bronescombe*, 59; D&C 3521, pp. 263–4.

20. There is no evidence that they existed as early as Bishop William Warelwast's charter of 1107–1137 (as note 11), or that they originally numbered eighteen.

21. *Reg. Bronescombe*, 60–2.

22. When benefactions were made to the vicars to celebrate masses for the dead, and by analogy with their colleagues at Exeter.

23. Oliver (as note 14), 82, 84.

24. *Reg. Bronescombe*, 60–2; D&C 3521, pp. 266–70.

25. *Reg. Grandisson*, ii, 752–4; D&C 3521, pp. 249–57.

26. Davidson (as note 16), 255–6.

27. *Reg. Bronescombe*, 60–2.

28. *Taxatio Ecclesiastica* (as note 14), 146.

29. Oliver (as note 14), 415–17; D&C 3521, 231–49.

30. *The Register of Walter Stapeldon, Bishop of Exeter, 1307–1326*, ed. F. C. Hingeston-Randolph (London & Exeter, 1892), 377–8; Oliver (as note 14), 86–7.

31. *Reg. Grandisson*, ii, 752–4; D&C 3521, pp. 249–57.

32. *Reg. Grandisson*, iii, 1325, etc.

33. In a separate document dated 30 September 1334 (D&C 3521, pp. 258–63).

34. *Valor Ecclesiasticus* (as note 10), ii, 324–5.

35. *The Register of Edmund Stafford, 1395–1419,* ed. F. C. Hingeston-Randolph (London & Exeter, 1886), 395.

36. *Reg. Stapeldon*, 446–56.

37. The cost of Grandisson's reforms of worship in 1334 was £13.0s.4d. The prebendaries contributed £7.12s., und the rest (£5.8s.4d.) came apparently from the two vicarships formerly held by the dean, hence the figure of £2.14s.2d. per vicar (*Reg. Grandisson,* ii, 752–4).

38. Ibid., iii, 1221.

39. A number around ten is suggested by dividing the approximate income of the vicars in 1361 (about £40 in 1522–3 values: Oliver [as note 14], 82, 84) by their stipends of £4.

40. *Reg. Grandisson*, iii, 1220–2; D&C 3521, pp. 271–9.

41. Kathleen Edwards, *The English Secular Cathedrals in the Middle Ages* (Second edn. Manchester, 1967), 276–8.

42. *The Register of Thomas de Brantyngham, Bishop of Exeter, 1370–1394*, ed. F. C. Hingeston-Randolph, 2 vols (London & Exeter, 1886), ii, 665.

43. *Ordinale Exon*, ed. J. N. Dalton, vol. i (Henry Bradshaw Soc., 37, 1909), 17; vol. iii (ibid., 63, 1926), 247–8.

44. D&C 3521, p. 261.

45. T. Westcote, *A View of Devonshire in 1630,* ed. G. Oliver & P. Jones (Exeter, 1845), 120–6; T. Risdon, *The Chorographical Description of the County of Devon* (London, 1811), 97–102.

46. E.g. Robert Froste in 1534 (Oliver [as note 14], 77).

47. *Calendar of Patent Rolls, 1408–13*, 96.

48. *Reg. Lacy*, ii, 140–3.

49. Lambeth Palace Library, Reg. John Morton, i, fo 123v.

50. Devon Record Office, Reg. John Veysey, ii, fos 10v–12.

51. Oliver (as note 14), 83–5.

52. For the biographies of these men see A. B. Emden, *A Biographical Register of the University of Oxford to 1500*, 3 vols (Oxford, 1957–9), ii, 1329–30, 1396–7; iii, 1947–8; *A Biographical Register of the University of Oxford, 1501–1540* (Oxford, 1974), 386–8; *A Biographical Register of the University of Cambridge to 1500* (Cambridge, 1963), 275–7.

53. *Reg. Stapeldon*, 126, 201, 267 (Walter Barber and John Sydemuwe); *Reg. Lacy*, v, 28 (Philip Brocke alias Broke) and 114 (Thomas Kene).

54. Davidson (as note 16), 256–7.

55. Oliver (as note 14), 417. For a glimpse of the college's accounting system in the early sixteenth century see ibid., 82, 84.

56. *Reg. Stapeldon,* 126.

57. *Reg. Stafford*, 344; *Reg. Lacy*, i, 191–2.

58. *Reg. Grandisson*, iii, 1222.

59. For a lengthy discussion of the building see R. J. King, 'The Church of St Mary and of the Holy Cross at Crediton', *Transactions of the Exeter Diocesan Architectural Society*, 2nd series, 4 (1878), 81–113.

60. *Reg. Grandisson*, ii, 754.

61. Devon Record Office, Reg. Stafford, ii, fos 225v–6.

62. Ibid.

63. *Reg. Stafford*, 411–13.

64. Ibid., 404–5.

65. Ibid., 420–1.

66. William Worcester, *Itineraries,* ed. J. H. Harvey (Oxford, 1969), 80–1.

67. *The Itinerary of John Leland in or about the Years 1535–1553*, ed. Lucy Toulmin Smith, 5 vols (London, 1907–10), i, 239.
68. *Reg. Grandisson*, ii, 752.
69. Public Record Office, Prob 11/16 fo 55 (will of Precentor Robert Cooke).
70. D&C 3521, p. 261.
71. Ibid., p. 260.
72. *Reg. Lucy*, ii, 142.
73. D&C 3521, p 261; *Calendar of Patent Rolls, 1446–52*, 162–3; H. M. Whiteley, 'Inventories of the Collegiate Churches of . . . Crediton and . . . Ottery', *Transactions of the Devonshire Association* 34 (1902), 559–62.
74. G. T. Windyer Morris, 'Will of Simon Slader', *Devon & Cornwall Notes & Queries* 13 (1924–5), 322–5; 'An Inventory of Goods belonging to the Parish Church at Crediton, 1559', ibid. 32 (1971), 15–17.
75. Westcote (as note 45), 120–6.
76. The slab of Treasurer Giles Colledale (d. 1517) survives in the north choir aisle, and an unidentified tomb chest in the south choir aisle. Westcote mentions a former brass in the choir in 1630 (as note 45), 120–6.
77. Windyer Morris (as note 74), 322–5.
78. The vestry is mentioned in 1312 (*Reg. Stapeldon*, 126).
79. *Reg. Lacy*, iii, 288.
80. King (as note 59), 87.
81. Oliver (as note 14), 84. For the origin of the name 'Kalenderhey') see Nicholas Orme, 'The Kalendar Brethren of the City of Exeter', *Transactions of the Devonshire Association* 109 (1977), 153–4.
82. *Calendar of Patent Rolls, 1547–8*, 43–5.
83. Oliver (as note 14), 82, 84.
84. *Reg. Grandisson*, iii, 1213–15; *Reg. Lacy*, iii, 387.
85. For the observances at Exeter Cathedral see *Ordinale Exon* (above, note 43), i, passim.
86. Oliver (as note 14), 415.
87. *Reg. Grandisson*, iii, 1222; *Reg. Lacy*, ii, 140–3.
88. *Reg. Grandisson*, ii, 752–3.
89. F. Ll. Harrison, *Music in Medieval Britain* (Second edn., London, 1963), 454.
90. I am grateful to Mr N. J. Sandon for these observations.
91. *Reg. Brantyngham*, i, 378–9.
92. *Reg. Lacy*, iv, 56.
93. *Calendar of Patent Rolls, 1547–8*, 43–5.
94. Above, note 11.
95. Davidson (as note 16), 256–7.
96. *Reg. Lacy*, iv, 28.
97. Ibid., 70.
98. Nicholas Orme, *The Minor Clergy of Exeter Cathedral, 1300–1548* (University of Exeter, 1980), 100.
99. Emden, *A Biographical Register of the University of Oxford to 1500* (as note 52), ii, 1191.
100. C. W. Boase, *Registrum Collegii Exoniensis* (Oxford Historical Soc., 27, 1894), 365.
101. D&C 3521, p. 260; Oliver (as note 14), 85.
102. Devon Record Office, Crediton Governors, 1660A-13.
103. D&C 3521, p. 260.
104. Ibid.
105. Ibid., pp. 261–2.

106. J. B. Davidson, 'On Some Ancient Documents Relating to Crediton Minster', *Transactions of the Devonshire Association* 10 (1878), 237–54.
107. Ibid., 240.
108. G. Oliver, *Lives of the Bishops of Exeter and a History of the Cathedral* (Exeter, 1861), 249.
109. *Reg. Stapeldon*, 126–7.
110. Oliver (as note 14), 82, 84.
111. For these wills see *Reg. Stafford*, 383–4, 395–6, 405, 419–20; *Reg. Lacy*, iv, 55–6; and Windyer Morris (as note 74), 322–5.
112. *Reg. Stafford*, 383–4.
113. Ibid., p. 395; *Calendar of Patent Rolls, 1446–52*, 162–3.
114. Ibid.
115. Windyer Morris (as note 74), 322–5. The guild did not feature in the Devon chantry certificates of 1546–8.
116. Davidson (as note 16), 260, 262; *Reg. Grandisson*, i, 509; D&C 3521, p. 262; *Reg. Stafford*, 274 (bis), 280. A church of St Edmund, which may be one of the above, is also mentioned in 1243–4 (H. M. Whiteley, 'Sanctuary in Devon', *Transactions of the Devonshire Association* 45 [1913], 307).
117. *Reg. Lacy*, i, 242.
118. Ibid., ii, 41–2.
119. Devon Record Office, Reg. Veysey, ii, fos 35v–38.
120. *Reg. Bronescombe*, 5.
121. Ibid., 62.
122. *Reg. Grandisson*, iii, 1291; *Reg. Brantyngham*, i, 41, 169; *Reg. Stafford*, 162.
123. D. Knowles & R. N. Hadcock, *Medieval Religious Houses in England and Wales* (Second edn., London, 1971), 205–7. The remarks on p. 354 need to be corrected.
124. *Reg. Stafford*, 162.
125. Ibid., 74.
126. *Calendar of Patent Rolls, 1408–13*, 237.
127. *Reg. Stafford*, 162.
128. *The Register of Edmund Lacy, Bishop of Exeter, 1420–1455: Part I*, ed. F. C. Hingeston-Randolph (London & Exeter, 1909), 281; *Reg. Lacy* (as note 13), ii, 405; iii, 59.
129. Oliver (as note 14) 82, 84.
130. *Reg. Grandisson*, ii, 673–4.
131. Above, note 56.
132. *Reg. Brantyngham*, ii, 640.
133. Devon Record Office, Reg. Veysey, ii, fo 31v.
134. Oliver (as note 14), 84.
135. *Valor Ecclesiasticus* (as note 10), ii, 324–5.
136. For the list of canons in 1545 see L. S. Snell, *The Chantry Certificates for Devon and the City of Exeter* (Exeter, 1961), 63–4. For Richard Bramston see Nicholas Orme, 'Two Schoolmaster-Musicians of the Tudor Period', *Somerset & Dorset Notes & Queries*, forthcoming.
137. Snell (as note 136), 62–3.
138. The proceedings at Ottery lasted three days, and those at Crediton ended on 27 May.
139. Snell (as note 136), 63–4.
140. Whiteley (as note 73), 559–62.
141. 'Translation of Charter Constituting the Board of Governors of Crediton Church', *Devon & Cornwall Notes & Queries* 5 (1908–9), 187.
142. *Calendar of Letters and Papers, Foreign and Domestic, Henry VIII*, xx

part ii, 223. For Darcy's career see G. E. Cockayne, *The Complete Peerage*, vol. iv, ed. V. Gibbs (London, 1916), 78.

143. *Calendar of Letters and Papers* (as note 142), xxi part i, 764.

144. *Calendar of Patent Rolls, 1547–8*, 43–5; 'Translation' (as note 141), 179–220.

145. *Calendar of Patent Rolls, 1548–9*, 16.

146. Devon Record Office, Crediton Governors, 1660A/13–14.

147. Ibid.,/16. For Deane's earlier career see Orme (as note 98), 125.

148. Devon Record Office, Reg. Turberville, fo 18v.

149. Crediton Governors, 1660A/9.

150. Ibid., /11.

151. *Calendar of Patent Rolls, 1558–60*, 417–18.

152. Crediton Governors, 1660A/42.

List of Principal Dates

c. 675	Wynfrith born in Wessex, probably near Exeter
714–741	Charles Martel ruler of the Franks
716	Wynfrith's first mission to Frisia
719	*May 15:* Wynfrith made missionary to Germany by Pope Gregory II and receives the name Boniface
719–721	Boniface undertakes missionary work in Frisia under Willibrord
722	Boniface's second visit to Rome; he is consecrated bishop by Pope Gregory II on *November 30*
723 or 724	Felling of the Donar oak at Geismar in Hesse
723–735	Boniface undertakes missionary work in Hesse and Thuringia under the protection of Charles Martel
731–741	Pope Gregory III
732	Boniface made archbishop
735–737	Boniface works in Bavaria at the invitation of Duke Hucbert
737–738	Boniface's third and last visit to Rome; he is made papal legate for Germany
739	Boniface organizes the Bavarian church
741–752	Pope Zachary
741–747	Pippin and Carloman joint rulers of the Franks
741 or 742	Foundation of bishoprics at Würzburg, Büraburg and Erfurt
742 or 743	*April 21:* Concilium Germanicum, Boniface's first reforming council in Francia
744	*March 12:* foundation of monastery at Fulda
745	Franks agree to the erection of four church provinces, including one under Boniface at Cologne
745–747	Plans for provincial organization dropped; Boniface becomes archbishop of Mainz without a province
747	Carloman abdicates and goes to Rome; Pippin sole ruler in Francia

749–751	Pippin receives Pope Zachary's sanction for the deposition of King Childeric III and his own assumption of the royal title (autumn 751)
752–759	Pope Stephen II
753	Boniface hands over Mainz to his disciple Lull with the agreement of King Pippin. He returns to missionary work in Frisia
754	*early spring:* Pope Stephen II comes to Francia to appeal for help against the Lombards
	June 5: Boniface killed by brigands at Dokkum in Frisia
754–768	Willibald writes his Life of Boniface at some point in this period, probably near the end of it

Bibliographical Note

Works in English

The sources for Boniface and his period are generally available in English. Willibald's Life, much of Boniface's correspondence, and Lives of other Anglo-Saxon missionaries are translated in Talbot. Bede's *Ecclesiastical History* and the *Anglo-Saxon Chronicle* are both available in a number of English versions; the latter is in *EHD* along with much other English material and good bibliographies. Two of the main sources for Frankish political history of the time are *The Fourth Book of the Chronicle of Fredegar*, ed. J. M. Wallace-Hadrill (Edinburgh, 1960), and the Royal Frankish Annals, translated in B. W. Scholz, *Carolingian Chronicles* (New York, 1970). There is much less secondary reading in English. The main works are, in chronological order: W. Levison, *England and the Continent in the Eighth Century* (Oxford, 1946); G. W. Greenaway, *Saint Boniface* (London, 1955); J. M. Wallace-Hadrill, 'A background to St. Boniface's mission', in his *Early Medieval History* (Oxford, 1975), 138–54. The Anglo-Saxon background is best covered in F. M. Stenton, *Anglo-Saxon England* (Third edn., Oxford, 1970). There is a good brief account of Boniface by E. Ewig in *Handbook of Church History*, edd. H. Jedin and J. Dolan (London, 1969), III, 7–25; this also has bibliographies.

Works in other languages

The standard guide to the sources is *Wattenbach-Levison. Deutschlands Geschichtsquellen in Mittelalter*, I, ed. W. Levison (Weimar, 1952) and II, edd. W. Levison and H. Löwe (Weimar, 1953). The standard biography of Boniface is T. Schieffer, *Winfrid-Bonifatius und die christliche Grundlegung Europas* (Freiburg 1954; reprinted Darmstadt, 1972); the reprint has a postscript reviewing literature which appeared between 1954 and 1971. References to more recent work can be found in the footnotes of the chapters above, especially those by Christopher Holdsworth and Timothy Reuter; in the bibliographies in *Deutsches Archiv für Erforschung des Mittelalters*; and in the *Hand-*

buch der europäischen Geschichte, I, ed. T. Schieffer (Stuttgart, 1976).

Index

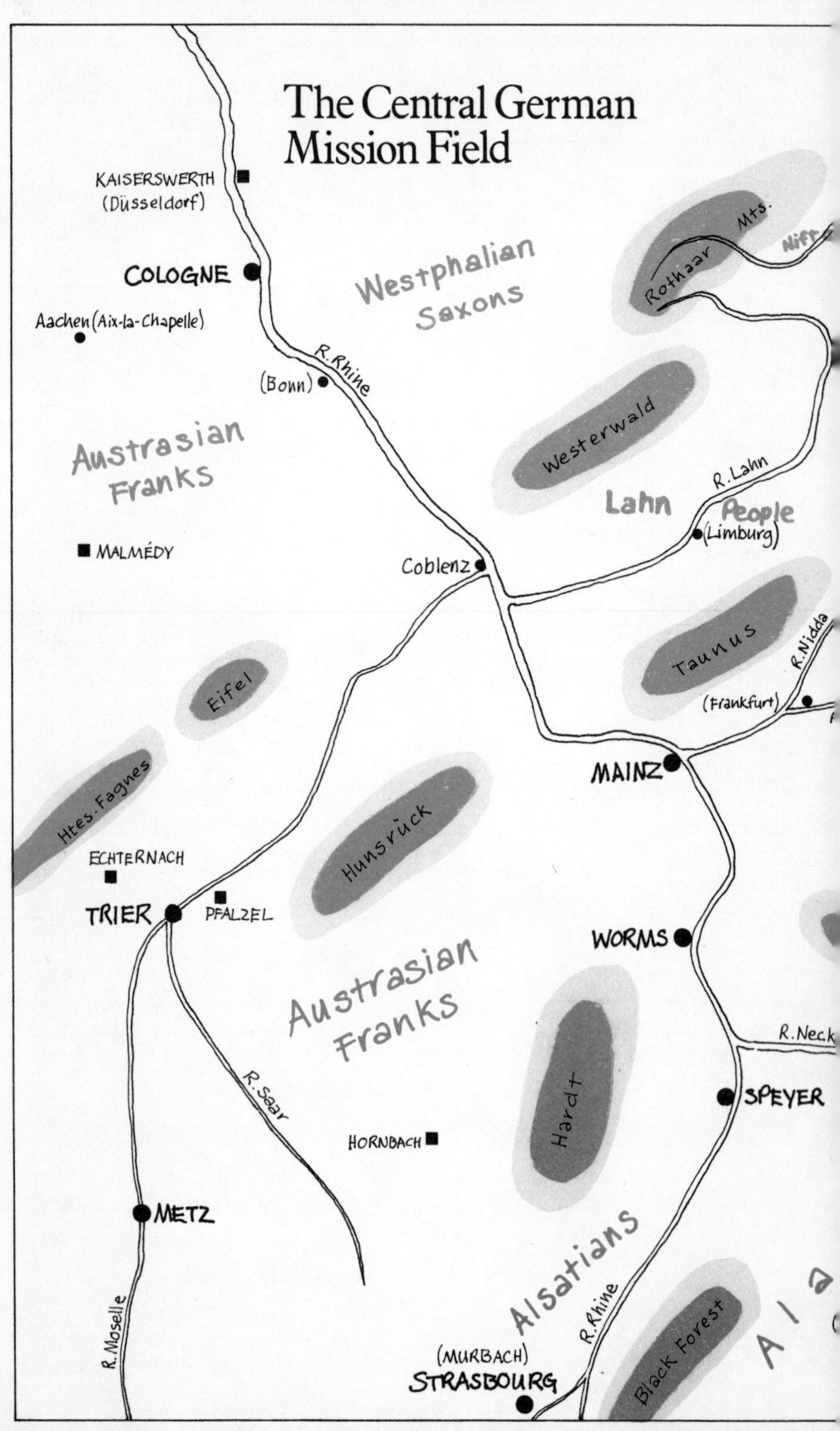

The Central German Mission Field
KAISERSWERTH
(Düsseldorf)
COLOGNE
Aachen (Aix-la-Chapelle)
Westphalian Saxons
Rothaar Mts.
R. Rhine
(Bonn)
Westerwald
Austrasian Franks
R. Lahn
Lahn People
(Limburg)
MALMÉDY
Coblenz
Taunus
R. Nidda
Eifel
(Frankfurt)
MAINZ
Htes. Fagnes
Hunsrück
ECHTERNACH
TRIER
PFALZEL
WORMS
Austrasian Franks
R. Saar
R. Neck
Hardt
SPEYER
HORNBACH
METZ
Alsatians
R. Moselle
R. Rhine
Black Forest
(MURBACH)
STRASBOURG